Praise for *The Song Machine*

A *Kirkus* Best Book of 2015
A *Publishers Weekly* Best Book of 2015
A *Library Journal* Best Book of 2015

"Revelatory. This thorough dissection of the anatomy of a hit belongs on any listener's bookshelf."　　　　　　　　　　　　　　*—FADER*

"A fascinating look at how the catchiest pop hits are manufactured. . . . You'll never hear Katy Perry the same way again."　　　　　*—People*

"A highly engaging narrative. . . . [Seabrook] paints vivid pictures of his protagonists. . . . And he brings little-known stories to life, from the con man who developed the Backstreet Boys and 'N Sync and is now in prison for fraud, to a singer who delivers a laugh-out-loud funny, profane tirade against Ms. Perry for ripping off her song title 'I Kissed A Girl.' "
　　　　　　　　　　　　　　　　　　　　　　　—Economist

"Seabrook spins a fascinating history, one that encompasses everything from the Brill Building and Phil Spector to Afrika Bambaataa to *American Idol*. Running underneath the human stories like a bassline is the inexorable flow of technology."　　　　　　　　*—Boston Globe*

"Copy editors will rejoice at Seabrook's well-written and deeply researched book. He is a staff writer for *The New Yorker* and his book fits into that magazine's penchant for telling very detailed stories about things you might not notice about pop culture."　　　*—Seattle Times*

"Well-researched. . . . [Seabrook] takes us inside the troubled modern music business."　　　　　　　　　*—New York Times Book Review*

"An absorbing new book which looks at the business of manufactured pop. . . . As a behind-the-scenes account of the pop business today, *The Song Machine* is an utterly captivating read. You'll never listen to Taylor Swift or Rihanna in quite the same way again." —*Independent*

"Seabrook pulls together both how and why the craft of hit-making has revved up to Internet speed. In alert close-up reporting, with financial savvy and historical perspective, he explains how Top 10 songwriting has become industrialized. . . . *The Song Machine* joins a strong tradition of hard-headed music-business reporting by music lovers." —Jon Pareles, *New York Review of Books*

"This is a fascinating tale about an amazing phenomenon: how hits get made. John Seabrook combines a love of music and an appreciation for personalities to take us on a starry journey from Stockholm and London to New York and Orlando, showing how creativity gets discovered, polished, and packaged. His book is a triumph of great writing and reporting, and the lessons reverberate far beyond the world of music." —Walter Isaacson, author of *The Innovators* and *Steve Jobs*

"Beneath the surface of today's pop music lies an industrial process as rigorous and bizarre as the one perfected by McDonald's. Seabrook shows what it takes to make a hit in a book that's beautifully written, revelatory, funny, and full of almost unbelievable details." —Eric Schlosser, author of *Fast Food Nation* and *Command and Control*

"Anyone who wants to understand how the clash of cultures has shaped what we listen to should read this important book. John Seabrook has a marvelous ear for language—and perfect pitch when it comes to music journalism." —Bob Spitz, author of *The Beatles: The Biography*

"In *The Song Machine*, John Seabrook tells of a cutthroat and fascinating industry, where readers discover the gifted musical maestros who orchestrate hit after hit but rarely get their names in print. The narrative shows not just how technology has upended the music business but of how—despite prattle about 'the long tail'—just one percent of artists generate 80 percent of the industry's profits."   —Ken Auletta,
author of *Googled: The End of the World as We Know It*

"Revealing, frightening, funny and unsettling—John Seabrook's account of the men and women who create the songs that poke at our ears all day really is terrific."   —Roddy Doyle, author of *The Commitments*

"The author covers a lot of ground—musical, social, economic, and even personal. . . . Seabrook is skilled at conjuring scenes and capturing characters."   —*Nation*

"Fascinating. . . . [T]he appeal of this superb book extends way beyond a curiosity about the machinations of the music business. Its colourful tales illustrate every point."   —*Sunday Times*

THE
SONG
MACHINE

Also by John Seabrook

Flash of Genius: And Other True Stories of Invention
Nobrow: The Culture of Marketing, the Marketing of Culture
Deeper: Adventures on the Net

John Seabrook

THE
SONG
MACHINE

Inside the Hit Factory

W. W. NORTON & COMPANY   NEW YORK · LONDON

INDEPENDENT PUBLISHERS SINCE 1923

Portions of this book originally appeared in *The New Yorker* in a different form.

For information about permission to reproduce selections from this book,
write to Permissions, W. W. Norton & Company, Inc.,
500 Fifth Avenue, New York, NY 10110

For information about special discounts for bulk purchases, please contact
W. W. Norton Special Sales at specialsales@wwnorton.com or 800-233-4830

Manufacturing by LSC Harrisonburg
Book design by Ellen Cipriano
Production manager: Louise Mattarelliano

Library of Congress Cataloging-in-Publication Data

Seabrook, John.
The song machine : inside the hit factory / John Seabrook. — First edition.
    pages cm
Includes bibliographical references and index.
ISBN 978-0-393-24192-1 (hardcover)
1. Music trade. 2. Sound recording industry.
3. Popular music—Production and direction. I. Title.
  ML3790.S382 2015
  781.6409'051—dc23

                                                                    2015022305

ISBN 978-0-393-35328-0 pbk.

W. W. Norton & Company, Inc.
500 Fifth Avenue, New York, N.Y. 10110
www.wwnorton.com

W. W. Norton & Company Ltd.
15 Carlisle Street, London W1D 3BS

4 5 6 7 8 9 0

For Harry and Rose:
The Melody and the Beat

CONTENTS

SECOND VERSE: Factory Girls: Cultural
Technology and the Making of K-Pop

CHORUS: Rihanna: Track-and-Hook

BRIDGE: Dr. Luke: Teenage Dream

CHORUS: Spotify

OUTRO: Songworm

A NOTE ON SOURCES

The Song Machine is mainly based on interviews I conducted over the course of several years; the interviewees are listed in the acknowledgments. In the text, interviews by the author are in the present tense (he "says"). Quotations drawn from supplementary material are in the past tense (he "said"). The magazines, books, and broadcasts used as sources are noted in the text at the point where that particular source first appears. Quotations and texts originally in Swedish were translated by Lisa Lonstron.

As a research tool, a premium subscription to Spotify was invaluable in making this book. I have created Spotify playlists of most of the songs referenced in the narrative, broken both into chapters and individual hit makers (Max Martin songs, Stargate songs, and so on). The Taylor Swift songs referenced are currently unavailable, but hopefully by the time you read this, the artist and Spotify will have worked it out.

THE
SONG
MACHINE

One cannot live outside the machine for more perhaps than half an hour.

VIRGINIA WOOLF, *THE WAVES*

Bring the hooks in, where the bass at?

IGGY AZALEA, "FANCY"

HOOK
THE
BLISS
POINT

1 | You Spin Me Round

IT STARTED WHEN the Boy got big enough to claim shotgun. No sooner seated up front than he reprogrammed the presets, changing my classic and alternative rock stations to contemporary hits radio, or CHR—what used to be called Top 40.

I was irritated at first, but by the time we had crossed the Brooklyn Bridge and arrived at school, where he was a fifth-grader, I was pleased. Hadn't I reconfigured my parents' radio to play my music when I was his age? And since there are only so many times you can listen to the guitar solo in Pink Floyd's "Comfortably Numb" without going a little numb yourself, I made the Boy my DJ, at least for the day.

Thumpa thooka whompa whomp Pish pish pish Thumpa wompah wompah pah pah Maaakaka thomp peep bap boony Gunga gunga gung

Was this music? The bass sounded like a recording of a massive undersea earthquake. The speakers produced sounds such as might have been heard on the Island of Dr. Moreau, had he been a DJ rather than a vivisectionist. What strange song machines made these half-brass, half-stringed-sounding noises?

It was the winter of 2009, and "Right Round," by Flo Rida, was the number-one song on Billboard's Hot 100. The song begins with a swirly sound that goes right 'round your head in a tight circle.

EEeeoooorrrroooannnnnwwweeeyyeeeooowwwwouuuzzzzeeEE

Sprays of words follow the jackhammer beats, sung-rapped by Flo and assisted on the hook by the barbaric yawp of the artist Kesha.

> *You spin my head right round right round*
> *When you go down when you go down down*

I missed the lyrics at first, but thanks to the repetitiveness of the CHR format—the playlist was closer to Top 10 than to Top 40—I didn't have to wait long for the song to come right 'round again. It concerned a man in a strip club watching the pole dancers spin. And the hook was a double entendre for oral sex! Now, in *my* day, songwriters used double entendre to *conceal* the real meaning of the song. But in "Right Round," the surface meaning—*From the top of the pole I watch her go down*—is as lewd as the hidden one.

The nation was near the bottom of its worst economic collapse since the Great Depression, but you wouldn't know that from "Right Round." Social realism is not what this song is about. Like a lot of CHR songs, it takes place in "da club," where Pitbull oils his way around the floor, calling "Dále!" to the women and remarking on their shapely behinds. The club is both an earthly paradise where all sensual pleasures are realized, and the arena in which achievement is measured: the place where you prove your manhood. Exactly what is the Boy doing in this place? Fortunately, I will be here with him now, to keep an eye on things.

"I WANT TO HOLD YOUR HAND," my first number one, came out when I was five; my sister had the 45. I heard pop music on the radio, on car-pool rides to and from the bus stop. ("Bus Stop" by the Hollies was one of the hits.) The mothers kept the radio tuned to WFIL, a Philadelphia Top 40 powerhouse in the mid-'60s. The Brill Building era, epitomized by professional songwriting teams like Gerry Goffin and Carole King, had given way to the Beatles. That led to the rock era, and I was fortunate enough to have lived my peak music-loving years during the glorious '70s and '80s up through the '90s with Nirvana and grunge. For me, rock came to a spectacularly violent end on April 5, 1994, although Kurt Cobain's body wasn't discovered until three days later. By that point I'd mostly moved on to big beat (The Chemical Brothers, Fatboy Slim), then to techno and EDM. Otherwise I listened to hip-hop, but only on my headphones—you couldn't spin that stuff around kids, and my wife hated the misogyny.

Around the time I stopped listening to rock, I began playing it. I rediscovered my teenage love of the guitar, and when the Boy came along, I gave him the gift of rock. By the age of three he had been treated to any number of intimate unplugged concerts, featuring me performing the folk and rock canon, during bath and bedtime. Why couldn't my dad have been this cool?

Yet the little gentleman showed an unnatural lack of affection for my music. "Don't play!" he'd say whenever I reached for my instrument. He'd leave the room when "Knockin' on Heaven's Door" came around again. In his displeasure with my music he reminded me of my dad.

And now, age ten, the tables were turned and for the first time I was treated to a full blast of *his* music, rudely shaking me from my long rock slumber. The songs in the car weren't soulful ballads played by the singer-songwriter. They were industrial-strength products, made for malls, stadiums, airports, casinos, gyms, and the Super Bowl half-time show. The music reminded me a little of the bubblegum pop of my preteen years, but it was vodka-flavored and laced with MDMA; it doesn't taste like "Sugar, Sugar." It is teen pop for adults.

Like the Brill Building songs of my youth, the hits on the radio are once again "manufactured" by songwriting pros. The hit makers aren't on the same team, but they collaborate and work independently for the same few A-list artists. Collectively, they constitute a virtual Brill Building, the place where record men go when they have to have a hit. The song machine.

MUSICALLY, THE SONG MACHINE makes two types of hits. One branch is descended from Europop, and the other from R&B. The former has longer, more progressive melodies and a sharper verse-chorus differentiation, and they seem more meticulously crafted. The latter have a rhythmic groove with a melodic hook on top that repeats throughout the song. But these templates are endlessly recombined. And the line between pop and urban is as blurry as it was in the '50s when the record business was in its infancy, and the distinctions between R&B and pop were still fluid. Sam Smith, Hozier, and Iggy Azalea are all white artists with a black sound.

Phil Spector, an early master at mixing R&B and pop, required dozens of session musicians to build his famous Wall of Sound. CHR hit makers can make all the sounds they need with musical software and samples—no instruments required. This is democratizing, but it also feels a little like cheating. By employing technologically advanced equipment and digital-compression techniques, these hit makers create sounds that are more sonically engaging and powerful than even the most skilled instrumentalists can produce. And it's so easy! You want the string section from Abbey Road on your record—you just punch it up. Whole subcultures of musical professionals—engineers, arrangers, session musicians—are disappearing, unable to compete with the software that automates their work.

Some instrumental sounds are based on samples of actual instruments, but they are no longer recognizable as such. And the electronic atmosphere and the dynamic changes in the density of the sound are more captivating than the virtuosity of the musicians. The computer is felt in the instrumentation, the cut-and-paste architecture, and in the rigorous perfection of timing and pitch—call it robopop. Melodies are fragmentary, and appear in strong short bursts, like espresso shots served throughout the song by a producer-barista. Then, slicing through the thunderous algorithms, like Tennyson's eagle—*And like a thunderbolt he falls*—comes the "hook": a short, sung line that grips the rhythm with melodic talons and soars skyward. The songs bristle with hooks, painstakingly crafted to tweak the brain's delight in melody, rhythm, and repetition.

The artists occupy a central place in the songs, but more as vocal personalities than singers. The voices belong to real human beings, for the most part, although in some cases the vocals are so decked out in electronic finery that it doesn't matter whether a human or a machine made them. On sheer vocal ability, the new artists fall short of the pop divas of the early '90s—Whitney, Mariah, Celine. And who are these artists? Britney? Kelly? Rihanna? Katy? Kesha? What do they stand for as artists? Their insights into the human condition seem to extend no further than the walls of the vocal booth. And who really writes their songs?

Yes, I could have reprogrammed the presets and gone back to "Comfortably Numb." I didn't. Now the Boy and I had something to talk about.

I HAD TRIED TO interest him in watching sports. He'd seen the pain the Philadelphia Eagles organization has caused me over so many years; naturally he wanted no part of that. But he was pleased to debate the merits of beats, hooks, choruses, and bridges. Like me, he knew where hit songs stood on the Billboard Hot 100—the fast risers and quick fallers-off; the number of weeks spent at number one; whether or not Katy Perry's *Teenage Dream* album would score its fifth number one and thus tie Michael Jackson's *Bad* for most number ones ever on an album. When Katy did it, he was proud; it proved his pop stars could compete with mine.

And yet he was reluctant to share his true feelings about his music. He sensed there was something unnatural about my interest in it, and probably there was. After all, the songs on CHR were *his*. I'd had my glory days with the Sex Pistols; shouldn't I step aside, take what pleasure I could in, say, Mark Knopfler's amazing pickless guitar playing on the live version of "Sultans of Swing" on YouTube, and leave him to it? What if my parents had said, "Hey, son, the Pistols are really groovy!" or "Sid Vicious seems like a *nifty* guy!"? They'd only approved of one rock(ish) song, and that was "Teach Your Children," by Crosby, Stills, Nash & Young. I could never listen to it with pleasure again.

Who *are* the hit makers? They are enormously influential culture shapers—the Spielbergs and Lucases of our national headphones—and yet they are mostly anonymous. Directors of films are public figures, but the people behind pop songs remain in the shadows, taking aliases, by necessity if not by choice, in order to preserve the illusion that the singer is the author of the song. I knew much more about the Brill Building writers of the early '60s than about the people behind current CHR hits.

They all have aliases—disco names. One of the most successful is called Dr. Luke. He and his frequent songwriting partner, a Swede called Max Martin (also an alias), have had more than thirty Top 10 hits between them since 2004, and Max Martin's own streak goes back a decade before that; more recently, he's become Taylor Swift's magic man. In both volume of hits and longevity, Max Martin eclipses all previous hit makers, including the Beatles, Phil Spector, and Michael Jackson.

"Did you know that 'Right Round,' 'I Kissed a Girl,' 'Since U Been Gone,' and 'Tik Tok' are all done by Dr. Luke?"

"Really?"

"I doubt he's a *medical* doctor!" I snorted. The Boy smirked uncertainly.

This became my mission: to find out more about who created these strange new songs, how they were made, and why they sounded the way they did, and report back to him. I shared tidbits I had gleaned about

the process, and the Boy seemed pleased to know them. Our car r...
together were full of song talk. It was bliss.

SOME WEEKS PASSED. A new song or two appeared, but for the
most part the same tunes played ad nauseam. There were few ballads,
and fewer rock songs. The music sounded more like disco than rock. I
thought disco was dead. Turns out disco had simply gone underground,
where it became House, only to eventually reemerge, cicadalike, as the
backing track to the CHR music and to bludgeon rock senseless with
synths. Weirdly, the only place I consistently heard new guitar-driven
rock music was on the girl-power cartoon shows my youngest watched
on Nick Jr. There, guitar gods were still aspirational figures, albeit for
five-year-old girls.

Taylor Swift was a welcome surprise. Her early hits—"Our Song,"
"Love Story," and "You Belong With Me"—were still playing on the
radio. They're sort of country rock songs with great rhythm guitar parts,
and Nashville polish and production added. And Swift was at least
recognizable as belonging to the old singer-songwriter tradition I grew
up with. She actually wrote her own songs. We both loved her.

Some of the pop hits had a definite rock *vibe*, and I dutifully pointed
out the spots where I heard it. The back beat in Kelly Clarkson's "Since
U Been Gone." The opening riff in Katy Perry's "I Kissed a Girl." The
baroque swoop of '80s guitar lines in Kesha's "Tik Tok," except that they
aren't actually made with guitars. These songs are musical chimeras—
rock bodies with disco souls. They have more melody than rap songs, but
less melody than most '80s music, and less chord complexity than songs
from the '60s and '70s; they're closer to punk that way. They get a lot of
song mileage from simple and repetitive chord structures, thanks to the
lush production.

You'd think that in an age when anyone with basic computer skills
can make a song on a laptop—no musical training or instrumental mas-

tery is required—the charts would be flooded with newbie hit makers. The barriers to entry are low. And yet it turns out that the same handful of top writers and producers are behind hit after hit—a mysterious priesthood of musical mages. They combine the talents of storied arrangers like Quincy Jones and George Martin, with the tune-making abilities of writer-producers like Holland–Dozier–Holland, Motown's secret weapon. On the pop side, there's Ryan Tedder, Jeff Bhasker, and Benny Blanco; on the urban side Pharrell Williams, Dr. Dre, and Timbaland. Bridging both genres are the über hit makers like Stargate, Ester Dean, Dr. Luke, and Max Martin.

THE MORE I HEARD the songs, the more I liked them. How could that be? If you dislike a song the first time, surely you should loathe it the tenth. But apparently that's not how it works. Familiarity with the song increases one's emotional investment in it, even if you don't like it.

This happens gradually, in stages. The initially annoying bits

> *If I said I want your body now*
> *Would you hold it against me*

become the very parts you look forward to most in the song. You quote lines like "No lead in our zeppelin!" as if they are hoary oaths. In the car, I steel myself against hearing the same song yet again, but once it starts, I feel oddly elated. Melody and rhythm are deliciously entwined; in Brill Building songs, melody and rhythm sleep on opposite sides of the bed. The beats produce delightful vibrations in the sternum. And the hooks deliver the aural equivalent of what the snack-food industry calls the "bliss point"—when the rhythm, sound, melody, and harmony converge to create a single ecstatic moment, one felt more in the body than the head.

At the PS 234 graduation the following summer, there was a DJ in the schoolyard who played Kesha, Pink, Rihanna—the whole posse of post-aught pop stars. And because I knew the music, I had a great time dancing. I outdid myself twirling around to Chris Brown's "Forever" with one of the younger moms, while the Boy looked on, mortified.

What can I say? Ordinary domestic life needs its bliss points, those moments of transcendence throughout the day—that just-behind-the-eyelids sense of quivering possibility that at any moment the supermarket aisle might explode into candy-colored light. The hooks promise that pleasure. But the ecstasy is fleeting, and like snack food it leaves you feeling unsatisfied, always craving just a little more.

2 | A Continuity of Hits

CLIVE DAVIS HAS a way of pronouncing the word "hits." If the word occurs in the course of conversation, as it always does, the record man will huff it out, like a lion.

"I'm talking about HITS!" he barks in his curious Brooklyn-by-way-of-Bond-Street accent. It's 2014, and Davis, who is the chief creative officer of Sony Music, has been talking about hits for fifty years, ever since he started at CBS Records as a music attorney in the mid-'60s. For a record man like Davis, hits are the whole ball game. A pop star is nothing without a hit, and a pop career depends on a "continuity of hits," a favorite Davis phrase.

Of course, there have been swings in popular taste over Davis's career. The pure pop center he aims for has periodically been purged by new, edgier styles, which, in turn, eventually become absorbed into the mainstream too, usually on a ten-year cycle. Teen tastes, which pop music has historically served, are the most fickle of all. But through all the cyclical changes, there have always been hits. Hits are the strait gate through which all the money, fame, and buzz passes on its way to heaven. Ninety percent of the revenues in the record business come from ten percent of the songs.

A recorded song has two principal sets of rights—the publishing and the master recording. The publishing covers the copyright of the composition, and the master is the sound-recording copyright. The master is the real estate; the publishing is the mineral rights under the land, and the air rights. In addition there are mechanical royalties, which are based on sales, and performance royalties, for when a song is played or performed in public, including on the radio. There are also synchronization rights, for use of a song in a commercial, ball game, TV show, or movie. In some countries (though not in the United States), there are neighboring rights, which are granted to non-authors who are closely connected to the song, such as the performers. The system is ridiculously complicated, as it's supposed to be. It takes a music attorney like Davis to understand all the complexities in royalties payments. Labels have lots of them.

A smash hit not only makes the songwriters a bundle on radio spins, it also moves the album, which generally benefits the label, and sells tickets to the world tour, which is how the artists make most of their money. A historic smash can be worth hundreds of millions for the rights holders over the term of its copyright, which, depending on when the song was composed, is the life of its composers plus fifty or sixty years. "Stairway to Heaven" alone was said to have earned its rights holders more than half a billion dollars by 2008.

With so much dough potentially at stake, it is no surprise the hits are the source of hard dealings and dark deeds. In the old days, artists were induced to give away the publishing rights of their hits, which ended up being worth more than the records. Today, a top artist can insist on a full share of the publishing even though they had nothing to do with writing the song. ("Change a word, get a third," the writers call this practice.) The music business, like the TV business depicted by Hunter S. Thompson, is a "cruel and shallow money trench . . . a long plastic hallway where thieves and pimps run free, and good men die like dogs," and that's how the hits have always been accounted for. (Thompson added, "There's also a negative side.")

Does it make sense, this all-or-nothing way of doing business, in which one song becomes all the rage and ten equally worthy songs are ignored, for reasons that no one entirely understands? As Clive Davis's former boss, the chairman of the Bertelsmann Music Group, Rolf Schmidt-Holtz, stated back in 2003, "We need reliable calculations of returns that are not based solely on hits because the way people get music doesn't go with hits anymore. We have to get rid of the lottery mentality." When Jason Flom, a top record man then at Atlantic Records, heard Schmidt-Holtz's remarks, he looked stunned. "That ain't gonna happen," he told me at the time. "If anything, hits are more important than ever, because stars can emerge practically overnight on a global scale. The day we stop seeing hits is the day people stop buying records."

THAT DAY HAS ARRIVED. The selling of records, which sustained the business for more than half a century, and made fortunes for a few record men, is coming to an end. David Geffen sold his label (Geffen) to MCA for more than $550 million in 1990, and Richard Branson sold Virgin to EMI for $960 million in 1992. And in 2001 Clive Calder's BMG-Zomba deal earned him $2.7 billion—placing the capstone on humankind's ability to make money from hits. But ever since Napster set music free in 1998, the customer has been able to get any hit he wants without paying for it. This presents a problem, if you're Clive Davis or Jason Flom, because making hits, as we will see, can be very expensive. "What would happen if shoppers had the option to get groceries or furniture for free?" Flom asks. "Those businesses would have to adapt rapidly, just as we've had to do."

Even on the legal streaming services, such as Spotify, music consumption is "frictionless"—a favorite word of techies. It means—well, not "free" exactly, but at least unburdened by the inconvenience of purchasing a product. You've gone from a world of scarcity to one of abundance. Nothing is for sale, because everything is available. For both the pirates and the paying subscribers, buying records is rapidly becoming a thing of the past. And yet the hits go on and on.

In *The Long Tail*, the 2005 techno-utopian argument for the coming triumph of niches in popular culture, author Chris Anderson posits that hits are a scarcity-based phenomenon. Record stores have limited shelf space, he explains, and records that move 10,000 units are more profitable to stock than records that move 10. But on the Internet, shelf space is infinite, and therefore record companies don't need to focus so much of their business on making hits. They can make money from the long tail of the artistic middle class—artists with small but loyal followings who will never be heard on CHR. Collectively these fans comprise what Anderson calls an "unseen majority," a "market that rivals the hits."

"If the twentieth-century entertainment industry was about hits, the twenty-first will be equally about niches," Anderson declares early in the book. Using data from Rhapsody, an early streaming music subscription service, Anderson foresees the coming age of the "micro-hit." He writes, "This is not a fantasy. It is the emerging state of music today." Among other things, this means that the cool indie music that thinking people like Anderson and his friends like will finally have a fighting chance against "manufactured" boy bands that appeal to the teen masses.

A long-tail record economy threatens the very vocation of the record man. Why bother to take on the risk of making hits, and endure the far more numerous failures, when the labels can make as much money licensing their back catalogue of hits, which are already paid for, so that the money goes straight to the company's bottom line? The record label of the future will be like a 1-800 number, Flom says sarcastically. "Dial one for pop, dial two for the blues."

But that's not what happened. Not even close. Nine years after *The Long Tail*, the hits are bigger than ever. Of the 13 million songs available for purchase in 2008, 52,000 made up 80 percent of the industry's revenue. Ten million of those tracks failed to sell a single copy. Today, 77 percent of the profits in the music business are accumulated by 1 percent of the artists. Even Eric Schmidt, the CEO of Google and an early supporter of long-tail theory, changed his mind. "Although the tail is very interesting, and we enable it, the vast majority of the revenue remains in the head," he said in a 2008 interview with McKinsey, the management consulting firm. "In fact, it's probable that the Internet will lead to larger blockbusters, more concentration of brands." In her 2014 book *Blockbusters*, Harvard Business School professor Anita Elberse showed how mega hits have become more important across the whole entertainment industry. "Smart executives bet heavily on a few likely winners. That's where the big payoffs come from," she writes.

The long tail is a lovely concept—more prosperity for a larger number of artists—and it makes sense in the tech world, where it is an article of faith that the fundamental logic of networks will foster a meritocracy. But the music business doesn't work logically, and merit doesn't always matter. Power, fear, and greed are the laws of the land.

How did the hits survive such severely disruptive forces as free music and infinite shelf space? There are many different reasons, some of which are discussed at length in the following pages. Specialized teams of songwriter-producers employ a method of composition I call track-and-hook to make songs that are almost irresistible. Record labels have figured out how to orchestrate demand for top artists like Katy Perry and Rihanna, relying on their close alliance and long history with commercial radio. And the public, given the ability to call up any song they choose, still wants to listen to what everyone else is playing.

It's telling that so many recent hits have been written by a Swede, Max Martin, and his Swedish-trained collaborators. The distinction between R&B and pop, which in the United States has as much to do with race as with music, is less pronounced in Sweden, a more racially homogenous country. Beginning with the Backstreet Boys and extending through major hits for Britney Spears and 'N Sync, Kelly Clarkson, Katy Perry, Kesha, and Taylor Swift, Max Martin and his fellow Swedish writers and producers have created a genre-bursting hybrid:

pop music with a rhythmic R&B feel. Their foreign-ness to English and American music allows them to inhabit, and in certain ways co-opt, different genres—R&B, rock, hip-hop—and convert them to mainstream pop using working methods developed in Stockholm in the '90s at a place called Cheiron Studios, where the song machine begins.

FIRST VERSE
CHEIRON: MR. POP AND THE METALHEAD

3 | Inside the Box

ONE DAY IN 1992, a demo tape addressed to Denniz PoP, a twenty-eight-year-old DJ, arrived at a Stockholm-based music company called SweMix.

So Californian-looking he could only be Swedish, Dag Krister Volle—Denniz PoP's given name; friends called him Dagge—wore his long blond hair with plenty of volumizer, loosely parted in the middle, Jon Bon Jovi–style, a reminder that the New Jersey rocker had started his career as a hair dresser. When it hung down in his eyes, as it usually did, Denniz would blow upward, puffing aside hair strands with wheezy gouts of smoky breath; he always had a Marlboro Menthol going. "Maybe two hundred and fifty times a day he'd do that," says Kristian Lundin, one of his later protégés, who Denniz called "Krille" (Dagge was big on nicknames). Denniz dressed like a teenager, in T-shirts and jeans, or in large green military-style trousers, and hoodies, everything worn loose. Seated in front of his Apple computer—he always had the latest Macs—his cigarette would stick straight up between the fingers of his right hand as he moved the mouse. He had a licentious-looking gap between his two front teeth that showed when he smiled. And he was always smiling.

SweMix was located in the soundproofed basement of a building on Kocksgatan street, in Södermalm. It was a collective of ten Swedish DJs led by René Hedemyr, who as JackMaster Fax spun records at Tramps, one of the city's biggest discos. When they weren't in the studio or working a club, most of them clerked at the Vinyl Mania record store in Vasagatan, close to the Stockholm train station. "They were all a bit cocky," Jan Gradvall, a prominent Swedish music journalist, remembers. "I was always a little nervous when shopping there. A bit like *High Fidelity* but with dance music." Apart from René and Denniz, the best known of the SweMix DJs was Sten Hallström, who goes by the name StoneBridge and is still active in Stockholm.

At Ritz, Stockholm's premier dance club, Denniz was much in demand as a DJ. Unlike his SweMix colleagues, who spun house and acid house at the Bat Club—as Thursday nights at Ritz were called—Denniz loved funk and soul. Parliament-Funkadelic, Cameo; "anything with a funky bass line Denniz loved," says Lundin. StoneBridge says, "I grew up with Chic and Nile Rodgers, but Denniz was never into disco; he was a bit younger than us." In 1986, when Hedemyr showed up with a stack of house records he'd gotten from Stax in Chicago, Denniz didn't like it; it threatened the funk and soul that was his true love. StoneBridge adds, "Denniz also hated jazz. It wasn't simple enough. He liked chords you could play with three fingers. Whenever I would play my complicated jazzy chords, Denniz would make a face. That was the thing that drew him to pop—the simplicity of it." Denniz much preferred the synth-pop bands coming out of London in the early '80s—Depeche Mode, Human League, OMD. He also adored Def Leppard, especially the production work by superproducer Mutt Lange. As Jan Gradvall notes, "Def Leppard were used as a blueprint when they made their own Swedish pop/R&B-mashups."

In 1987, Denniz was in the booth at Ritz one night in November, that month Stockholm descends into its long winter darkness, when on the club's small stage, for the first time ever in Sweden, Public Enemy appeared, in their trademark military uniforms, followed by LL Cool J. Gradvall, who was also in the club that night (in later years virtually every significant music figure in Sweden would claim to have been in the club that night) recalls, "It was like seeing the light: visual proof that exciting music didn't have to be played on guitars, bass, and drums, but with only a Technics 1200," a high-fidelity turntable favored by DJs.

SweMix remixed US and UK hits for European audiences, working largely by hand. StoneBridge says, "The very first mixes were pure edits with added samples. Then, about 1987 we got various take-outs from the original mix session tapes. It could be drums and vocal or dubby parts, but still the original music. We still had very limited sampling time, but sometimes there were a cappellas on the vinyl and we simply synced them manually."

"We sat and cut by hand, razor blades and stuff like that, and spliced the songs in real '80s fashion," Denniz said in an interview in the mid-'90s:

> Nowadays we use digital, but when we first started it was tape that you'd measure. You took the tape in your hand and then you'd just listen. *Tuk, tuk, tuk.* OK there's the first stroke. Then you'd manually fast forward until you found the second stroke, and mark the tape . . . then fold the tape in the middle and made a line where you ended up, which gave you a half rhythm or half stroke. Fold it one more time and you got one quarter. If you were really talented you could do one eighth. Then you'd take a bunch of different strokes, sounds or yells, and cut these incredibly small segments into different formats. Finally it turns into long segments of sounds —*drrrr tuk tuk tuk tang-eeeee*—typical '80s hysterical sounds. . . . You'd sit with tape parts around your neck, meters and meters all with little notes jotted down on them, like, 'kick backwards,' and then you'd take a chance and cut them together with Scotch tape. If I were to do the same thing now, I'd do it on the computer. It's a completely different thing.

Some of the mixes merely extended songs for dancers by adding instrumental sections and long drum breaks, like Tom Moulton's pioneering disco remixes at the Sandpiper Club on Fire Island a decade earlier. But Denniz got far more creative than that, as in his remix of Soul II Soul's track "Keep On Movin'," which he combined with Donna Summer's "Love to Love You Baby," creating a sort of proto-mashup. He slowed down the tempo of Michael Jackson's "Billie Jean" (without changing the key, which is hard to do), and he rearranged Philip Oakey's and Susan Ann Sulley's voices in Human League's 1981 smash "Don't You Want Me," to create more of a dialogue between the man and the woman. He would often debut his sonic concoctions at Ritz, from where they would make their way around clubs in Sweden, then to Germany, the Netherlands, and Italy. Eventually, twelve-inch "white label" vinyl discs would be offered for sale, which was how SweMix made money.

Remixing was a lucrative and growing business, but that success had kindled larger ambitions in Denniz. Instead of merely remixing US and UK hits for Europeans, he dreamed about making his own hits. "In the end," he said, "you have remade an original song so much that you've now made your own song and just added the vocals from the original. And that's where the idea that, 'Dammit now we can make our own song!' came from." He would regale his fellow SweMix DJs with his vision of the gold and platinum records from the UK and the United States that would one day decorate the walls of the studio, signaling Sweden's global power in pop music. No one believed him.

THE '80S WERE A good time to be in the record business. The post-disco doldrums were over, and the modern music "industry" was about to explode. In 1983, the president of PolyGram, Jan Timmer, introduced what he hoped would become the new platform for the sale of recorded music—the compact disc—at a recording-industry convention in Miami. On a CD, music takes the form of digital strings of ones and zeros, which are encoded on specially treated plastic disks. The high-tech allure of the CD would allow the industry to raise the cost of an album from $8.98 to $15.98 (even though CDs were soon cheaper to manufacture than vinyl records), and the record companies got to keep a larger share of money. The industry would even persuade artists not to raise royalty rates, arguing that the extra money was needed to market the new format to customers.

Sure enough, in spite of costing almost twice as much, CDs turned out to be extremely popular with record buyers. Fans who already owned music on vinyl dutifully replaced their records with CDs. By the early '90s hit albums on CD were selling in far greater numbers than hit albums on vinyl had sold. CDs also turned out to be a brilliant way of repackaging a label's catalogue—all the recordings that were no longer in production on vinyl. CDs spawned a generation of record executives whose skill was in putting together compilations of existing music rather than in discovering new artists. Through the stock market crash of 1987 and the recession of the early '90s, the CD market grew steadily.

But these thin plastic disks, which brought so much treasure to record labels, were the seeds of their downfall. Because digitized songs had to be compatible both with CD players and computers (CDs would soon replace floppy disks as the standard storage medium), they weren't copy-protected. Songs could be "ripped" from the labels' CDs and "burned" onto blank CDs with home computers. Homemade CD compilations didn't pose any greater threat to the music business than homemade tapes had. But when it became possible to compress these digitized song files into much smaller packets of bits known as MP3s, and share them over the Internet, the record business would face its extinction.

"GIMME SOME MO' (BASS ON ME)" is the first track to have "Denniz PoP" listed as the artist. PoP was a double entendre: an acronym for "Prince of Pick-ups," which was a reference to his prowess with a stylus arm, and also a sardonic jibe at his colleagues' rarefied musical tastes. "During that time 'pop' was almost like a swear word," he said in a 1998 interview with Anders Löwstedt on Swedish Radio. "Everything was hip-hop and break, and you weren't allowed to say 'pop.' It was no fun at all." And Dagge was all about fun. So "I took 'Denniz' from the cartoon character"—Dennis the Menace, whose refusal to do anything that didn't strike him as fun echoed Dagge's spirit—"and then I just added Pop to that. And now I've had to live with it. Overseas they only call me "Denniz." But here, 'Ah, Mr. Pop!' is what I get when I register at the hotel under that name."

Denniz loved games almost as much as he loved music. Not just computer games, although he was certainly devoted to those, and would spend hours playing Broken Sword, an adventure game, and Marathon, an early first-person shooter, producing detailed walk-throughs for his buddies; gaming would become a big part of Cheiron culture. He also delighted in board games and practical jokes. One time, Denniz turned all the lights in the studio off, wrapped himself in toilet paper like a mummy, and spent three hours waiting for his best friend Anders Hannegård, whom he called "Snake," to come downstairs so that he could scare him to death. His office looked like an *Indiana Jones* movie set. "Denniz was a guy who didn't want to grow up," observes Andreas Carlsson, a Swedish songwriter and producer who became a Cheiron "disciple." "He was the Steven Spielberg of pop." He got bored easily, and his friends invested a lot of energy in keeping him happy. Jeanette von der Burg, a Swedish backup singer who later worked for Denniz as a secretary, says, "You wanted so much to please him—everyone did."

Each year Denniz would organize an elaborate annual scavenger hunt for colleagues and friends, hiding clues all over Stockholm. E-Type, one of the artists Denniz would eventually produce, remembered in the documentary *The Cheiron Saga* by Fredrik Eliasson on Swedish Radio, "We'd run around town like clowns, counting the number of wine bottles at the liquor stores, say, and driving cars too fast and ending up with speeding tickets, and there were boats, and we'd borrow things, and try to mess each other up. And then Dagge would sit there for hours trying to determine the winner."

His parents, Anna and Jan Volle, were originally from Norway; eventually they settled in Tullinge, a suburb of Stockholm. His mother thought Dagge's interest in collecting and playing records was "very much fun," his older sister Ann-Katrin told documentarian Fredrik Eliasson. "But not my dad; he didn't think it was good." She added, "Because it wasn't a real job. He thought that Dagge should become something real, like for example a civil engineer." Curiously, although he was obsessed with music, Dagge wasn't interested in learning an instrument, even though the Swedish educational system made it very easy to do so. Forced to pick up the recorder, he quit after three lessons. "It was really boring," he said. "Really my only interest was to purchase the records, and sit at home playing them."

He was far less engaged in the practical necessities of the day-to-day world. He ruined the engine in his Nissan Micra by letting the oil run dry. ("Was I supposed to put oil in it?" he innocently asked.) His best friend Snake said, "If he had a nice car and you commented on how cool it was, and asked him about the horsepower, he'd be like, 'I have no idea.' He'd stop the car just to open up the hood to check if it had a six- or eight-cylinder engine."

Although his music eventually made him extraordinarily rich, Denniz never cared about the money. At one point in the mid-'90s his bank called him up and said, "Mr. Volle, are you aware that you have ten million dollars sitting in an ordinary checking account?" He had no idea. His business partner, Tom Talomaa, handled the financial side of things, leaving Denniz free to dream up new sounds, and new ways to have fun.

But in spite of his devotion to fun—or perhaps this was the reason for it—Denniz also had a morbid fixation on the idea that he wouldn't live very long. He couldn't imagine himself being old—he literally couldn't conjure up a mental picture of what he would look like. When Snake's father died of cancer in 1991, Denniz became convinced that he'd die of cancer too.

Denniz frequently visited a fortune-teller named Emmy. She told him he was "an angel" who was put on Earth to do great things. But she also saw something else. She didn't tell him what it was, except to say, "You have a third eye, but you have chosen to keep it closed."

PRIOR TO DENNIZ POP, hit songs in the United States and the UK, the world's two largest music markets, had come almost exclusively from American and British songwriters and producers, along with the occasional Aussie. New directions in popular music often combined American and British elements. A new beat would emerge in the States from black music and make its way to the UK, where the heavy rhythmic grooves would be sweetened with progressive European melodies. Then the music would return to the States and mainstream chart success. It was a global conversation about African and European culture, transacted in song.

This ping-ponging of musical styles across the Atlantic had been going on at least since the early '60s, when British musicians discovered the blues. In the late 1980s, around the time this story begins, it was occurring in the dance-driven genre known as house, which had come from Chicago and Detroit and crossed the Atlantic to become a fixture in British clubs and raves. But in the United States it remained a mostly underground phenomenon. You had to go to clubs to hear it.

On the rare occasions when a hit came from outside the English-speaking world, the group that sang it was likely to be from Sweden. Sweden has one of the highest percentages of English-speakers of any non-English-speaking country, and with only 9.5 million people in the whole country, Swedish performers have a long tradition of singing in English, in the hope of reaching a wider audience. Blue Swede had scored a number-one hit in April 1974 with the 1968 B. J. Thomas song "Hooked on a Feeling," to which they added the ooga-chaka ooga-chaka refrain from Jonathan Martin's 1971 version of the song. ABBA had created a series of top-ten hits in the second half of the '70s, and the rock duo Roxette was just beginning their US chart success in the late '80s; they would achieve no fewer than four Billboard number ones.

But those were performing acts. Denniz's vision was entirely different: a factory of Swedish writers and producers who would create hits for British and American artists. Andreas Carlsson says, "That idea seemed absurd, because Sweden was very disconnected from the international music market at that time. The profession of songwriting wasn't even invented yet in Sweden."

Denniz wasn't sure what these Swedish-made hit records should sound like, but he knew that somehow they had to meld the beat-driven music that people danced to inside the clubs with the pop music people listened to on the radio. The music would combine the hard-hitting breakbeats and bass lines of reggae and hip-hop with the singsongy melodies that the Swedes have such a gift for, and the big choruses of '80s hits like "Beat It," "Livin' on a Prayer," and "The Final Countdown" by Sweden's own, the hair band Europe. The trick was to come up with a melody that worked with the beat, not against it. In the United States, melody was kept at arm's length by the DJs who were the producers of house music, because in the clubs, whenever a strong melody came over the speakers, the dancing stopped. But in Sweden, it was different. As Jan Gradvall observes, "In discos in small towns all over Sweden in the '80s, people danced to the biggest hit song rather than the funkiest songs or best mixes. When the chorus came around, that's when the dance floor boiled. Those kind of choruses, not unlike those of songs sung in hockey arenas or soccer stadiums, have always been loved in Sweden. So when Denniz PoP and the others DJed at these places, they realized the importance of BIG choruses."

. . .

DENNIZ POP WASN'T A musician in the usual sense of the word. He didn't play an instrument, he couldn't sing, and he didn't write music. He was a pop pioneer in a whole new way of making music—electronically programmed sounds, tracks, and beats. He mixed machine-generated sounds with samples of existing music. He was a prototype of a new kind of producer, one that would change the way songs are made, and how they sound. By the early '90s he was making tracks exclusively on the computer, using an early version of Logic Pro, the music-production software that is native to the Mac.

Machine-made music has been a part of the pop world since the mid-'70s, with Kraftwerk's *Autobahn* (1974), a twenty-minute track created with electronic drums, a Minimoog, a Farfisa organ, and an ARP Odyssey synthesizer. Kraftwerk's predecessors in electronic music weren't musicians at all; they were avant-garde German visual artists such as Conrad Schnitzler, who were interested in "noise sounds"—steam shovels, jack hammers, trains, birdsongs—and were as far removed from pop music as you could get. (Schnitzler commented in the film *Kraftwerk and the Electronic Revolution*, "I was never liking melodies, because a melody is like a worm in your head. You hear this melody and the whole day it rattles in your head.") Their work inspired Karlheinz Stockhausen, a German composer, to create electronic compositions, such as his *Prozession* (1967) for live performance. Kraftwerk carried Stockhausen's methods into the pop realm, adding costumes and cool stage effects. They created electronic tracks that had simple, repetitive, major-chord melodies, and some of them became hits: first "Autobahn," and then "Trans-Europe Express" (1977). Live, the band presented their songs as a manifesto for the music of the future, and they really did seem revolutionary. The guys looked more like technicians than musicians, with their short hair and dress shirts and ties, standing expressionless before their song machines, fiddling with dials and pushing buttons. Their work inspired the British synth-pop bands, as well as Devo and Talking Heads in the United States. But when Kraftwerk pushed their sound further into the realm of pop, with "The Model," (1978), the hit from the album *Man Machine*, their core fans were turned off, branding them sellouts.

Donna Summer's "I Feel Love," the 1977 disco hit made by the Munich-based Italian producer Giorgio Moroder, is the other seminal work of electronic pop. The track is a complex tapestry of rhythm patterns and swooshy synth sounds, joined to a sinuous Moog-made bass line. Summer's icy vocals suit the chilly ambience of German electronic music—that synth-made landscape of urban alienation. "I Feel Love" was unloved by mainstream rock fans and pop-culture highbrows, but whereas Kraftwerk would remain a rarefied interest of the relative few, Moroder's sound was the music of the future—almost forty years later, Daft Punk's Grammy-winning album *Random Access Memories* would feature his work. And the future was on the dance floor.

By the early '80s, drum machines and controllers made it possible to create beats by drumming with your fingers on keypads, also known as beat boxes. The Roland TR-808, the first programmable drum machine, provided the reverb-drenched bass line of early hip-hop. Hip-hop producers as well as house music DJs could sample preexisting sounds from records, program their drum machines to play them, loop rhythmic sequences, and thus build up richly layered tracks. Libraries of prerecorded samples gradually became available to those who didn't want to dig through crates of old records looking for their own sounds. There were bass samples, piano samples, string samples—any instrumental or vocal sound could be sampled, and if you wanted to record the ticking of your radiator, that could be a sample too. The fact that the sounds and samples were often used without permission added outlaw glamour to the producers, many of whom were Jamaicans and African Americans living in New York City. One of the greatest of them, Afrika Bambaataa, sampled Kraftwerk (without permission) in his 1982 song "Planet Rock" combining the melody of "Trans-Europe Express" with the rhythm of Kraftwerk's song "Numbers," and those 808 beats. His Kraftwerk mashup birthed hip-hop.

Other song-making machines arrived—Roland and Prophet polyphonic synths, the Linn drum machine, Fairlight and Synclavier samplers. The "MIDI" interface between a keyboard and the computer, created in 1983, allowed producers to see the notes played on keyboards rendered graphically on a computer screen. A producer could play a little keyboard riff and then swap in any number of other sounds or instruments, cut and paste bits of music anywhere inside the composition, and change the tempo, pitch, and the timing of the beats through a technique called quantization to eliminate imperfections. Synthesizers and filters distorted sounds into unearthly warbles and trills; compressors squeezed the loud and soft sounds within a track into a dynamic midrange, making the quietest whisper as powerful as a booming drum.

Taken all together, these tools transformed the role of producers like Denniz PoP from musicians' midwives into musical masterminds. Ever since Phil Spector, Brian Wilson, and George Martin began working their studio magic in the mid-'60s, the producer's job had been growing beyond mere fidelity in recording—from creating records that reproduced the sound of the musicians playing in the studio to full creative partnership. Around the time SweMix started, producers like Denniz could do away with the musicians altogether. Everything could be made "inside the box."

When Swedish journalists interviewed the increasingly well-known Denniz PoP, they always expressed doubt about electronically made songs. Wasn't it cheating, if you didn't actually play an instrument? In a documentary that appeared on Swedish national television (STV) in 1997, Denniz told a reporter, "It's easy to say producing this music is equal to pushing a button in the studio. But that's like saying writing a novel is a simple push of a button on your typewriter." Denniz liked to say that no matter how technically adept you were at programming, sometimes you just had to "let art win."

But the reporter was still skeptical. "So tell me," she asked, "do you start with 'cool beats' from your computer?"

"Yeah first you lay down 'cool beats' and they just come out of nowhere," Denniz replied sarcastically. "No work done, of course. That's what people seem to think, they just pop out from somewhere. Then you add some 'fancy leads' and bring in a cool rap artist and a cool chick."

No matter how successful Denniz became, this critique would continue to dog him: programming music required less skill than playing it.

4 | "The Sign"

IN 1990, DENNIZ POP began to have hits as a producer of original songs, partly by employing cool rap artists and cool chicks. The first was with a Nigerian dental student in Stockholm who went by the name Dr. Alban. The dentist also worked as a DJ in the Alphabet Street club where Denniz spun records. Alban was a loquacious young man who wore his dreads in a bunch at the front of his head, a style that, together with his cocky attitude, earned him the nickname "The Rooster."

"I would talk over the records while I was playing them in the club," Alban recalls, "and Denniz liked the way my voice sounded, and so invited me over to SweMix to make a record." They cut two English-language tracks together: one was a heavily percussive number that starts with that most hated instrument from Dagge's childhood, the recorder, and, curiously, has no bass in it. It was called "Hello Afrika." The other tune, which ended up on the B side of Denniz PoP's first 12-inch as an artist, was a funky dance-hall reggae-style track called "No Coke."

Denniz's fellow DJs at SweMix hated these songs, with their obvious hooks and their craven desire to please.

"No way are we doing that shit," StoneBridge told him.

"What do you know, with your jazz chords?" Denniz shot back.

So a competitor, BeaTek, put out the Dr. Alban record, and it became a big hit across Europe. StoneBridge: "That's when we realized our mistake and let Dagge back in with us again. We still thought it was trash, but it was nice to have the money."

"Another Mother," by a Swedish singer and dancer named Kayo, combined a chill reggae backbeat with a hard hip-hop vocal style. It was another hit in Sweden, which was how two young men from Gothenburg, the industrial city to the west of the capital, came to hear it playing in a record store one day.

Ulf Ekberg and Jonas Berggren were school friends who, together with Berggren's sisters, Jenny and Malin, had a four-person techno group. They made their music in the basement of an auto-repair shop in Gothenburg. It was "a shithole studio," Ekberg recalls, but they were the masters of their basement space, which is how they settled on their name: Ace of Base. Berggren was a decent keyboard player, and Ekberg could play passable guitar, but they made most of their music with synthesizers and drum machines.

When Ekberg and Berggren heard "Another Mother," they knew right away, Ekberg says, "that this was the sound we wanted. It was a fantastic sound. We just had to meet this Denniz PoP."

They hitchhiked to Stockholm, a five-hour drive, and turned up at SweMix, hoping to persuade Denniz to produce them.

"They said, 'Denniz isn't here,'" Ekberg remembers.

"Where is he?"

"He's in the studio with a dentist," Ekberg was told. "We couldn't understand why a dentist was more interesting than we were."

So they went back to their basement in Gothenburg, made a demo tape, and sent it to SweMix, care of Denniz PoP. They attached a note: "Please listen to our tape and call us! Ace of Base."

ONE NIGHT, AS DENNIZ left SweMix, he took the demo tape with him, and popped it into the cassette deck of his Nissan Micra for the short drive across the water to his apartment in downtown Stockholm. (Although a night owl by inclination, Denniz had a young son, Daniel, with his girlfriend, and was trying to keep more regular hours.) It wasn't a luxurious car and it always needed a wash, but Denniz relied on it to test songs in; he knew that one of the keys to popular success in the United States was making songs that sounded good in the car. Later, his disciples would institutionalize this practice as "The L.A. Car Test": songs written in Stockholm are sent out to California, inserted into a car stereo, and driven up and down the Pacific Coast Highway to make sure they sound right.

The first track was called "Mr. Ace." It began with a reggae back-beat played on a pianolike synth. After four bars, a crude dance rhythm enters the mix: it sounds like someone is dropping a box of apples on the floor, in 4/4 time. Somewhere inside the demo were great hooks, but the songwriters hadn't properly placed them. The track trailed off with some whistling, which was perhaps the catchiest part of the whole mess.

Even before he was home, Denniz had decided he had no interest in producing the group. However, when he tried to remove the tape, it wouldn't come out of the Micra's dashboard. It was stuck, and no amount of mashing the Eject button would dislodge it.

The next morning, when Denniz arrived at the apartment of his co-producer, Douglas Carr, to give him a lift to SweMix, "Mr. Ace" was playing.

Carr recalls, "We were joking in the car, laughing at the quality of the demo." However, because Denniz's car radio also happened to be broken—typical Denniz—"we couldn't listen to anything else except for that demo." Every morning when Denniz picked Carr up, "Mr. Ace" would be playing, and they'd listen to it on the way to work. This went on for two weeks or so, until one day Denniz heard something in the song. He saw a way to marry the melody to the beat by breaking everything down into basic elements and then layering it all together.

The next morning, after Carr had climbed into the car and heard the now annoyingly familiar tune, Denniz turned to him excitedly and said, "I think I'm going to produce this!"

Pop music would never be the same.

ANYONE WHO ASPIRES TO make pop music in Sweden stands in the shadow of ABBA, the '70s foursome who broke through with their song "Waterloo," the winner of the Eurovision Song Contest in 1974. ABBA took the flowing melodic element in Swedish folk songs and hymns (even the national anthem, "Thou Ancient, Thou Free," sounds a bit like a pop song) and added elements of Schlager music, the Polka-based European popular music from the '50s and '60s, most often heard in German. Listening to Schlager gives you some notion of what American pop music might sound like without the African influence—in a word, cheesy. Benny Andersson and Björn Ulvaeus, ABBA's songwriters, kept the Schlager influence at arm's length, but you can hear it clearly in, say, the wheezy organ sound in "Take a Chance on Me." An air of melancholy pervades the superficially happy-sounding ABBA songs, another uniquely Swedish quality that would cast a long shadow over the future of pop music. Their happy songs sound sad, and their sad songs that sound happy. They appeal to listeners in a broad variety of moods.

ABBA set a high bar when it comes to excellence in the studio. Virtually every moment in an ABBA song is exquisitely crafted, packed with studio-made ear candy—harmonies, countermelodies, and a variety of synthetic sounds—all of which became standard in pop music thirty years later. It's hard to believe that songs so pleasing could be revolutionary, but then again a band that was deemed revolutionary, the Sex Pistols, acknowledged their debt to ABBA. In the 2013 BBC documentary *The Joy of ABBA*, Glen Matlock admits borrowing the hook in "Pretty Vacant" from "S.O.S."

ABBA showed that teen pop could be about adult subjects. Both "When All Is Said and Done" and "The Winner Takes It All" are about

Björn and Agnetha's and Benny and Anni-Frid's respective divorces, and there they are in the videos, singing about their mutual pain together onstage. That's not something you saw every day in the pop world.

In addition to ABBA's influence, contemporary Swedish songwriters speak of growing up with the music that accompanied the popular Pippi Longstocking TV series that ran on Swedish TV in the late '60s and early '70s, and was later dubbed (badly) into English. In particular the theme song, "Here Comes Pippi Longstocking," written by Jan Johansson, and also the jazz musician Georg Riedel's contributions to the series, have a sweet-sad sort of innocence about them that would later inform many a Swedish-made Billboard hit.

Klas Åhlund, a Swedish songwriter and producer in his forties, who is also a performer (in the rock band Teddybears), says: "Swedes are very musical, and they love to write songs. But it's a big country, and it has very few people in it. So you had these farmers out there who were good at writing songs, but had no one to sing them. Songwriting was just a thing you did on your own when you were watching the cows, a kind of meditation. You didn't focus as much on your ability as a performer as you did on the structure and craft of the songs. Which is really not the case in the US, where your charm and your voice and your powers as a performer come immediately into play."

A nation of songwriters endowed with melodic gifts, and who were meticulous about craft, but who were reluctant to perform their own songs, was a potential gold mine for a nation of wannabe pop stars who don't write their own material. And Denniz PoP would hook them up.

IT WAS NOT UNTIL July of 1992, after Ace of Base had a minor hit with "Wheel of Fortune," that Ekberg and Berggren worked up enough nerve to call Denniz PoP and ask him what he thought of their demo.

The producer was pleased to hear from them. "I've been waiting for you guys to call!" he declared. "I really want to work with you guys, and

I have time in August." A month later they were in Stockholm to record "Mr. Ace," which now had a new title: "All That She Wants."

Denniz had fixed his tape player by then, and he got the songwriters to ride around Stockholm with him, listening to an instrumental version of the song, over and over again. He had moved the whistled melody, which had been at the end of the demo, to the front of the song. It is followed by a kick drum, which gives the track guts, and a softly bubbling bass. Major chords carry the verses, but with the chorus, the chords turn minor—a Swedish touch.

"Jonas and I are good at melodies, but there were too many things happening on the track," Ekberg recalls. "Denniz was very good at erasing things, and making the sound picture cleaner, and simplified. I think he took away maybe fifty percent of our instrumentation." As Denniz once said, in response to a question about how hard could it possibly be to write such simple songs, "it's much more difficult to make it simple, especially achieving a simplicity without having it sound incredibly trivial."

Lundin says, "Denniz was an arrangement genius." He adds, "like Steve Jobs, he knew what to take out. 'You can get rid of that, that. Keep it simple.'" As Denniz put it, "A great pop song should be interesting, in some way. That means that certain people will hate it immediately and certain people will love it, but only as long as it isn't boring and meaningless. Then it's not a pop song any longer; then it's something else. It's just music."

Ekberg recalls, "He always said, 'I don't care how we do it, as long as it sounds good.' He didn't know how to write songs, but he knew what worked." Martin Dodd, who was head of A&R at Mega Records, says, "Denniz had a childlike wonder about him, and was a very social being, which reflected strongly in the music, where nothing was ever allowed to be "nice" or boring; absolutely every note, word, and beat had to have purpose or be fun." Always, Denniz's point of reference was not what made sense compositionally but what sounded good on the dance floor. "He was a DJ in the evenings," Ekberg says. "So he always took the sounds, played them on the floor, and checked what worked."

Lyrically, "All That She Wants" strains sense. It's written in English, but it lacks a colloquial touch. The vocal hook, which comes in the first line of the chorus—"All that she wants is another baby"—sounds at first as if the woman wants another child, an odd desire to hear in a pop song. Of course, "baby" means "boyfriend," but the usage is slightly off. The first verse sounds vaguely as if it has been translated from another language:

> It's not a day for work
> It's a day for catching tan

"Catching tan"? One's inner copyeditor cringes.

Though it's rare to have a pop hit without lyrics, the lyrics don't need to mean anything much; the disco era had shown that. Lyrics that command too much attention are likely to kill the dancing. And Dylan not withstanding, song lyrics don't need to be poetry; they need only to tell you what you are supposed to feel when you hear the music they accompany. But whereas disco lyrics, such as "More, More, More" (1976) by Andrea True Connection, were written only to enhance the beat and the sexy ambience of the song, Denniz had something more sophisticated in mind. In addition to working rhythmically, the sound of the words had to fit with the melody, an approach to songwriting that Denniz's great protégé, Max Martin, would later call "melodic math."

Grammar and usage didn't matter much to Denniz, and wit and metaphor, Brill Building staples, aren't even in the picture. "I think it was to our advantage that English was not our mother language," Ekberg says, "because we are able to treat English very respectless, and just look for the word that sounded good with the melody." Freed from making sense, the lyricists' horizons are boundless.

Denniz asked for a second verse, and Ekberg and Berggren supplied one.

"And then Jenny and Malin came up to Stockholm and put the vocals on," Ekberg goes on, "in about a half day of takes."

"All That She Wants" was released on Mega Records in Denmark in the fall of 1992. The record went to number one on the Danish charts. Kjeld Wennick, who was the head of Mega, wanted the album, *Happy Nation*, in stores by Christmas, so the band rushed to complete and mix their remaining demos. In early 1993, "All That She Wants" made charts around Europe, and spent three weeks at the top of the UK charts in May. But when Wennick tried to interest US labels in an American distribution deal for *Happy Nation*, he got a resounding "No!" from everyone. "'No, no, no, no,'" he recalled. The reason was always the same: "This band will never work in the States.'"

Certainly, it was not a propitious time to break a foreign synth-pop band in the United States—when is? Grunge dominated the radio. Popular song themes included alienation, suicide, and despair, accompanied by searing guitar solos, crashing drums, and burnt-out sounding vocals. In videos bare lightbulbs illuminate foul-looking basements, while the singer moans amid the debris. Electronics were certainly used to enhance these records—Nirvana's *Nevermind* wouldn't have been the sonic masterpiece it is without digital compression—but Butch Vig's production magic is well hidden behind the real instruments.

On the urban side, a new generation of R&B stars like Whitney Houston and Boyz II Men were making huge hits, and, although it wasn't played on the radio very much, hip-hop was going mainstream. Ace of Base, in offering mindless fun and the pleasures of "catching tan," set to an electronically produced ragga-lite dance track, seemed like the absolute worst possible sound for the times.

After making the rounds of most of the US labels, "All That She Wants" reached the celebrated ears of Clive Davis, then the head of Arista Records. Although he likes to remind people of his rock credentials—his first signing was Janis Joplin, after seeing her perform at the Monterey Pop Festival—Davis's greatest contribution to the record business has been in identifying R&B singers who can fit into the pure pop mainstream. Whitney Houston and, later, Alicia Keys are among his signings. He is on surer ground with female artists, but he also signed Barry Manilow. He has an international palette, and, for better or worse, he brought the Australian duo Air Supply Stateside, which gave the world "All Out of Love," and "Making Love Out of Nothing at All."

Davis comes from a time when A&R really did involve both artists and repertoire—discovering and developing artists *and* choosing the songs for them to sing, because in the pre-rock era it was not expected that the singers would write their own material. Although this approach to A&Ring a record went out of fashion in the singer-songwriter era, it became more important as the era waned, and it would serve Davis especially well in his work with *American Idol*.

Davis happened to be vacationing on a yacht in Europe when he listened to "All That She Wants." He prides himself on knowing a hit as soon as he hears one, and he was so sure of "All That She Wants" that he directed the ship's captain to make haste for the nearest port, so that he could call Kjeld Wennick and make a deal. On reaching his Danish colleague, Davis declared, "Kjeld, I want this band!"

Upon returning from his vacation, Davis flew the band to New York and had them brought straight from the airport via limo to his offices atop the BMG Building in Manhattan. Before meeting the great man, the Swedes watched a forty-minute film about Davis's storied career in the music business. ("You really don't do that in Sweden," Ekberg observes drily.) Finally, they were ushered into Davis's palatial office, lined with photographs of the musical superstars whose careers the record man had shaped.

Davis told the awed Swedes that he wanted to release their album in the United States but that it needed at least two more potential hits on it. He suggested recording a cover; the band objected, but eventually agreed to record "Don't Turn Around," an Albert Hammond and Diane Warren song, which became the album's second single. Still Davis wasn't satisfied. Wasn't there something else? Berggren said he had been working on a new song, but it was for the band's next album. Davis insisted on hearing it, and on a subsequent visit Berggren played it for Davis in his office. It was called "The Sign."

IN 1992, DENNIZ POP quit SweMix. His move to pop, although it enriched the collective, was never accepted by the other DJs. It was *dum*—crass. "Finally, Denniz couldn't take our shit anymore," Stone-Bridge says, "and he said to Tom, 'I want out.'" Tom Talomaa saw Denniz was making all the money anyway, so he sold SweMix to BMG. "We all got twenty thousand crowns, which we thought was a bloody fortune, but in fact the Alban publishing was worth a million at least." With BMG's backing, Talomaa and Denniz built a new studio on Fridhemsplan. Denniz named it Cheiron, after the wise centaur in Greek mythology who teaches Dionysius how to sing and dance.

The studio was inside a white-brick building with a large metal gate in front. (Later, when Cheiron Studios became famous, the white bricks filled up with messages written by fans to the artists who made records there.) Denniz's large oak desk was on the ground floor, under a very high ceiling that went up to the roof. On the mezzanine was Talomaa's office. Next to Denniz's desk hung several paintings of anime-like characters brandishing big swords—prototypes for a computer game he would not get to build, "The Cheiron Adventures." A pair of six-foot movie-prop totem poles stood on either side of the desk—a Polynesian touch.

Down belowground were the heavily soundproofed recording studios—studios A, B, and C—which were all connected to the same vocal booth, in an ingenious design. Denniz had commissioned Snake to build a pair of speakers capable of blasting out the massive low-end sounds he required to test his beats. They were the "Snake speakers."

Cheiron was initially conceived as a record label and a studio. "We were going to go out and find new artists and distribute a bunch of stuff," Denniz said, including rock music, which he hated but Talomaa liked. One of the label's first signings was a local hard-rock band called It's Alive, fronted by a glam-rock singer who called himself Martin White, a move that would have huge consequences for Cheiron, and the future of pop music, but not in a way anyone could have guessed.

The label side of the operation quickly foundered. "I guess you could say that wasn't our thing," Denniz recalled. "To be a record company when you're small is incredibly expensive. . . . We realized that we should only work with the stuff we know how to do, and that's making and producing the songs."

Clive Davis gave "The Sign" to Denniz, hoping for the same magic the producer brought to "All That She Wants." Douglas Carr, again Denniz's co-producer on the track, recalls, "The demo we got was very basic; it sounded like one of those preprogrammed tracks on a cheap family keyboard where you press a button and the band starts playing." Unlike "All That She Wants," Denniz knew from the beginning what he wanted to do with "The Sign." "Denniz's skills for making and mixing fat beats is here in full blast," Carr goes on. "He knew what the dance floor needed, and we had the speakers and the volume to know what was going to happen in the clubs."

The track starts out with four bars of a dance beat made with a kick drum, hand clap, and snare, struck so closely together that the ear hears them as one sound; this would become Cheiron's sonic signature. The sound incorporates fragments of a sample from "Shack Up," a song by Banbarra, a US funk group from the '70s. A synthetic log drum plays on the off beats, making a woody, *thwoka thwoka* sound. Mixed in with the electronically made music is a track of Carr playing timbales and cymbals, to lighten the robotic feel. Then comes the first melodic hook, a wheedling synth flute made with an EMU vintage module that is out of phase—a mistake that sounded cool so they left it. Underneath the flute is the bass, which is actually two sounds mixed together: a Moog sub-bass and a Korg M1 bass on top. "The bass took some figuring out," Carr says. "I remember us talking a lot about the space that the reggae bass players always make in their music, and how important that is—that sense of air."

Then the singing starts. A reggae rhythm guitar sound made on a Yamaha TG77 synthesizer plays a Nile Rodgers guitar riff. A dry tap of a snare, and then comes the hook:

> *I saw the sign*
> *And it opened up my eyes*
> *I saw the sign*

with a chilly silvery sound in the vocal. At the bridge, voices go up an octave, and the soaring, joyous Europop sound lets the ecstasy in. The song is a three-minute, thirty-second sonic thrill ride of Swedish funk.

Carr: "I remember Denniz one night standing in the doorway, about to leave after a long day and night's work. And he asked me, 'So what do you think?' Meaning, 'Do you think it's a hit?' without saying it out loud. And I looked at him, and after a moment I nodded. And we both knew what that meant."

"All That She Wants," released as a single in the United States in September 1993, was a huge hit, although it only got as high as number two on the Billboard Hot 100 (it couldn't dislodge "Dreamlover" by Mariah Carey). But "The Sign," released in the United States in December 1993, was a historic smash. It spent six weeks at number one and was the top-selling single of the year. Remarkable in light of the fact that the band had virtually no following in the States, had never toured, and made music that was far from the reigning grunge sound. The album, which was also called *The Sign*, sold over 23 million copies, making it one of the bestselling debut albums of all time, and earning Arista $42 million.

. . .

THAT TRIUMPH WAS SHORT-LIVED. The band's next album, *The Bridge*, sold far fewer copies than *The Sign*. The Denniz PoP track, "Beautiful Life," was the most successful single on the album, peaking at number fifteen on the Hot 100. Worse still, Ulf Ekberg turned out to have belonged to a neo-Nazi party in his younger days, and although he apologized when the facts came to light, suddenly Ulf wasn't exactly the stuff of *Tiger Beat*. Also, Malin, one of the two Berggren sisters, disliked flying, and the band's 179 flights in 1995 disenchanted her of touring. On top of all that, a crazy fan with a knife broke into the Berggren family's home in Stockholm. Still, the group managed to put out a third album, the Motown-inspired *Flowers*. When that stiffed, they were more or less finished. As quickly as Ace of Base had risen to the top of the charts, they disappeared.

If Cheiron was going to be a legitimate hit factory, the studio needed an American act—a solo artist or a group who could carry its electronic pop sound deep into the bars, malls, and sports arenas of America. Not accidental stars with baggage, but lifers who would do whatever it takes to get to the top and stay there.

An urban act would be cooler. But what black American star was going to record music written by Swedes? The gold standard in songwriting for early '90s urban acts was Babyface, the writer-producer behind Boyz II Men. Or, there was Teddy Riley, the creator of the New Jack Swing sound, a fusion of R&B and hip-hop that got Bobby Brown to number one in 1988 with "My Prerogative."

But who needed Sweden? The answer lay not in the usual spots—L.A., New York, Miami, Atlanta—but among the theme parks, water slides, and thirty-six-hole golf courses of Orlando, Florida.

5 | Big Poppa

IN THE EARLY '90S, Orlando was home to a fleshy, cherubic entrepreneur, a jovial rainmaker named Louis Jay Pearlman. An only child, Lou was born into humble circumstances in Flushing, Queens. His father owned a dry cleaner, and his mother was an aide in a school lunchroom. The family lived next to Flushing Airport (which closed in 1984), engendering in the boy a lifelong interest in aviation. In particular, the dirigibles that took off and landed at the blimp port fascinated him, and he dreamed of building one of his own.

But his first passion was music. Pearlman's cousin, the son of his father's sister, was Art Garfunkel, of Simon and Garfunkel fame. Lou remembered Cousin Artie singing in Yiddish at the extended family's Passover seders. He was thrilled when his famous cousin, thirteen years older, attended his bar mitzvah in 1967. Lou took guitar lessons, saved up for a Fender, and started a band, which he called Flyer. It played around the city, but Lou, short and roly-poly, wasn't made for the stage, and eventually he set his dreams of stardom aside.

After enrolling in Queens College, Pearlman put together a business plan for a helicopter taxi business in Manhattan. Then, still in his early twenties, he launched Airships International, and approached the Jordache brothers, founders of the jeans empire, about advertising on the side of one of his blimps. In fact, Pearlman had no blimps, but upon securing Jordache as a client, he used their money to build one, and, to make certain that it stood out, he had the entire hull painted in gold leaf.

On October 8, 1980, the blimp took off from Lakehurst, New Jersey, with as much media fanfare as Pearlman could muster (which wasn't much), bound for Battery Park City in Manhattan. But the gold paint weighed the dirigible down; it traveled only a few hundred yards before crashing into some pine trees, near a garbage dump. *That* got the media's attention. It was not exactly the exposure the Jordaches had been looking for; however, as Pearlman wrote in his 2003 how-to-be-a-millionaire memoir, *Bands, Brands, and Billions*, "As I told the Jordache brothers, their name was all over the news that night."

By the early '90s Pearlman had leveraged his blimp business into a luxury airplane charter enterprise, which he grandly christened Trans Continental Airlines. Among his clients were rock and pop acts, which Lou liked because it connected him to his first love, music. One of the acts that chartered a Trans Con plane was a boy band called New Kids on the Block. Pearlman had never heard of them, and he was surprised that the group had the means to afford the $250,000 monthly charter fee. On asking around, he learned that a Boston-based producer who called himself Maurice Starr (his real name was Larry Johnson) had created the group.

Starr had discovered the R&B group New Edition, which was fronted by Bobby Brown, at a talent show in 1982, and signed them to his Streetwise Records label. Their first album, *Candy Girl*, was a major hit, and New Edition became the pivotal act in the transition from traditional R&B vocal groups to modern-day, MTV-friendly boy bands. But New Edition and Starr fell out over money (the guys' final take after all the expenses were deducted reportedly worked out to $1.87 each in royalties) and parted company in 1984.

That year, Starr created a Caucasian version of New Edition, which was New Kids on the Block. Whereas New Edition had been a singing ensemble before Starr discovered them—they had come together on their own, in the tradition of street-corner doo-wop groups—New Kids was invented from scratch by Starr and his business partner, Mary Alford, which gave them much more control. (Three of the five knew each other from Dorchester, Massachusetts, but they had never sung together.) They auditioned boys from around Boston, and eventually assembled a quintet that was fronted by Donnie Wahlberg (his brother Mark, soon to be known as Marky Mark, was briefly a member but dropped out). Success came slowly, but thanks to MTV, which magnified the appeal of five good-looking young guys in ways that their sound alone, which was bubblegum pop, could not, they eventually broke through and had a number-one hit with "I'll Be Loving You (Forever)" in 1989, the year Pearlman met them. Their popularity peaked in the early '90s with their triple-platinum album *Step by Step*. (They performed in the Super Bowl half-time show in 1991, the first pop group to do so.)

Through the New Kids' manager, Dick Scott, Pearlman arranged to see a show. He remembers it vividly fifteen years later, in straitened circumstances—while serving a twenty-five-year prison sentence for fraud in the Texarkana Federal Correctional Institution. "I was blown away by the concert," Pearlman says over the phone from the warden's office. "Seeing all these mothers dropping the little kids off at the show, it was just such a nice market—a win-win. The kids were going crazy, loving it, and parents were liking it because it was clean, wholesome family fun."

Pearlman did some research. He discovered that in 1990 the New Kids raked in $800 million in merchandise sales, to go along with $200 million in ticket sales. They were the highest-paid entertainers in the United States in 1991—the boys made more than Michael Jackson and Madonna. In malls, Pearlman "watched the kids snatching up New Kids posters, book bags, jackets, T-shirts, lunch boxes, magazines, diaries, journals, tapes, and CDs." He quizzed Dick Scott and Maurice Starr on the New Kids' business model. "They told me exactly how it worked, the marketing of it. Our target market was always going to be young teenage girls, because boys are into sports, and they like buying jerseys and caps and so on, for baseball or football, things of that nature, whereas the girls are totally enthralled with the band. . . . They don't have money, but they have access to a large supply of it: their aunts, uncles, grandmas, grandpas, who would spend money on them for a concert or merchandise sooner than they would spend it on themselves."

When Pearlman took some friends to a New Kids concert at the Nassau Coliseum in Long Island, they thought he had lost his mind. However, "While they were talking about calling the guys in the white coats," he writes, "I was studying the responses of ten thousand teenage girls who screamed at every raised eyebrow and every waggled hip. The New Kids weren't the greatest singers, but they were slickly packaged. They sold their songs well." Pearlman also analyzed the composition of the group. He noted that in addition to the five voices—bass, baritone, second tenor, first tenor, and lead—there was a significant demographic component to the range of ages, which gave the New Kids an appeal to both tweens and teens, as well as a mix of personality types. There was a bad boy to appeal to the demographic Pearlman called the "Cutting Edgers," a normal-looking one for the "Mainstreamers," a jock for the "In-Crowders," a poetic type for the "Individualists," (and a hunk for the moms who brought their daughters to the shows).

Once, when Lou was at a party at Cousin Artie's sensational apartment overlooking Central Park, he brought up the subject of the New Kids with the singer. Garfunkel knew all about the group: they were on his record label, Columbia. The word on the street about the New Kids, Artie confided to his cousin, was that not all of them could actually sing. Maurice Starr himself sang on a lot of their records, it was said. In 1992, Gregory McPherson, a director-producer who worked on the *Hangin' Tough* album, claimed that the group merely lip-synced to prerecorded vocal tracks by real singers during their shows. The group hotly contested this accusation, and sang a cappella on the *Arsenio Hall Show* to disprove it. But although McPherson later withdrew the charge, the public remained skeptical. The scandal that had erupted over Milli Vanilli's faking of their vocals two years earlier, which cost the duo (another of Clive Davis's signings) their Grammy Award, was still fresh in people's minds. A New Kids backlash set in, and, with popular taste shifting toward harder-edged, more "authentic" music—grunge and gangsta— the group disbanded in 1994.

Pearlman wondered what an urban-sounding group of five white boys who really could sing might do in the marketplace. Orlando, where he had relocated his blimp business by 1991, offered a ready supply of talent for a would-be boy-band Svengali. The city's theme parks were a magnet for young entertainers of all kinds—stuntmen who impersonated Teenage Mutant Ninja Turtles, performers who dressed as spooks in the *Beetlejuice Graveyard Revue*, actors who played Disney creations in character parades, and the lucky few, such as Justin Timberlake, Christina Aguilera, and Britney Spears, who were chosen for the Disney Channel's *Mickey Mouse Club* show. No other city in the world is more dependent on popular culture than Orlando, and while it wasn't hard to find kids in any town who had mainlined pop culture by growing up in front of MTV, only Orlando offered a lot of young people whose job was to bring pop culture characters to life. In addition, Orlando was blessed with a ready supply of talent scouts, vocal and dance coaches, and experienced star makers who could help a neophyte like Pearlman assemble and train a pop group.

After many months of study, Pearlman decided he was ready to make his move. In 1992, he placed an ad in the *Orlando Sentinel*.

PRODUCER SEEKS MALE SINGERS THAT MOVE WELL, BETWEEN 16–19 YEARS OF AGE. WANTED FOR NEW KIDS-TYPE SINGING/ DANCE GROUP. SEND PHOTO OR BIO OF ANY KIND.

Together with several local talent scouts, who included Gloria Sicoli and Jeanne Tanzy, Pearlman began auditioning candidates at his home. They saw about forty guys, but no one they liked. Sicoli had access to the Orlando Civic Theater's archives, and she pored over résumés and head shots of kids who had auditioned for parts there. She found about a dozen possible candidates, and another round of auditions was held in August. This time they found two keepers: A. J. McLean, and Howie Dorough, who would one day be known to the world simply as AJ and Howie D.

Pearlman placed another ad, which produced more than a hundred callbacks, leading to a third round of auditions in the warehouse in Kissimmee where he kept his blimps (there was no air conditioning, but Lou thoughtfully kept the blimps' props running to help cool the place). That netted three more guys, including Nick Carter, the baby of the bunch, at age twelve. But one of the remaining two dropped out and the other wasn't really good enough. Eventually one of Pearlman's employees at Trans Con suggested Kevin Richardson, and Richardson suggested his cousin, Brian Littrell.

"See, you had five different personalities," Pearlman explains, "and so five different types of fans, all in one group. It makes a real phenomenon." He goes on, "You needed a younger anchor, as Joey McIntyre was to New Kids and Nick Carter was to [us]. Then you needed an edge on it. Donny Wahlberg was a little edgy, so we got AJ to be edgy. And I thought it would be nice to add a little Latino spice, because Menudo was out there too, so Howie D added that, then Kevin was the big brother, and Brian had the sweet melodies."

And with that Lou had his group, which he named the Backstreet Boys.

MALE VOCAL GROUPS HAVE been singing together in religious settings for thousands of years. In a secular context, college a-cappella groups and barber-shop quartets were well known in the 1920s and '30s, and white male vocal groups, such as the Gotham City Four, made early Tin Pan Alley standards popular. Black male vocal groups also have

deep roots, especially in gospel settings. But lacking the secular insti-
tutional opportunities available to white singers, they were more of a
street-corner phenomenon when removed from church. The first black
harmony groups to achieve nationwide recognition were the Ink Spots
and the Mills Brothers, whose peak years were in the 1940s. Their Tin
Pan Alley ballads, originally made popular by white singers, gave them
enormous crossover appeal.

Some younger singers, coming of age in the '40s, thought the Ink
Spots' sound wasn't "black" enough, and these vocal harmony groups—
the Ravens, the Orioles, the Clovers—began to mix blues and bebop
songs with the Tin Pan Alley standards in their repertoires. They also
began to incorporate dance steps into their routines, and franker sexual content (or at least more suggestive metaphors) into their lyrics.
In the late 1940s, the record industry began to promote these groups
under the label "rhythm-and-blues," a term invented by a white *Billboard*
writer, Jerry Wexler—later a partner in Atlantic Records—to replace the
derogatory trade name "race music." (He later regretted he hadn't called
the music "R&G," for rhythm and gospel, instead; such R&B staples as
falsetto singing and hand claps derived from gospel music.) R&B was, as
Stuart Goosman points out in his 2005 book *Group Harmony*, a marketing term that became a badge of black musical identity. By definition, a
black group would always be labeled R&B even if they sang pop.

In the '50s, acts such as the Imperials and the Twilighters achieved
prominence as so-called doo-wop groups. The optimism of the decade
was embodied in the soaring quality of their harmony singing. In the
late '50s and early '60s came the Drifters, the Four Tops, the Temptations, and, a bit later, the Jackson 5, who, along with girl groups like
the Marvelettes and the Supremes, achieved crossover pop success on
Berry Gordy's Motown label. By the end of the '60s, the classic era of
vocal harmony was on the wane, but with the rise of "oldies" stations
on the radio, harmony groups were preserved in the amber of nostalgia,
the sound of sweeter, simpler times (which came to sound progressively

sweeter still as rap ensembles took up the banner of group singing in the '80s).

By the time New Edition achieved fame, in the mid-'80s, R&B harmony groups had been dormant, as an innovative musical form, for more than a decade. Bobby Brown and his band members reinvented the genre for the MTV generation, giving birth to the modern boy band in the process, by adding slicker choreography, a hipper fashion sense, and more pop-oriented melodies; the gospel that Jerry Wexler had savored in the music was all but gone from New Edition's sound. New Kids took over where New Edition left off, achieving even greater chart success, and then came Boyz II Men. Sonically and visually, the stage was set for the Backstreet Boys. All they needed was a record deal, some hit songs, and luck.

PEARLMAN—"BIG POPPA," as he instructed the boys to call him—bought the group clothes and jewelry, feted them at fancy restaurants, and chauffeured them around in his cornflower-blue Rolls Royce Phantom (and, later, his Gulfstream II jet), neglecting to mention his expenses would all be recouped from their later earnings. He was physically affectionate with them, roughhousing and head patting, and exhorting the guys at every turn, "You're going to be huge, huge I tell you." A later member of one of Lou's groups, the late Richard Cronin (he died of leukemia), accused Pearlman of impropriety, but those allegations were challenged by other of Lou's recruits, and Pearlman, for his part, has always steadfastly denied them. "None of that stuff is true," he says from prison, adding, "When you're down, people kick you because you're down."

Pearlman brought in Johnny Wright, who had been the New Kids' tour manager, to help manage Backstreet, together with his wife, Donna. After four months of vocal and dance training, the group made their debut at SeaWorld, Orlando's famed aquarium, in May 1993. Their opening number was a R&B classic, the Temptations' "Get Ready." The stage floor, in Shamu Stadium, was wet from the eponymous killer whale who lived beside it (in Shamu's Happy Harbor), and the guys had to take care when dancing that they didn't slide into Shamu's tank.

Pearlman sent around a video of the SeaWorld gig to various labels; none showed interest. He had the group record a demo of a song of his (Lou wanted in on the publishing, too), "Tell Me I'm Dreaming," but that got no takers either. In Orlando, they opened for visiting acts, including Brandy and En Vogue. They performed at festivals, theme parks, and any other venue that would have them. In the fall of 1993, the group did a national tour of high schools, and every performance featured at least one a-cappella performance, to prove the boys really could sing (they did the same thing when they visited radio stations). One night toward the end of '93, when the group was playing a show in Cleveland, a friend of Donna Wright's, who went by the name Azra, called a guy she knew at Mercury Records, Bobby Duckett, and held up the phone to record the performance, and the fans' reaction to it. Duckett wasn't home at the time, but the call was recorded on his answering machine, and he liked what he heard well enough to tell Mercury's A&R manager, David McPherson, about the group. McPherson was intrigued by their sound, and also by the fact that the guy who put them together was a multimillionaire who seemed willing to pay for substantial upfront marketing out of his own pocket. Pearlman, on hearing of Mercury's interest, offered to fly the two men first-class down to Hickory, North Carolina, to meet the group.

"At the airport we were met by Donna Wright and Azra," McPherson recalls, "and we were driven to a Holiday Inn in Hickory and brought into a banquet room, where there was a performance scenario set up— mikes, sound and video equipment . . . Donna and Azra introduced us to Lou, and we saw the Backstreet Boys perform. The first thing in my mind was, this is a group like New Kids. But the knock on New Kids at the time was that they couldn't really sing, and these guys *could* sing.

They sang a cappella, and they also performed to track. They were very developed for a group that didn't have a record deal—they had clothes, choreography, and songs. I was excited. . . . I thought, This could work."

The next day, Duckett and McPherson were brought by bus to nearby Bunker Hill High School, to watch the boys perform. "I was surprised by how well they were received," McPherson goes on, "because this was at a time when grunge rock was popular, and that New Kids stuff just wasn't cool. . . . But I saw the performance, and saw the reaction, especially from the female population, and I was like, These guys definitely have something."

On returning to Mercury, McPherson recommended signing the group, and the label did. However, because there were minors in the band, Mercury had to go through a lengthy court-approval process before money could be made available for recording.

"I don't want to wait for that; I'll just pay for the recording," Pearlman said.

"That could get pretty expensive," McPherson pointed out.

"How expensive?" Pearlman asked.

"A million, maybe more?"

"That's nothing!" Big Poppa exclaimed.

Several months of recording took place at the end of 1994, stretching into early 1995. As the demos came in, McPherson played them for his colleagues at Mercury. They were not impressed. "There was concern that something like this wasn't going to work in the US," McPherson said. "That it would get laughed at, because it was too corny. So they decided not to move forward with the group."

McPherson conveyed the bad news to Pearlman, who was naturally disappointed. However, as it happened, McPherson was being courted by another label, Jive Records, which was headed by a brilliant South African music entrepreneur named Clive Calder. Calder had been talking to McPherson for several months, asking him about the acts he was working with, and of all the artists on McPherson's plate, the Backstreet Boys seemed to interest Calder the most. That struck McPherson as odd, because Jive was known as a rap label. "I couldn't believe this guy would be interested in the Backstreet Boys," McPherson says. "But Clive said, 'Man, if I could have a group like that, it would be huge. Because even if America wasn't into a group like that right away, Europe is into boy bands right now, and that would help me with some business endeavors I have over there.'"

So, when Mercury dropped Backstreet, McPherson called Calder. "I told him, 'They don't want the Backstreet Boys, do you?' And he was like, 'Yeah, and I want you to come work for me over here too.'" Mercury released the group from their contract. Jive paid Pearlman the $35,000 he had already incurred in recording costs, and the Boys were back in business.

6 | Martin Sandberg's Terrible Secret

JIVE WAS THE label side of a music publishing company called Zomba, founded by Calder in London, in the early '70s. Calder—who is and for the foreseeable future will be the single richest man the music business ever produced—started out as a bass player in several Motown cover bands in South Africa, in the 1960s. Under apartheid, whites could only listen to music made by whites, and blacks were restricted to black music, but American R&B was the exception. In an interview with *Music Business International*, Calder recalled how, as a long-haired white teenager, he performed Motown songs nightly with various groups (one band was called In Crowd, another Calder's Collection), and did session work during the day, using the money to support his mother and sister, after his father died. In 1969, he got an A&R job at EMI South Africa, and eighteen months later started his own record label, Clive Calder Productions (CCP).

Calder modeled CCP on Motown; indeed, Motown would become a touchstone for Calder in all his future endeavors. Like Berry Gordy, Calder insisted on controlling every aspect of the process of making a record: the artists, the songwriters, the producers, the production facilities, the session musicians—even the instrument rentals. Also like Gordy, he was involved with every step of the process, from deciding what key a song should be played in to mixing the record to making deals with manufacturers and distributors to putting together set lists for live shows.

In his early twenties, Calder and a white Rhodesian session musician named Robert John "Mutt" Lange began making versions of US and UK hits, and putting them out on CCP before the originals could arrive in South Africa. Lange made the music and sang on the tracks (his wife at the time sang the songs performed by female artists), while Calder oversaw A&R and production. This experience—taking hit songs apart, figuring out how they worked, and putting them back together again— gave both men a keen appreciation for what went into making a hit, knowledge that served them both very well later on. Lange became a hit maker for artists ranging from AC/DC to the Cars to Shania Twain, whom he married.

In 1974, accompanied by Lange and his business partner, Ralph Simon, Calder moved to London, where he eventually became a British citizen. After a brief spell as a manager, he and Simon started Zomba in 1977. Their business plan was unusual. Initially Calder wasn't interested in making records, which was where the big money was at the time. He was interested in owning the publishing rights to songs, where the money would be thirty years later.

The people Calder signed to Zomba weren't artists but producers and songwriters, the most successful of whom was Mutt Lange himself. Calder opened a Zomba office in New York in the late '70s, where he formed a partnership with Clive Davis, supplying songs for Arista artists.

Calder also started a label, Jive Records, in London in 1981. The label established itself with New Wave rock bands, notably A Flock of Seagulls. Calder also signed Billy Ocean, the British R&B artist, with whom Jive had a major international hit in 1984 with the now classic "Caribbean Queen (No More Love on the Run)," as well as the dance-pop singer Samantha Fox (a former "Page 3 girl," known for taking her top off in the Rupert Murdoch–owned tabloid, *The Sun*). Calder's years in London had bred a streak of Europop into his R&B sensibility.

Jive also opened its New York office in 1981, relying on Arista for distribution. To run its US operation, Calder hired Barry Weiss, a young Cornell graduate whose father, Hy Weiss, had been the owner of Old Town Records, an independent label that put out R&B hits in the 1950s. For his job interview, Calder asked Weiss to take him on a tour of clubs around New York City, and Weiss arranged a night-long odyssey, hitting hot spots in the burgeoning rap scene, including Better Days on Forty-Eighth Street, where they spent time with DJ Tee Scott, and Mystique on First Avenue, before finishing in the early morning hours at Paradise Garage on King Street, where DJ Larry Levan was in the process of reinventing disco as house music. By morning, Weiss had a job and Calder had a new direction for his US operation: hip-hop.

In the '80s Jive became the home of classic rap artists such as Schoolly D, DJ Jazzy Jeff & The Fresh Prince, KRS-One and A Tribe Called Quest. Calder also later signed R&B superstar R. Kelly and his protégée (and child bride), Aaliyah. But Calder's emphasis on hip-hop provoked a split with Clive Davis, who had never liked the genre. "He used to ask me why I was wasting my time with all this," Calder later said, "when I should be looking for more rock bands like A Flock of Seagulls." But rock groups, who generally wrote their own stuff, didn't fit into the Motown business model Calder embraced.

A musical act is a small entrepreneurial business. Making a hit requires a lot of different services that not all bands can provide for themselves. Calder was looking for acts that would accept his involvement and partnership. A music-industry insider told *Billboard*, "The idea of a rock group that is self-contained, produces itself, and does all that is not the kind of business model that he tends to join with. It's not that he wouldn't be able to have success with Creed or Korn or Limp Bizkit—I just don't think it's where his business model is. It's more, 'I'll sign this artist, I've got this producer, they'll record in my studio.'"

In 1991, the Bertelsmann Music Group, a division of the venerable German publisher, Bertelsmann, approached Calder about buying Jive.

Calder had no interest in selling, but he needed BMG's sales network. Distribution—getting the records into the stores—was the one aspect of the record business in which an independent label could not compete with the majors. He agreed instead to sell BMG 25 percent of his publishing company, Zomba, and in return BMG became Jive's worldwide distributor. In 1996, BMG deepened its involvement with Calder by purchasing 20 percent of Jive. As part of that deal, BMG agreed to give Calder the option (known on Wall Street as a "put" option) to sell the rest of Zomba to BMG at any time before the end of 2002, for three times whatever the company's most recent year's earnings were. BMG felt secure in this potentially risky clause because Zomba was Calder's baby, his obsession, and his life's work. "I never wanted to be David Geffen or Richard Branson," he once said. "I respected these people but I wanted to be Donny Hathaway"—that is, a brilliant musician like the American jazz and blues player and vocalist best known for his duets with Roberta Flack. Michael Dornemann, then the chairman of BMG Entertainment, told *Billboard* in 2000, "I cannot believe he would sell his company—it's outside my imagination."

CALDER'S INTEREST IN THE Backstreet Boys, so surprising to McPherson, actually had less to do with their music than with his business relationship with BMG. Calder was unhappy with the German company's distribution because BMG was unable to break his R&B and hip-hop acts in Europe. Calder felt that BMG "had seriously stunted the growth of our record business," he told BMG executives. BMG's Heinz Henn noted that Calder "was always fairly critical of us when it came to the work we did on the black roster. . . . Clive felt that we didn't try hard enough. We'd ask, 'Could you please give us a little bit of pop mixed in with the urban stuff? Then we'll deliver.' And look what happened when he gave us the Backstreet Boys."

But that gift was a Trojan horse. Building up Jive's pop roster also made the label more attractive to other regional European distributors. Calder formed alliances with smaller distributors such as Pinnacle, Southgate, and Rough Trade, who gave Jive more favorable terms, and later allowed him to sever his European distribution ties with BMG. Eventually, Calder was able to buy those smaller European distributors and thus bring Jive's European distribution under his own control.

Big Poppa was also a significant inducement to signing the Backstreet Boys. He represented himself as a man for whom money was no object, a high roller willing to bankroll the cost of recording and touring out of his own pocket. Pearlman had already spent more than a million dollars on the boys—no small consideration to the frugal South African. "He said that was one of the reasons he wanted to sign the group," Pearlman recalls. "And he said, 'I'm going to help you take it from here to the next level.'"

Jive brought Lou and the boys, together with AJ's mom, Denise McLean, to New York to sign the record contract, in May 1995. They assembled at the Zomba headquarters, an eleven-story brick building at 137 West Twenty-Fifth Street that was formerly a branch of the New York Public Library. Calder had a small, unpretentious office at the top of the building, which had airtight doors, sealed windows, and its own AC system, to relieve the allergies that plagued him. He did not attend the signing, leaving Barry Weiss to oversee the proceedings.

The band was presented with a contract, which "their lawyer," who had been hired by Pearlman, had already signed off on. There were some peculiar terms in it. For one thing, Pearlman was recognized not only as the band's nominal manager (Johnny Wright was their actual manager), but also as a sixth Backstreet Boy, entitling him to participate in their record sales, merchandising, and touring income. When AJ's mom balked, asking if she could take the contract back to Florida and have her own lawyer look it over, Pearlman told her this was a one-time offer, take it or leave it.

In her memoir, *Backstreet Mom*, McLean wrote, "By that point we had put all of our trust in Lou. He had taken a big risk financially and, by that time, we felt that we owed him so much. On more than one occasion, Lou told the boys how he was going to make them into millionaires. The way he lived was the way we all wanted to live. Nice house, nice car, fame, fortune. What parent would turn that down for their child?" Not Denise: they took the deal. That evening Lou brought everyone to the Copacabana to celebrate, and they ended the night in front of the Virgin Megastore in Times Square, harmonizing for passersby on Broadway.

Jive quickly set about looking for songs. The boys thought of themselves as R&B singers, a white version of Boyz II Men, not as pop artists. Barry Weiss recalls, "They wanted to make an R&B record, but we saw them more in a pure pop vein." However, the American songwriters and producers the label reached out to for material, including Jive's in-house producer, Eric Foster White, were unable to come up with anything that sounded to Calder like a hit. When they were half a million dollars deep into recording, most of it Pearlman's money, McPherson began to worry. "I thought, Uh-oh, what if they get dropped again?"

Meanwhile, Johnny Wright, who had connections to promoters in Germany, was arranging shows for the boys over there, and German fans were going nuts for the group.

"Johnny was sending us videos from Europe of the band performing and people going crazy," McPherson says. "He was saying, 'You don't get it. This is going to be huge! We got to put this out!' But Clive said, 'Yeah, but we have to get this right.'"

Desperate, McPherson even reached out to black songwriters and producers for material. "Most of them looked at me like I had three heads," he recalls. "'Are you kidding, man? You want me to write for *this*? A *pop* group?'"

Finally, Calder turned to Martin Dodd, the man who brought Ace of Base to Mega Records, and who now headed Jive's A&R in Europe. Dodd had himself been searching for the missing ingredient that would join contemporary R&B to pop, and work the alchemy that Berry Gordy had pulled off at Motown. He later recalled this mid-'90s quest in a rare interview with *Music Headline*: "I remember that I sat in a park in Amsterdam, looking at these children who were playing and they had baggy jeans and the whole hip hop thing going in style. In the evening I went to listen to R&B in a club, but there was no melody that stuck with me." Because of that, he went on, "Very few of the R&B records broke through over the world, but in terms of style, vibe, and fashion it was there. It just lacked melody lines."

Calder wondered if Dodd had any ideas about who could write material for the Backstreet Boys. Dodd did: Denniz PoP, the producer behind the Ace of Base hits. Moreover, Denniz happened to be in L.A. at that very moment with his young protégé, a former hard-rock singer who went by the name of Max Martin.

BY 1995, DENNIZ HAD recruited a number of young Swedish writers and producers to the Cheiron hit-making team. They included Kristian "Krille" Lundin, who had taught himself how to be a producer by reverse-engineering songs he liked. He joined the rest of the core group: Andreas Carlsson, Herbie Crichlow, Jake Schultz, David Kreuger, Per Magnusson, Jörgen Elofsson, John Amatiello, and Martin Sandberg. A strong part of Denniz's vision for the studio was that songwriting should be a collaborative effort; no one was supposed to be proprietary about his work. Songwriters would be assigned different parts of a song to work on; choruses would be taken from one song and tried in another; a bridge might be swapped out, or a hook. Songs were written more like television shows, by teams of writers who willingly shared credit with one another. The Swedish artist E-Type (Bo Martin Erik Eriksson) recalled, "I get this feeling of a big painter's studio in Italy back in the 1400s or 1500s." In a STV documentary, *The Nineties*, he told producer Jens von Reis, "One assistant does the hands, another does the feet, and another does something else, and then Michelangelo walks in and says, 'That's really great, just turn it slightly. Now it's good, put it in a golden frame and out with it. Next!'"

In assembling his team, Denniz PoP sought out protégés with different skill sets. E-Type said, "I mean, I had been around to a bunch of different record studios and everyone said, 'You're nuts, what would we do with you . . . ? You're not good-looking, you can't sing, and you write really strange songs.' Dagge told me the opposite: 'How fun that you look so odd, and sound so strange, and make music that I believe could become something in the future.'"

Andreas Carlsson was a gifted lyricist. Lundin had excellent technical skills. Jörgen Elofsson was adept at flowing melodies, while Rami Yacoub, a later Cheiron recruit, made sick beats. But of all the talents Denniz gathered around him, no one could match the genius for crafting melodies that fit both dance tracks and ballads possessed by the baby-faced, long-haired metalhead named Karl Martin Sandberg.

Sandberg was born in Stenhamra, a suburb of Sweden, in 1971. His father was a policeman. His older brother was a glam-rock fan, and "he brought home old Kiss cassettes," Sandberg recalled in a *Time* magazine interview; listening to them made young Martin want to be a rock star. Like many of his colleagues at Cheiron, Sandberg learned music through Sweden's excellent state-sponsored music-education programs, receiving free private lessons in the French horn. "I first began with the recorder in our community music school," he remembered in the Swedish Radio documentary. "After that I played horn, and participated in the school orchestra. I remember that I started playing brass not so much because I had a calling but because I thought it looked cool." Eventually he moved on to drums, then keyboards.

In the mid 1980s, Sandberg dropped out of high school to become the front man and main songwriter of a glam-metal band called It's Alive, adopting the stage name Martin White. The band was very Iron Maiden–esque. In the video for the group's song "Pretend I'm God,"

Sandberg plays Jesus and enacts a pseudo-crucifixion, doing his best Ozzy Osbourne imitation.

But Martin Sandberg had a terrible secret, one he couldn't share with the rest of the band. He loved pop music. At home he listened to Depeche Mode's "Just Can't Get Enough" and The Bangles' "Eternal Flame," which he later told *Time* was an all-time favorite. "I couldn't admit to my friends that I liked it," he said.

Denniz signed It's Alive to the studio's short-lived label, Cheiron Records, in 1993, and produced an album with the group called *Earthquake Visions*, which came out in 1994. It did poorly, and the band was soon dropped; the label itself folded not long after. But Denniz heard something in Sandberg's songwriting, and permitted him to hang around the studio and watch the more experienced Cheiron writers and producers at work. "I spent two years, day and night, in that studio trying to learn what the hell was going on," he later recalled. "I didn't even know what a producer did."

Unlike Denniz PoP, or any of his collaborators at that time, Martin Sandberg knew music theory and musical notation. "Martin was very schooled; he could read the notes, write partitions, and do musical arrangements," E-Type said in *The Cheiron Saga*. "Dagge would say, 'We need a new influence, so Martin, make us something pretty while E-Type and I run out for some sushi.' We'd come back and find something so gorgeous that we both almost fell backwards."

Sandberg worked by theory, Denniz by feel. "Dagge was driven by his instincts," E-Type said. "If there was something that worked, well then that's what he'd do, always. Martin was the musician, and he got the principles around funk, and with those abilities was able to take it a step further."

"We thought he wrote really good songs, so we simply approached him and asked if he'd write songs for us," Denniz said. However, he added, "He really needed a new name, I mean, 'Martin Sandberg' wasn't exactly a disco name, so you couldn't really talk to him."

The name "Max Martin" appears for the first time on Barbados-born Herbie Crichlow's 1995 album, *Fingers*. The first single was "Right Type of Mood." "I arrived at the studio one day," Sandberg recalled, "and the single had just been cut and I was looking at it, and it was such an amazing experience to be holding it. It read 'Produced by Denniz PoP and Max Martin.'

"Hmmm. Who's that?" Sandberg asked.

"It's *you!*" they replied.

"Oh, OK," Sandberg said. "And that was my name from that point on."

With success, the dynamic in the studio changed, which is what happens in hit factories, when people begin to realize just how rich a hit can make them. Douglas Carr, for one, did not care for the new careerist vibe. "I walked out," he says, and adds, "A lot of new things came with the money and success."

TRUE HIT FACTORIES HAVE occurred only rarely in the history of the record business, and they don't last very long, for a variety of reasons. The hits stop coming, or competitors copy the factory's sound, or listeners' tastes change. Throughout the rock era, critical opinion and popular taste have turned against "manufactured music" at regular intervals. It happened in the mid-'60s with the Beatles and Stones, and again in the mid-'70s with the birth of punk, and it happened a third time in the early '90s with grunge.

Another common problem hit factories suffer is that the balance of power between the artists and the writers and producers tends to change over time. At the beginning, the artists are regarded as mere hired hands by the writers and the producers, who are the real artists in the operation. But with success, the artists come to feel that they are, in fact, real artists—everything about the way they are sold to the world confirms it. They demand, at a minimum, more respect from their songwriters and producers, and they usually insist on more creative control over the songs. Some want to write their own material, often with disastrous results.

The very first hit factory was T.B. Harms, a Tin Pan Alley publishing company overseen by Max Dreyfus. With staff writers like Jerome Kern, George and Ira Gershwin, Cole Porter, and Richard Rodgers, T.B. Harms was the dominant publisher of popular music in the early twentieth century. Dreyfus called his writers "the boys" and installed pianos for them to compose on around the office on West Twenty-Eighth, the street that gave Tin Pan Alley its name, allegedly for the tinny-sounding pianos passersby heard from the upper-story windows of the row houses. The sheet-music sellers also employed piano players in their street-level stores, who would perform the Top 40 of the 1920s for browsing customers.

But T.B. Harms was a publishing company, not a record label; records and phonographs were still rarities in its day. To find the first hit factory of the record era, you'd have to head up-century thirty years and uptown thirty blocks, to the section of Broadway that stretched from the Brill Building, at Forty-Ninth Street, where Jerry Leiber and Mike Stoller had an office, to 1650 Broadway, at Fifty-First, where Don Kirshner's Aldon Music was located. In the warrenlike offices, publishers, writers, agents, managers, singers, and song pluggers formed hit-making's vibrant and colorful subculture. Although "Brill Building pop" is the catch-all term for the period in which songwriting teams like Goffin and King, and Barry Mann and Cynthia Weil flourished, in fact most of the rock-'n'-roll hits of the mid-1950s and early 1960s were written outside of the Brill Building itself.

Jerry Leiber and Mike Stoller were the first hit makers of rock 'n' roll, penning R&B hits for black artists such as Big Mama Thornton ("Hound Dog") and the Coasters ("Yakety-Yak"), among others. When a white kid named Elvis Presley wanted to record "Hound Dog," the songwriters were at first dismayed—they thought they were writing for cool black people, not white hillbillies—but the first royalty check changed their perspective, and they went on to write "Jailhouse Rock" and other hits for the King. Leiber and Stoller also produced their own songs, which was unusual; eventually they formed one of the first independent production companies in the record business, Red Bird Records. And they were the first producers to add strings to a R&B record, on the 1959 Drifters hit "There Goes My Baby," thus inventing a key component of soul music; the song also features a Brazilian *baion*, and the beat is kept by a timpani instead of a snare drum. Hearing these orchestral elements, which were familiar in pop music, employed on a R&B record would inspire a younger songwriter-and-producer wannabe named Phil Spector, who apprenticed with Leiber and Stoller in their Brill Building office, to create his famous Wall of Sound. But not for a few more years.

Aldon Music, headed by Don Kirshner, was an early '60s Broadway hit factory. His "Magnificent 7," the songwriters, worked on the sixth floor of 1650 Broadway. Writing in little cubicles with upright pianos in them were Neil Sedaka, Howie Greenfield, Gerry Goffin, Carole King, Barry Mann, Cynthia Weil, and Jack Keller. Kirshner was the go-between who placed his writers' best songs—"The Loco-Motion," "Up on the Roof," "On Broadway"—with leading local act such as the Shirelles and the Drifters. Kirshner also established the "demo"—short for "demonstration record"—as the basic working method of turning written compositions into sound. A demo was a rough draft of a record. In the Tin Pan Alley days, songwriters had done live "demos" by playing their songs for publishers, but in the era of recorded music, demos pressed onto acetate proved to be a more efficient way of working, one that gave producers much more control over the feel and sound of the record.

These songs were written for the new teen market, which had been created by the long postwar boom, both reproductive and economic. The lyrics embodied teen themes—young love, fun, fast cars, dancing—and they were generally less sophisticated than, say, the songs T.B. Harms published. My parents' feelings about a song like "Da Doo Ron Ron"—a lyric that was originally intended only as nonsensical placeholder until the songwriters, Jeff Barry and Ellie Greenwich, thought of real lyrics—was roughly equivalent to my feelings about "Right Round."

> *Tutti frutti, au-rutti*
> *Bop bopa-a-lu bop a whop bam boo*

No, this wasn't Cole Porter. (Though Cole might have enjoyed the original version of the lyric, which was supposedly "Tutti frutti, good booty," Little Richard's homage to gay sex, and contained the line "If it don't fit, don't force it.") But then, these songs weren't meant for playing on the piano in the parlor; they were for dancing or making love, and the beat, not the lyrics, was the essence of the song.

Phil Spector learned production from Leiber and Stoller, and had early hits within the Brill Building system in New York. But after several years he moved his operation to L.A., where he had grown up. Spector established his own label, Philles Records, and began making records in Gold Star Studios, near the corner of Santa Monica and Vine. Musically, Phil could do it all: write, produce, play guitar (he did the solo on Ben King's "Spanish Harlem"), and even sing backup. Unlike Kirshner, who only had business relationships with most of the artists to whom he sold Aldon's songs to, Spector had them under contract to Philles, his label: the Crystals, the Ronettes, the Righteous Brothers; he even put together his own group, Bob B. Soxx and the Blue Jeans, which featured Darlene Love.

Working with songwriters Jeff Barry and Ellie Greenwich, the arranger Jack Nitzsche, and the engineer Larry Levine, and employing top studio musicians such as the drummer Hal Blaine and other members of "The Wrecking Crew" who were familiar with his "Wall of Sound" recording methods (many of the same kind of instruments played in unison and recorded in an echo chamber), Spector went on a hit-making tear. His "little symphonies" began appearing in 1962, with the Crystals' "He's a Rebel," and ended 1966, when the failure of his masterpiece, Ike and

Tina Turner's "River Deep—Mountain High," drove him to early retirement and seclusion in his Sunset Boulevard chateau. He made several comebacks, with John Lennon and also with George Harrison, and later with the Ramones, but never recovered his spectacular hit-making form of the mid-'60s.

Spector not only changed pop music; he also established an archetype: the driven, obsessive, autocratic producer, who will stop at nothing to get the sound he hears in his head onto a record, even if it means screwing over his collaborators. He used Darlene Love's vocal on "He's a Rebel," but he gave the credit to the Crystals because he thought they'd sell more. He married Veronica Bennett, who supplied the timeless vocal on "Be My Baby," and turned her into Ronnie Spector, making her a virtual prisoner in his mansion, which he filled with guns after the murder of Sharon Tate in the summer of 1969. He kept a gold coffin in the cellar for Ronnie, saying that was the only way he would ever let her leave him—in a box. Today, the maestro is behind bars for the murder of actress Lana Clarkson, serving a nineteen-years-to-life sentence in Corcoran State Prison, where his fellow inmate (and songwriter) is Charlie Manson.

Motown was the ultimate hit factory. It combined a stable of writers like Kirshner's Magnificent 7 with Spector's control over the artists and the production. At Hitsville USA, as its Detroit headquarters was called, the artists, producers, writers, musicians, booking agents, managers, publishers, and recording studios were all under one roof and one man, Berry Gordy. He had worked on the production line at Ford's Wayne Assembly Plant, and he envisioned a hit factory that worked according to similar methods, with crews of writers and producers continually turning out product for Motown's singing groups. Writers such as Smokey Robinson and Marvin Gaye would bring their demos to Friday production meetings, and Gordy would decide which songs to produce and which artists would sing them.

But while Gordy was a shrewd judge of talent, he could be unscrupulous about exploiting it. He was known for keeping copyright in his writers' songs for himself. This often caused resentment that lasted for years. Barrett Strong, who was originally listed as a co-writer on the song "Money (That's What I Want)," claimed that Gordy stole the copyright and denied Strong credit. (Gordy maintained that the original listing was the result of a clerical error.) Holland–Dozier–Holland, the songwriting team who created more than a dozen number ones for Motown, brought an epic series of lawsuits against Gordy and Motown that stretched over twenty years before ultimately settling. The notoriety, along with the failure to adequately credit the Funk Brothers, the label's house band (its famous rhythm section was made up of Benny Benjamin on drums, James Jamerson on bass, and Earl Van Dyke on piano) for their role in making the Motown sound, may help explain why even Motown's magic period lasted only about six years—roughly the same length of time Kirshner's and Spector's factories endured.

Philadelphia International Records, the hit factory run out of 309 South Broad Street in Philly by Kenny Gamble and Leon Huff, made crossover R&B hits that featured strings, pianos, and vibraphones, to which they added some sweet Philly soul while keeping the bass quietly ascendant. They created a pop R&B sound that would influence the '90s boy bands. Starting with "Back Stabbers" and "Love Train" for the O'Jays, and "Me and Mrs. Jones" for Billy Paul—all from 1972—and followed by "You Make Me Feel Brand New" (1973) for the Stylistics and "The Love I Lost" (1973) for Harold Melvin and the Blue Notes, there was no stopping Gamble and Huff until "Ain't No Stoppin' Us Now" (1979) for McFadden & Whitehead, by which time their best writers and artists had stopped working with the producers, disillusioned by their hard-nosed business tactics.

The British hit makers Stock Aitken Waterman (SAW) had a hit factory in London in the second half of the 1980s. SAW also wrote and produced all songs in-house and then chose the artists to perform them. Kylie Minogue, SAW's biggest star, was an Australian soap-opera actress who had scored a hit Down Under with her cover of the

Goffin-King classic, "The Loco-Motion." SAW invited her to record in London. In a slip-up that revealed the low esteem in which artists were held around the studio, they forgot Minogue was coming and had nothing prepared when she arrived. They told her to wait outside while they wrote "I Should Be So Lucky," which became a number-one hit in the UK and Europe. They also created "You Spin Me Round (Like a Record)" for Dead Or Alive in 1984—the hook would come 'round again in Flo Rida's "Right Round"—as well as Bananarama's 1986 dance-floor remix of the Dutch band Shocking Blue's hit "Venus," and Rick Astley's worldwide 1987 smash "Never Gonna Give You Up." They racked up more than one hundred UK Top 40 hits and sold more than 40 million records. But although they had a last hurrah with Steps, a big UK act in the 1990s, SAW's hot streak also lasted barely more than six years.

DENNIZ POP AND MAX MARTIN'S first success as co-producers in the United States came in 1994, with the songs they wrote and produced for the R&B group 3T. The group was composed of the three sons of Tito Jackson, an older brother of Michael's. Michael himself was executive producer of their first album, *Brotherhood*, which was released toward the end of 1995. The Gloved One wanted to change the key in one of the songs, and asked Denniz and Max to fly to L.A. to work with him in his studio. At first, the Swedes declined. "We don't want to travel all that way just to go record four bars of music, especially since we thought it was really good just like it was," Max Martin said. But on reflection, the opportunity to meet the King of Pop and work with him in his own studio was too great to pass up, and they flew west, early Nordic navigators of what would become a popular trade route of Swedish song Vikings for decades to come. Expecting a state-of-the-art facility, "instead we went to this little studio out in the country, although not far from Hollywood, but it was like a shack," Max Martin said in the Swedish Radio documentary. "Our studio was like a dream studio compared to where we went to record over there. So there we sat, pretty much on a rotten sofa, sharing some coffee, just like usual." But when Michael went into the booth to add his vocals, Max was overcome. "That's when I lost my mind and started laughing; you know, like the hysterical kind of laughter at funerals when people just can't help themselves."

That was what they were doing in L.A. when Martin Dodd called, asking if they were interested in working with the Backstreet Boys. McPherson, who was also in L.A. at the time, was dispatched to meet with the Swedes. He brought along a recording of the Backstreet Boys performing at SeaWorld in Orlando. Although Denniz wasn't sure the world needed another boy band, he agreed to send Jive a demo of a tune he and Max had been working on, which was called "We've Got It Goin' On." Clive Calder loved it, and Denniz was hired to produce the song.

Calder told Pearlman about Denniz PoP during a trip to Orlando. As Pearlman recalls, "Clive and Barry had come down to Orlando to see the blimps." Pearlman asked Calder and Weiss to imagine, if they could, the promotional value of enormous images of the Backstreet Boys on the side of blimps hovering over the biggest theme parks in America. "Also we'd give rides to radio people," Pearlman says, "so that if they'd give us some airplay we'd give them a free ride." As always with Lou, it was a win-win situation.

"We were talking," Pearlman goes on, "and Clive mentioned Denniz PoP, who had done something with Michael Jackson, and he said he's a great guy and it would be really great if he would give us some songs." How would Pearlman like to pay for the group to go to Sweden? That sounded just fine to Big Poppa. The band was Pearlman's baby, and yet he was oddly disinterested in the details of making their debut album. The terrifically complex process of making records, which Calder was obsessed with, didn't seem to interest Pearlman much at all. He just wanted the group to be massive, one way or another.

The Backstreet Boys and Pearlman arrived in Stockholm in the summer of 1995. They first met Denniz and Max Martin at their hotel, the Strand, which looks out across the water at the picturesque old city. Although the plan had been to spend the whole week on "We've Got It Goin' On," Denniz and Max finished recording the boys' vocals in only two days, and so they brought out two more songs they had written together, including a midtempo ballad called "Quit Playing Games (With My Heart)." "Max asked us if we wanted to do those songs as well," Pearlman remembers. "He said, 'It's not going to cost you anything unless you want to use them.' And we said, 'Why not?' And we recorded those, too." As the entourage departed Stockholm for some German concert dates, both the band and the label felt they had what they needed to go to US radio in the fall.

"We've Got It Goin' On" showcased for the first time the genre-busting combination of influences that converged in Max Martin. The song combines ABBA's pop chords and textures, Denniz PoP's song structure and dynamics, '80s arena rock's big choruses, and early '90s American R&B grooves. On top of all that is Max's gift for melody, which is timeless, and owes as much to Edvard Grieg's dark Norwegian musical fable "In the Hall of the Mountain King" (aka the *Inspector Gadget* theme song) as to any contemporary influence.

Max Martin also sang on the demo, brilliantly; Denniz PoP produced the song; and Herbie Crichlow contributed to the lyrics. The beat borrows from New Jack Swing, with its characteristic triplet pattern on the eighth notes. The trademark Cheiron snare and kick-drum combo is also present, and, between the beats, there is the same sense of air that distinguished "The Sign." The main riff, which also makes up the chorus melody and contains the hook, is made with synth trumpets (a nod to "The Final Countdown"), played at a startlingly fast tempo. It almost feels like ragtime, but the horn sound has a distinctively European flavor, like the military band in Sgt. Pepper's on speed. The riff plays through twice, followed by a verse sung by Brian Littrell. The second verse is rapped, and is about as urban a sound as Cheiron would ever achieve with the Backstreet Boys. Then, as if to compensate for that temporary surrender to Dionysus, the beat drops out for the bridge, and the boys harmonize; the song briefly becomes a ballad, and an air of Scandinavian melancholy enters the music, blowing in from the hall of the mountain king himself. The beat rejoins the song for a final chorus.

The lyrics contain typical Swedish neologisms like "crazy wildin' static" and lines like "Keep it ruthless when I get wet." Melodic math had pretty much taken over from lyrical logic. But did anyone care?

Musically, everything that happens in "We've Got It Goin' On" seems to happen for a reason; the song never fails you. Savan Kotecha, who co-wrote with Max Martin "DJ Got Us Fallin' In Love," a number-one smash, and apprenticed in the Cheiron songwriting method, thinks this quality is uniquely Swedish. "With the Swedish people, what is expected to happen is going to happen," he says. "A Swede will not let you down, and neither do their songs. If you expect the song to blow here, it will blow here, and if you expect it to be chill there, it's chill there."

"We've Got It Goin' On" was released in the United States in September, 1995. It got only to number sixty-nine on the Billboard charts, and there it stalled; radio refused to play it. It sounded suspiciously . . . European. However the song was big hit in Germany, Austria, and Switzerland, and Jive sent the band on a six-month European tour, paid for in part by the glad-handed Pearlman, who, again, seemed only interested in the magnitude of the group's success, not the economics of it. Although they didn't speak French, the boys learned how to sing in it, as well as in Spanish, and recorded versions of "We've Got It Goin' On" in those languages. The song soon became a hit in France, and then jumped the Atlantic to French-speaking Quebec (a Montreal-based program director had heard the song on the radio while on a vacation in France, and brought it back to Canada). From Montreal the song spread to the English-speaking Canadian provinces. By the end of 1996, Backstreet Boys were a sensation in Canada, but almost no one back home knew who they were.

"Imagine how crazy it was," McPherson says. "The boys would play three sold-out shows in the Molson Center, and then come back to New York and no one cared. So we started flying program directors, writers, and tastemakers up to Canada to see the shows. And what happened was that radio in the cites that were closer to Canada, like Rochester, and Chicago, started to play the record." Still, it was slow going. Jive kept pushing the video on MTV, but the channel wouldn't play it, and eventually issued a ban: Don't send us the Backstreet Boys.

The band stayed on the road in Europe for most of 1996. They also did an extensive Asian tour, visiting Japan, and South Korea, where fans went crazy for them; their visit helped galvanize the nascent phenomenon known as K-pop, which would later sweep through much of the Asian world. But as 1996 came to a close, the boys' future at home remained cloudy at best.

1996 WAS THE YEAR the US Congress passed the Telecommunications Act, a major piece of legislation aimed at deregulating the media industry. The Internet had created previously unimagined opportunities for new media companies, but only if deregulation allowed them to flourish, went the argument.

One of the many changes the law brought was to raise the number of radio stations a single entity could own. Before the Telecommunications Act, radio-station ownership was capped at forty—twenty AM stations, and twenty FM stations—with no more than two stations in any one market. The act did away with the national market cap entirely, and raised the local cap to a maximum of eight, depending on the size of the market. Part of the rationale was that by creating large nationwide radio networks, individual stations would be able to command higher national advertising rates, which would assist financially struggling broadcasters.

Within only a few years of the passage of the act, two broadcast companies, Clear Channel and Infinity Broadcasting, had grown into Goliaths, acquiring hundreds of stations across the country. By 2001, Clear Channel had swelled from forty stations to 1,240. Advertising rates did indeed rise, but the interest on the debt that these companies took on to make acquisitions offset the increased profits.

Prior to the act, programming a radio station had been a regional art. Local disk jockeys and program directors took seriously their responsibility as curators, introducing under-the-radar songs to their listeners. Taste and instinct were as important as research in choosing what songs to play. But with the creation of coast-to-coast chains, national playlists could be devised for all stations within a particular format. This one-size-fits-all approach led to widespread complaints about homogenized programming and research-driven playlists.

Was that critique really true? An academic study commissioned by the FCC five years after the Telecommunications Act passed found that the number of unique songs played on a representative sampling of radio stations actually increased in some formats—namely urban, country, and alternative. But other formats saw a significant decrease in diversity, and one of the least diverse was contemporary hits radio—that is, Top 40. "You can get in a car in Maine and drive all the way to California and hear the same Top 40 songs on the same chain broadcasters," bemoaned the report.

The Top 40 format was invented by Todd Storz and Bill Stewart, the operator and program director, respectively, of KOWH, an AM station in Omaha, Nebraska, in the early '50s. Like most radiomen of the day, Storz and Stewart programmed their station like a variety show—a little something for everyone (network TV is still programmed that way). As Marc Fisher writes in his 2007 book, *Something in the Air*, "The gospel in radio in those days was that no tune ought to be repeated within twenty-four hours of its broadcast—surely listeners would resent having to hear the same song twice in one day." The eureka moment, as Ben Fong-Torres describes it in his 2001 book, *The Hits Just Keep on*

Coming, occurred in a restaurant across from the station, where Storz and Stewart would often wait for Storz's girlfriend, a waitress, to get off work. They noticed that even though the waitresses listened to the same handful of songs on the jukebox all day long, played by the customers, when the place finally cleared out and the staff had the jukebox to themselves, they played the very same songs. The men asked the waitresses to identify the most popular tunes on the jukebox, and they went back to the station and started playing them, in heavy rotation. Ratings soared.

The rise of FM radio and album-oriented rock, in the late '60s and early '70s, hit Top 40 hard. Rock, with its heady artistic aspirations, didn't fit the nakedly commercial format. Pop music began to splinter into "Adult Contemporary," "Easy Listening," and "Oldies," among other formats. Rock, meanwhile, gave birth to "Classic," "New Wave," and "Modern." Top 40 never went away—Casey Kasem's syndicated radio countdown, *American Top 40*, kept the concept alive—but by the early '80s, Top 40 could no longer claim to be America's soundtrack.

The tide began to turn back toward Top 40 in 1983, when the New York area's WHTZ, popularly known as Z-100, switched formats. Scott Shannon, the newly hired programming director, combined rigid playlists—heavy rotation of only the biggest hits of the day—with the renegade spirit of pirate radio, which he had been fascinated by as a boy, when offshore ship-based broadcasters in the UK sent their signals to terrestrial British listeners who otherwise were stuck with the staid BBC.

Success was swift and dramatic. On August 2, 1983, shortly after Shannon arrived at the station, Z-100 was dead last among the city radio stations as measured by Arbitron, the radio ratings company. But within seventy-three days of its launch, Shannon's Z-100 was the number-one station in the number-one market in the country. With Michael Jackson, Madonna, Prince, the Police, Cyndi Lauper, and Bruce Springsteen supplying the hits, and Shannon, Elvis Duran, and their pirate band of men and women (but mainly men) troweling the music with attitude,

Z-100 became the de facto sound of New York, and Top 40 was reborn as CHR, a potent commercial format.

Clear Channel acquired Z-100 as part of its post–Telecommunications Act expansion. Soon Z-100-esque clones were popping up across the country. Changes in popular music also aided CHR's spread. Standardized playlists magnified the impact of a hit, superheating the lottery mentality of the hit makers. But the ubiquity of the hits also magnified the backlash against them. By the end of 1996, grunge, the genre Nirvana and its Seattle cohort inspired, had come to seem to pop program directors like ratings poison, with its buzz-killing themes of alienation and despair. Z-100 lost more than one-third of its audience. Radio men like Tom Poleman, a whiz-kid program director Z-100 brought in to turn things around, pined for some sweet, middle-of-the-road "pure pop" that would bring back the masses.

Clive Calder had just the band.

7 | Britney Spears: Hit Me Baby

THE FIRST SIGN that teen pop was going to be massive came from the Spice Girls, a five-member group from the UK. Music entrepreneur Simon Fuller managed the band. Like the Backstreet Boys, the Spice Girls were a group made up of different personality types, to appeal to different psychodemographics. Peter Loraine and his colleagues at *Top of the Pop*s came up with nicknames to go along with the girls' supposed identities: Sporty, Scary, Posh, Baby, and Ginger Spice. When the Spice Girls first blew up in England, in 1996, they were viewed by American A&R guys like David McPherson as a weird British enthusiasm that would never make it big in the States. That notion was proven wrong in January of 1997, when the group's single "Wannabe" hit number one in the Hot 100 and stayed there for four weeks. Their debut album, *Spice*, sold 7.4 million in the United States, and a whopping 28 million world-wide, equaling Ace of Base.

Next came Hanson, a band of three adorable blond brothers (Isaac, Taylor, and Zac Hanson, in descending order of age) from Tulsa, Oklahoma, whose infectious song "MMMBop" topped the Hot 100 in May 1997, and remained there for three weeks. It featured a fuzzed-out guitar vibe, and hip-hop-style scratching on the chorus, which makes "Da Doo Ron Ron" sound like Shakespeare.

Mmmbop, ba duba dop
Ba du bop . . .

By the summer of 1997, Clive Calder judged the time was finally right to bring the Backstreet Boys back from their two-year international crusade, and try again to crack the US market. A second single, "Quit Playing Games (With My Heart)," was selected from the batch that had been recorded back in June 1995 at Cheiron. (Calder, in a rare error of judgment, had pressed the group to go out with his friend Mutt Lange's song "If You Want It to Be Good Girl" as the single, but both the boys and Lou were dead set against it, and Calder eventually relented.) Before the song was released, Nick Carter, the baby of the bunch, recorded a second verse. Carter's voice had changed and he was now one of the strongest vocalists in the group, and Calder wanted to feature him on the record.

"Quit Playing Games" was released to radio on May 19, 1997, and as a CD single on June 10. By the end of June, the song had hit number two on the Hot 100, and it remained on the chart for forty-three weeks. "Quit Playing Games" was followed by the singles "As Long as You Love Me," "Everybody (Backstreet's Back)," and "I'll Never Break Your Heart," all enormous hits.

"And with that," McPherson says, "the world knew all about Backstreet, Max Martin, and Cheiron Studios." In his 2009 memoir, *Live to Win*, Andreas Carlsson writes, "For a long time Martin was actually the Backstreet Boys' sixth member. He sounded more like Backstreet then they did themselves, or it was they who sounded like Max Martin."

When the group returned to Sweden toward the end of that year, the boys were mobbed. Max was amazed by the number of fans in the street, including "the thousands of young girls who would camp out and sleep on the bus-stop benches outside the Cheiron studios. They had to hire a company to provide bodyguards, and park limousines as a barrier in front of the studio, as the façade contained only glass windows. Otherwise things could have really gone sideways."

But although the boys were a gigantic success around the world now, selling millions of CDs and playing sold-out shows, the band saw very little of the money. Pearlman explained that plenty of dough would be forthcoming, after he had recouped the funds—$3 million altogether, he claimed—he had invested in creating, training, housing, feeding, clothing, adorning, grooming, recording, transporting, and promoting the group. But the boys and their parents began to suspect Lou was never going to part with their money. And to make matters worse, a new boy band—'N Sync—had appeared on the scene, threatening Backstreet's market.

IT HAD TAKEN LONGER than expected for the Backstreet Boys to break through in their own country, but Lou Pearlman hadn't been idle while waiting. He figured it was inevitable when the group finally did take off that someone else would come along and piggyback off their success by offering a product that was basically the same but just different enough to gain market share. "My feeling was, where there's McDonald's, there's Burger King," Pearlman says over the phone from prison, "and where there's Coke there's Pepsi and where's there's Backstreet Boys, there's going to be someone else. Someone's going to have it, why not us?" So, without telling the Backstreet Boys, Pearlman had set about creating another boy band, which he eventually named 'N Sync.

As luck would have it, the Disney Channel's *Mickey Mouse Club*, a reliable teen talent finder since 1989, was canceled in 1996, and one of the Mouseketeers, sixteen-year-old Justin Timberlake, was interested in joining Pearlman's new group. Others members were JC Chavez, Chris Kirkpatrick, Joey Fatone, and Lance Bass. Johnny Wright, Backstreet's manager, became 'N Sync's manager too, again without the boys being told. Ariola, a BMG label, signed the group, and Cheiron wrote and produced songs for them, including the first single, "I Want You Back," and the second, "Tearin' Up My Heart." Like Backstreet Boys, the group first caught on in Europe. BMG was delighted to have its very own boy band to compete with Jive.

Once 'N Sync was launched, Pearlman's next move was to manufacture a girl group to complement his two boys bands. Spice Girls were huge, and just as Lou's boy bands had proven even more popular than the comparable British offerings, so Lou thought he could do Simon Fuller one better on the distaff side too. In 1997, working with Lynn Harless—Justin Timberlake's mother—Lou began auditioning girls for his group, which was to be called Innosense. Harless suggested another former cast member of the Mickey Mouse Club. Not only could she dance and sing, Harless said, she could also act, and she had been schooled in the same clean-cut and wholesome Disney values that had shaped Justin. Her name was Britney Spears.

BORN IN DECEMBER 1981, in Mississippi, Britney Spears grew up in Kentwood, a small town in southern Louisiana. She was fifteen when Pearlman auditioned her. She had been in show business for half her life at that point. Her mother, Lynne, was a day-care supervisor and her father, Jaime, was a boilermaker and construction worker whose problems with alcohol plagued the family. Britney found order and control, both absent in her home life, by performing at local talent shows, where she first made a name for herself with the power of her voice. When she was eight, Britney auditioned for and was awarded a spot on the *Mickey Mouse Club*, in recognition of which her hometown would later declare a "Britney Spears Day."

But the Disney producers eventually decided Britney was too young to be a Mouseketeer, and so, on the advice of a Disney talent scout she went to New York, where she was taken on by an agent, Nancy Carson of the Carson-Adler talent agency, who specialized in child performers. Lynne and her daughter lived in a small apartment in the theater district, and Britney attended the Professional Performing Arts School. She was cast as the understudy to the star, Laura Bell Bundy, in the off-Broadway musical *Ruthless!* In 1992, before the musical premiered, she got to the finals of *Star Search*, the Ed McMahon–hosted television talent show. But she finished second, which crushed her, and after four months of long nights backstage at the theater, she and Lynne called it quits and went back to Kentwood. Britney was replaced by another unknown child actor named Natalie Portman.

The following year she auditioned for the *Mickey Mouse Club* again, and this time secured a spot among the seven new mice on the show; her cohort included Timberlake, Ryan Gosling, and Christina Aguilera. She and Lynne moved to Orlando in the summer of 1993, and Britney's show-biz career began in earnest. In addition to acting, singing, and dancing, she learned to smile for the paparazzi, sign autographs, and how to conduct herself in interviews and "meet-and-greets." Britney was a model student of these show-business mores, and a dutiful if unimaginative pupil in the school Disney created for Mouseketeers (where controversial subjects, such as evolution, were avoided). As the principal of the "Mickey Mouse School," Chuck Yerger, later recalled in *Britney: Inside the Dream* by Steve Dennis, "In all that she did, Britney gave the distinct impression that if an adult says do something, you do it. She truly felt that all adults and people in authority were good people, who had her best interests at heart."

After the show was canceled, Britney went back to Kentwood, where she tried to reenter normal American teen life: proms and homecomings (she was voted "Junior High Most Beautiful"), shopping and movie dates. But she did not give up on her show-biz dreams. In 1996, she contacted a New York–based entertainment lawyer named Larry Rudolph, who represented the Backstreet Boys and Toni Braxton, and, it so happened, Lou Pearlman. Upon meeting her, Rudolph sensed "a certain inexplicable quality" about the thirteen-year-old, and agreed to represent her. She auditioned for Innosense; Pearlman liked her and had a contract ready for her to sign. But Britney backed out of the contract at the last minute, deciding she would rather try for a solo career.

Not long after that, Rudolph sent Spears a tape of a song written for his client Toni Braxton, which Braxton had recorded but ultimately rejected for sounding too young. Rudolph advised Spears to sing it just the way Braxton sang it, and to make her own demo and mail it back to him. Upon receiving the demo, Rudolph sent it around to various labels, and garnered the interest of three: Mercury, Epic, and Jive. He arranged for Britney to audition for each of the three respective A&R teams, and in July 1997, Lynne and her now fifteen-year-old daughter flew to New York.

AT THE SONY BUILDING, a Philip Johnson–designed postmodernist skyscraper with a distinctive "Chippendale" top, Britney met Epic's vice president of A&R, Michael Caplan. He was joined by Polly Anthony, a veteran of radio promotion, and several other key Epic personnel. Rudolph, who escorted Britney and her mother to the meeting, had assured Caplan that his client was "the next big thing." But upon meeting her, the forty-year-old A&R man was unimpressed. "I was expecting a true artiste," he later told Steve Dennis, "and in walked a shy little girl." Britney performed a clutch of Whitney Houston songs for the Epic execs. "She came in," Caplan went on, "warbled 'I Will Always Love You,' and I couldn't wait for it to end. Her complexion wasn't great, her voice wasn't great and when the song ended, it was Larry, not Britney, who did all the talking. Seated beside me was Polly—more the pop connoisseur—and I don't think she was impressed either, so we passed." He added, "I believe in artistes, I believe in the art within music. Call me old-fashioned but I'm looking for true talent and a hell of a voice. I'm not looking for someone I can reinvent in the age of the celebutante that seems to have transcended the musical artiste." Noble sentiments—and possibly the worst business decision Caplan ever made.

Mercury also passed. That left Jive.

Rudolph had sent Britney's "Toni Braxton" demo tape to Jeff Fenster, a senior vice president of A&R for Jive in the United States. Besides Fenster, no one at the label liked it, except for A&R man Steve Lunt, who heard something in the demo. "It was in the wrong key," he remembers. "Britney was trying to sing like Toni Braxton, which was way too low for her. It sounded pretty awful in places. But when her voice went up high, you could hear the girlish quality, and there was something really appealing about that." Some snapshots of the fifteen-year-old accompanied the demo, showing a cute all-American teen in pigtails, sitting on a ramshackle wooden porch in Kentwood, and playing with her dog on the lawn. "I said, 'This is something we should look at seriously.'"

Britney and her entourage turned up at the Jive offices. There was nothing fancy about the place. "Clive was all about what went on between the walls," says Lunt, "and not the walls themselves." Britney met the entire A&R department, along with Calder, in a conference room. It was July, and the teenager wore a mid-thigh sundress. She sang two Whitney Houston songs, a cappella: "I Will Always Love You," and "I Have Nothing."

"Her eyes were rolling back in her head as she was singing," Lunt noticed, "and I remember thinking to myself, 'That is really weird but it's going to look great on video.' It was old-school church meets modern-day sex. But in fact it was because she was so nervous." When she was finished, Fenster asked her if she knew anything else, and Britney sang the national anthem. Everyone thanked her and said they would be in touch. Lynne and her daughter flew back to Kentwood that night.

As with all A&R matters at Jive, the decision about whether to sign Britney rested with Calder. Eric Beall, then the creative director of Zomba, observes, "Clive Calder was always searching for his Whitney or Mariah, but he never found her. We must have listened to a hundred auditions, but Clive's position was always that artists like Whitney or Mariah are the single most expensive and risky investment that a label can make, and you had to be prepared to spend millions in promotion." Such an investment wasn't a problem for Clive Davis, who had major-label backing. But Jive, an independent, did not have those resources, and besides Calder was congenitally frugal. "He could never find anyone that he felt was enough of a natural talent to warrant the risk," Beall says.

Calder was on surer ground with a girl like Britney, who was inexpensive to sign, and so evidently eager to please. She was hardly the type to engage in the divalike histrionics that made the Whitneys and Mariahs of the music world so difficult and costly to handle. Calder had the idea that Britney could be an American Robyn—a Europop teen queen, with an added dash of girl-next-door.

Calder offered Britney a contract with a "get-out" clause, stipulating that Jive could cancel the deal within ninety days, with no further commitment to Spears, if A&R decided the album wasn't going to work. Lunt was designated to be her A&R guy and to oversee the writing, the demos, and the musical direction. "It was my brief to either make this work within the ninety-day period, or to let Clive know that we should look elsewhere for our female pop star."

WITH THE CLOCK TICKING, the label brought Britney back to New York and installed her in a Jive penthouse. She was accompanied by a chaperone, a family friend named Felicia Culotta. Because Jive was still a predominantly rap and R&B label, almost all of its in-house songsmiths were urban writers. They had only one pop producer, Eric Foster White, signed to Zomba, Calder's publishing company.

Almost every day, Britney and Culotta, often accompanied by Lunt, would be driven out to White's studio, 4MW East Studios in New Jersey, where they worked on developing the teenager's sound. Spears had originally envisioned doing "Sheryl Crow music, but younger," but Lunt and White pushed her in a teen-pop direction, which Britney liked "because I can dance to it—it's more me." White also got her to sing higher, to bring out the girlish quality that Lunt had heard in her voice. They recorded a handful of original songs together, some of which, like "From the Bottom of My Broken Heart," ended up on her debut album. But Calder didn't hear any hits in the demos, and he debated not picking up the option. With time running out, Lunt suggested that Britney cover a hit from the '80s, "You Got It All," by the Jets. On hearing that demo in an A&R meeting, Calder said, "OK we have a project, let's pick up the option and get going on an album. If the Backstreet Boys are the New Kids on the Block, then this is Debbie Gibson."

In October, Lunt flew down to New Orleans, and made the hour drive north to Kentwood, to get a better idea of where their new artist was coming from. He showed Britney Robyn's video of "Show Me Love." He recalls, "She said, 'The record is really good, but the video is all wrong. It's in boring black and white and no one is dancing. If it was me I'd be wearing a miniskirt and I'd be dancing.'" Dancing, it turned out, was the teenager's passion: Jive had no idea. In his notes Lunt wrote, "She says she can dance and she really wants to be able to entertain." Lunt also noted that Britney told him the only thing she was afraid of was "failing, and having to go back to Louisiana and face all the people."

Everyone agreed that Max Martin had to be involved with the Britney project, and shortly after the label picked up the option Max was flown to New York to meet the girl.

"I was scared of him!" Spears said of first meeting the hirsute Swede. "I thought he was someone from, like, Mötley Crüe or something." Though he was rapidly becoming the genius of teen pop, Max Martin still looked like Martin White, the front man of It's Alive: very long lank hair, a fleshy grizzled face, skinny tees and jeans, and the sallow skin of a studio rat.

The label left them alone together for a couple of hours, and Max came away impressed. Lunt says, "I remember Max saying from the first meeting, 'I get it, I know what to do.'" He adds, "Robyn was a forceful artist, and Max couldn't always get her to do it his way." (Robyn herself later commented, "I became quite associated with Max Martin and Denniz PoP during that time, which I didn't always find so amusing as I really wanted to stand on my own two feet.") Lunt continues: "But with Britney, Max said, 'She's fifteen years old; I can make the record I really want to make, and use her qualities appropriately, without her telling me what to do.' Which is kind of what happened."

MAX MARTIN HAD A song in mind for Britney. He had composed it in Stockholm the year before with Rami Yacoub, the Swedish-Moroccan beat maker who was now part of the Cheiron team. The song, which was initially called "Hit Me Baby (One More Time)" had been written for TLC, the three-woman American R&B group. Cheiron sent TLC a demo of the song, which featured Max doing four-part harmonies all by himself. (As E-Type said, "With his own demos, Max Martin singing himself, those would have sold ten million or more, but he wasn't an artist, he didn't want to be an artist.") TLC rejected it. Years later, T-Boz recalled their decision: "I was like, I like the song but do I think it's a hit? Do I think it's TLC? . . . Was I going to say 'Hit me baby one more time'? Hell no!"

"Max at that point in his career thought he was writing a R&B song," Steve Lunt says, "whereas in reality he was writing a Swedish pop song. It was ABBA with a groove, basically." There is a funky bass slap in the song, which sounds urban, and on the trace vocal Max did that cowboy-sounding "owww" made famous by Cameo and beloved by Denniz. "But all those chords are so European, how could that possibly be an American R&B song?" Lunt continues. "No black artist was going to sing it." He adds, "But that was the genius of Max Martin. Without being fully aware of it, he'd forged a brilliant sound all his own, and within a few weeks every American producer was desperately scrambling to emulate it."

When TLC rejected the song, Max offered it to Robyn, but nothing came of that, either. After meeting Britney in New York, he went back to Stockholm, worked on the song a little more with her in mind, made a copy, and mailed it to Jive. As was Max's method of demo making, all the hooks in the song were worked up to their finished state, but most of the verses were unfinished, often mere vowel sounds. There was no bridge yet, because, as Lunt puts it, "Max would say, 'If you don't like the song by then, fuck you'—in his polite Swedish way, of course." When the demo reached Jive, everyone thought, "Holy shit, this is perfect," according to Lunt.

"Hit Me Baby (One More Time)" is a song about obsession, and it takes all of two seconds to hook you, not once but twice, first with the eighth note "Da Nah Nah" and then with that alluring growl-purr Britney emits with her first line, "Oh baby bay-bee." Then the funky Cheiron backbeat kicks in, with drums that sound like percussion grenades. Next comes Tomas Lindberg's wah-wah guitar lines, which signal to one's inner disco hater that it can relax: it's a rock song, after all. In terms of sheer sonic drama, "Hit Me Baby (One More Time)" belongs to the theatrical rock tradition of Queen, mixed with Mutt Lange's work with Def Leppard. It marries melody and rhythm in a way that Denniz PoP had been seeking since his DJ days—a catchy pop song that doesn't stop the dancing.

And yet the vocal hook, irresistible as it was, sounded odd. You weren't sure it was OK to sing it out loud. It's hard to imagine that anyone for whom English is a first language would write the phrase "Hit me baby" without intending it as an allusion to domestic violence or S&M. That was the furthest thing from the minds of the gentle Swedes, who were only trying to use up-to-the-minute lingo for "Call me." Jive, concerned that Americans might get the wrong idea, changed the title to ". . . Baby One More Time."

8 | "I Want It That Way"

EVEN BEFORE HIS health began to decline, Denniz PoP had been getting bored. By 1997, Cheironite Per Magnusson says, "I think Denniz was tired of the pop music. So he started working on his own computer games. If he had lived, I think he would have become a game designer or something like that." He adds, "He'd sit there, and smoke, and turn a knob—it seemed like nothing was going on." Denniz did put some work into an epic he called *The Cheiron Saga*, a sort of Wagnerian disco opera, which he never finished.

Denniz hadn't been feeling well for some time. Kristian Lundin recalls, "In 1997, I noticed he was having trouble swallowing. The food was getting stuck, even the pasta he liked to eat, which wasn't hard to swallow, really. It just dawned on him, 'Oh this is how I'm going to go.'" He refused to go to the doctor, but he did consent to go back to Emmy, the fortune-teller. Lundin accompanied him. Emmy began a Tarot-card reading, but five minutes into it, Lundin says, she became flustered. "Her whole demeanor changed. She got nervous, and Denniz saw that. He was almost like, 'Oh so you saw it too?' She wouldn't tell him what she saw, but he knew."

After that, Denniz would still come into the studio, but he didn't work much. "Day and night he would sit in front of the computer,"

Lundin remembers, "searching his symptoms, sweating with anxiety, and so afraid to go to the doctor because he knew." Max Martin said, "I'm the one who's the hypochondriac usually, so I was like, 'Go check it out,' but he was dragging his feet for a very long time. He'd start feeling better, and I guess he discovered a way to eat food without it bothering him so much."

Finally, in December 1997, Denniz agreed to an examination. His secretary Jeanette accompanied him to the doctor's office. Lundin and Max Martin remained at Cheiron, working. "And we were so nervous, waiting to hear the results," Lundin says. "It took them about three hours. We didn't think he was going to come back to the studio, so when we heard the door open upstairs, we thought, Oh it can't be that bad, because he came back! And then we went upstairs and saw Jeanette's face and we knew it was bad. And that was the moment when everything changed."

The sonogram had shown a tumor growing in Denniz's esophagus. He had surgery soon afterward at Karolinska Sjukhuset Hospital in Solna. "The tumor was positioned fairly close to the surface and was easy to operate [on]," Max said. "The most important thing would be that the cancer hadn't spread, but in fact it had already spread." It was in his brain, and Denniz had another operation in January. His girlfriend, Katarina, cut off Denniz's beautiful hair because she thought the radiation treatments would make it fall out anyway and that would crush him. But in the end his hair didn't fall out.

"I was at the hospital every day," Lundin goes on. "It was weird, because there was so much good work happening right then in the studio—everything was happening. We were writing the songs to record with Britney. But I just remember all of us, especially me and Martin, getting these huge panic attacks."

Denniz was too ill to attend the Swedish Grammys in February 1998, where he and Max received a special prize for their success in promoting Swedish music abroad. But he did appear in the studio in the early spring to work on the debut album of Jessica Folcker. "I was so incredibly in love with him, it was absolutely fantastic," she later said. "He was larger than life, a huge heart, incredibly generous, and an amazing gift of humor. Just being in his presence made you happy."

Britney, accompanied by Culotta and Lunt, arrived in Stockholm in late April. Before recording ". . . Baby One More Time," on May 2 and 3, they tackled Jörgen Elofsson's "Sometimes," a midtempo ballad that would be the second single. Lunt says, "Between 'Sometimes' and '. . . Baby One More Time,' you had the template for Britney's whole career—the innocent girl on the one side, and the sexy Lolita on the other."

Denniz didn't come into the studio while Britney and Steve Lunt were there, in May of 1998. Britney never met him. Max Martin was in charge. In spite of the emotional strain he was under, Max appeared to Lunt to be "totally on his game," during the Britney sessions, although Lunt did notice tears in his eyes from time to time. With the Cheiron all stars on hand—Max Martin, Rami Yacoub, Kristian Lundin, Per Magnusson, David Kreuger, Jörgen Elofsson, and Andreas Carlsson—they managed to record no fewer than six songs in ten days with Britney, including all four of the singles from the debut album.

Several weeks after the Britney sessions ended, Denniz miraculously returned to the studio. "Seventy kilos lighter and no hair—he was like a shadow of the former Dagge," according to Carlsson. "His trousers hung like sacks to the ground because of the big change in weight, and he wore a black cap to hide his head. It was heartbreaking, and all you wanted to do was to hug him."

In mid-June, when Sweden celebrated Midsummer, Denniz seemed fine, but later that summer he took a turn for the worse. Max and Lundin went over to his house, and spent hours playing games until they had to excuse themselves to go to the studio and complete all the work Denniz's brilliance had started. "It was not fun," Lundin says.

Denniz's sister, Ann-Katrin, recalled, "He was worrying a lot about his son, of course, since he was still pretty young." Daniel was ten. "I think that worry was the most challenging for Dagge—that he may not be around for his son." Daniel said, "You'd go see him, and even in the end he'd still want to play games and [do] puzzles, at the hospital, but he'd slip in and out of sleep because of the morphine. These are all very difficult memories I carry from around those times. I try to force away the pictures in my mind of his shaved head; he had gotten so skinny, and his lying in the bed involuntarily shaking. I work hard on trying to remember the joyful dad that I had."

Denniz died on August 30, 1998. A minute of silence was held on the following Friday by DJs all over Sweden. The funeral took place a week later in the church in Kungsholmen. The Swedish media, which had never given Denniz much credit for his success, now treated him like a national treasure. He was buried in Solna; his gravestone is shaped like an eighth note—a symbol he had no use for because he never learned to read music.

THAT SUMMER, AS DENNIZ was dying, Britney went on a US promotional tour. Jive chose shopping malls as the venues to introduce their new product to the American public. Britney, accompanied by two backup dancers, hit twenty-six malls in the course of the summer, performing a four-song set that included ". . . Baby One More Time." Johnny Wright, the manager of both Backstreet and 'N Sync, was brought in to manage Britney as well.

To make the video of ". . . Baby One More Time," the label hired a veteran video director, Nigel Dick. His concept was to animate Britney as a sort of proto–Power Puff Girl. Dick recalled in *Britney: Inside the Dream*, "Britney hated my idea, and Jive hated it, so they rang me and passed the phone to Britney. She said, 'Let's do a video where I'm a girl in school looking at lots of hot boys.' Dick had an unsettling thought: "Good God, I'm a grown man taking instructions from a sixteen-year-old girl." But the disquiet soon passed, followed by "this moment of clarity—she knows more about this world of girls and boys than I do."

Britney also suggested Catholic-schoolgirl uniforms. "The outfits looked kind of dorky," she said, "let's tie up our shirts and be cute."

As Willie Dixon puts it in "Back Door Man":

> *The men don't know*
> *But the little girls they understand*

MTV CULTIVATED AN EDGY IMAGE, but the pioneering video channel actually followed a traditional Top 40 strategy: carpet bombing viewers with a small number of hit videos, to achieve maximum saturation. Only five new videos were added each week. The jockeying at the labels to be one of the five was intense, and every week label honchos made personal visits to MTV headquarters, at 1515 Broadway, to lobby for their artists.

The Backstreet Boys and 'N Sync had been kept at arm's length by MTV for years, because that kind of pure pop threatened to blow the channel's cool cover. Andy Schuon, the wunderkind DJ from KROQ in L.A. who took charge of programming at MTV in the early '90s at the age of twenty-seven, recalled Barry Weiss coming into the office with Backstreet's first video, "We Got It Going On."

"I remember watching it," Schuon says. "And it was just so different from anything we played. And while we would sometimes find things and lead with them, like No Doubt—we broke them—we looked at that Backstreet video and said, 'That doesn't feel right.' Right-straight-down-the-middle pop from a group that wasn't an established act—that was hard for us." He went on, "We had success putting music into boxes. We had *MTV Jams* as a proving ground for rap, and then we had *Alternative Nation* for grunge. But we didn't have a pop zone. I mean, the whole channel was Top 40, but we were the arbiters of cool, and that made it harder for us to play that stuff." New Kids on the Block were never a major force on MTV.

But by 1998, it was hip to be square again. No show made that clearer than *Total Request Live*, which made its debut in September of that year. *TRL* played the top ten most requested videos, from tenth to first. Aired on weekday afternoons, it was broadcast from a glassed-in studio on the second floor of the Viacom Building, in Times Square, causing crowds of twelve-year-old girls to gather out on the sidewalk. The show's effusive host, Carson Daly, had none of the acerbic qualities of Kurt Loder, the dour face of MTV during the grunge years.

Schuon goes on, "What changed was when *TRL*, a countdown show, was launched, then you could say, 'Here's what's most popular, let's put it on, we didn't pick these things—you did!' That's what allowed us to play pure pop."

BRITNEY'S FIRST SINGLE, ". . . Baby One More Time," came out on November 3, and sold 500,000 copies *that day*. It was the soundtrack of everyone's holiday party that season, in heavy rotation with Prince's "1999." It got to number one right after New Year's. (It probably would have gone to number one sooner, but Top 40 stations rarely change their playlists during the holidays.) The production genius was undeniable. The sound leaps out of the speakers, from Britney's vocal fry to her belted lines. The Cheiron boys had produced a masterpiece of digital compression.

The video also dominated MTV. Ten years later, when *TRL* closed down, ". . . Baby One More Time" was honored as the most requested video of all time.

The song was Max Martin's first Billboard number one (the first of twenty-two, so far, including his 2014 number ones for Taylor Swift, "Shake It Off," "Blank Space," and "Bad Blood"). "I don't really think we understood what we had done," he said. "I actually remember that specific moment, I remember sitting in the studio when they called me to let me know that my song had made number one in the USA. And that was incredible, but I also remember that I had so much going on with everything else right then, I didn't really grasp the meaning of it." Britney's debut album went on to sell 30 million copies worldwide, eclipsing *The Sign* by Ace of Base as the bestselling debut of all time.

Meanwhile, as Britney was blowing up around the world, the Backstreet Boys came out with their album *Millennium* in May 1999. The first single, a midtempo ballad called "I Want It That Way," is arguably the prettiest of all Max Martin's tunes. The melody is a lambskin glove of the softest leather that fits perfectly over the rhythmic knuckles of the song. Although it never reached number one in the United States (no Backstreet Boys song did), "I Want It That Way" was a worldwide smash that became the group's best-known tune.

The second single, "Larger than Life," didn't do as well, but the third, "Show Me the Meaning of Being Lonely," another classic Max Martin earworm, was a smash. The video of the song was dedicated to Denniz; the bus driver in the video is a Dagge lookalike who drops AJ off at "Denniz Street." The album sold 1.1 million copies in its first week (a record only 'N Sync would break) and became the bestselling album of 1999. Today it ranks among the bestselling albums ever in the United States.

For Britney's second album, Max and Rami came up with "Oops! . . . I Did It Again," released in March 2000. Here that most distinctive of Cheiron sounds, the kick drum and snare, is programmed to perfection. The bliss point comes when the chorus melody meets the beat, and Britney growl-purrs the hook in that swampy Cameo-inflected Louisiana twang—"I did it again." The chord progression is reminiscent of sixteenth-century music, as Richard Thompson points out in his live cover version of the song.

With all this chart success, the word "Cheiron" had become a talisman in the record business. As a hit factory, the studio had surpassed Don Kirshner, Phil Spector, and SAW. Cheiron was approaching the standard set by Motown, at least in number of hits, though not in the development of artists.

Denniz PoP, the man who had started it all, was gone, but his disciples kept his legacy alive and reaped the benefits. Andreas Carlsson writes in his memoir, "All of our lifestyles expanded. We had become millionaires in a very short time. The seemingly never-ending lineup of new cars—Porsche, Jaguar and Mercedes—would be parked outside the studio. We gifted each other with expensive trips and birthday presents." Key West became a popular destination, almost a home away from home for the Cheironites. "We were the most expensive production machine in the world," Carlsson goes on, "with an eight percent production royalty." Typically, songwriter-producers got between 3 and 4 percent of the master recording proceeds from a song, along with a hefty percentage of the publishing. "But since Cheiron produced the singles that ensured that the album would sell as a whole, it must have been worth it."

Carlsson continues, "When the Backstreet Boys came to Stockholm, they would stay in the Sheraton Hotel, which turned into a teenage hangout zone. Us Cheironites had pretty much the same status as the band, and could take advantage of life as rock stars, if we wanted. The magic word 'Cheiron' became a door opener at all the clubs around town."

BACK IN THE USA, all was not well at Trans Continental, Lou Pearlman's company. The Backstreet Boys had finally figured out that the people behind 'N Sync were none other than their very own management team and Big Poppa himself. That didn't sit at all well with them. "Mr. Pearlman was always speaking loyalty and preaching loyalty," Kevin Richardson said later. "'I love you guys; you're like my sons.' And I'd lost my father to cancer. So I looked at Lou like a father figure. But I was naive, and he's a liar."

As the bands traveled around the country and the world, they kept meeting friends of Lou's who seemed to have a special claim on their time. These "friends" would eat with the guys, accompany them on tour buses, and sometimes even ride with them in airplanes and helicopters to gigs. Lou explained they were "investors"—not investors in the bands, exactly, but in one or another of his Trans Con companies with which his musical endeavors were commingled.

"He would pick us up at the airport in a Rolls Royce," Dave Mathis, one of Lou's investors, remembered in the CNBC show *American Greed.* "He would take us to his steakhouse"—Pearl Steakhouse, in downtown Orlando. "We would be driven around on a bus, which on the side said 'Backstreet Boys.' And when the door opened, we had kids all over the place!"

Is it possible that no one who was associated with Pearlman suspected his whole operation was in reality a giant Ponzi scheme? Pearlman was using the money from Backstreet Boys and 'N Sync to pay off investors in his other fraudulent businesses—the blimps, airplanes, and a massive insurance business scam. The forty-seven planes Pearlman claimed to own didn't actually exist. In fact, he had only one plane, and the fleet depicted in the brochures for Trans Con (the name took on a whole new meaning, when Pearlman's scheme finally came to light) was actually made of model airplanes, photographed to look real.

Dave McPherson, of Jive A&R, says, "Looking back on it, there were always these people around who weren't music people. . . . I knew Lou was getting them to invest, but I didn't think he *needed* them to invest. Lou was so nice and nonthreatening. I just assumed, he's this rich guy with all these connections to Wall Street, he's really into music, and he's proud of the Backstreet Boys and wants to show them off to his friends. I believed he had airplanes. I myself had been up in one of his blimps. I had flown on his private jet with him. He drove a Rolls, and he took me out to so many dinners at Peter Luger's, and the money covers everything up."

In 1998, with their careers peaking, Backstreet Boys sued Pearlman for fraud and breach of fiduciary duty. They accused him of keeping $10 million of their recording and touring revenues, and giving them only $300,000 all together. The suit also said Pearlman had treated them like his "indentured servants." Kevin Richardson, explaining the decision to sue, said, "There came a point that we'd done five tours in Europe and none of us had a significant amount of money to show for it. We started looking at each other, going, 'You know what? Our managers are driving Jaguars, and we're sharing hotel rooms. Something's not right.'"

Jive managed to get the lawsuit settled quickly. The terms were not disclosed, but Pearlman had reportedly received $30 million, and one-sixth of whatever the Backstreet Boys earned in the future, which was what allowed him to keep his Ponzi scheme afloat for another eight years. "It's ridiculous," Brian Littrell said, of the settlement. "He's doing no work." The band in return got to break its contract with Big Poppa. By the time *Millennium* came out, they were free. Henceforth, in the official Backstreet Boys press-kit bio, there would be no mention of Pearlman. He was expunged from their history.

'N Sync also suspected Pearlman was stealing from them. By 1998, even though 'N Sync had sold 15 million albums, they were still forced to make do on a $35 per diem. After much complaining from the band, in late 1998, Pearlman and Ariola Munich, their label, which had taken in millions in album sales, magnanimously gave each member a check—for $25,000. Lance Bass tore his up on the spot.

The band hired Adam Ritholz, a well-known music-business attorney, to examine their contract, and he discovered that Big Poppa was helping himself to half their CD and merchandise revenues, and to 20 percent of their touring income—far more than the typical manager received. Ritholz negotiated with Larry Rudolph, Pearlman's lawyer, to get the band a fairer deal, but Pearlman refused to alter the contract. So 'N Sync decided to go to court to break their contract with Pearlman, and asked the chairman of BMG's North American operations, Strauss Zelnick, to help. But Zelnick, whose wife, according to Steve Knopper's book *Appetite for Self-Destruction*, called him MKIA—Mr. Know-It-All—loyally but foolishly sided with Pearlman, telling Ritholz, "This is the girl I brought to the dance—she may not be the prettiest girl, but she's the girl I'm going home with."

Pearlman fought to remain as the band's manager, and the case eventually wound up in front of a Florida judge. Pearlman's attorney argued that as the sixth member of 'N Sync, his client was entitled to more than the typical manager's share. The judge responded, "So you're telling me that *Mr. Pearlman* is 'N Sync, and these guys over here, my daughter has a poster of on her wall, are *not* 'N Sync?" Not long afterward, the parties settled, resulting in another big payday for Pearlman.

Had Pearlman called it quits then, and made do with the assets he had, he might have avoided the calamity that later befell him. He had scored two huge successes with the Backstreet Boys and 'N Sync, and although both acts had eventually fired him, he had earned a lot of money from them. Had he paid back his investors, he might have gotten away with his scheme. But he did not. As Assistant US Attorney Roger Handberg later said, "When he made it big, when he made his money with 'N Sync and the Backstreet Boys, [Pearlman] didn't turn away from his fraud. . . . Instead . . . he used his newfound celebrity as another weapon against people, a weapon that he used to lure people into investing more and more money."

Although he had missed out on having Britney as a member, Pearlman forged ahead with Innosense, his girl group. Their first album, *So Together*, did not produce a hit. "What everyone was telling me was they wouldn't be super-huge," Pearlman says from the Texarkana Federal Penitentiary. "Boys aren't going to run around with an Innosense T-shirt, or run to all the concerts." They toured in Europe, but the trip didn't go well, and the members squabbled constantly. "It got to be catfights, so to speak," Big Poppa reports. "You know, guys have a fight and ten minutes later it's all over. But when girls have a fight, it's never over!"

Pearlman also developed a three-boy group called LFO, who enjoyed some success; their song "Summer Girls" hit number three on the Hot 100. Natural, a quintet, did well in Europe. Two more boy groups, Take 5 and C-Note, failed to chart. Pearlman also came up with an influential concept for a TV reality show, at a point when reality TV was a new format. "I was thinking of doing a reality show with music," he says, "so I suggested, 'How about watching me put together a band—just bring the camera and watch.'" That idea became the first reality show on network TV, ABC's *Making the Band*, which later became an MTV staple anchored by Puff Daddy.

Could Pearlman have stopped at some point, paid people back out of his bands' proceeds, and gone clear? "I did actually start doing that," he says, "but it got out of hand. Like a dyke that starts sprouting holes, and once there are too many you can't plug them. Don't forget it costs money to develop these bands, and once I recouped that money back, you have to pay the artist. So I started paying people back, but I knew that just one more band would take things to another level, and get me whole, and everybody else whole, and I was trying to get to that next band, but that just wasn't happening at the time."

Instead, Pearlman doubled down, buying a chain of TCBY yogurt franchises; Chippendales, the male striptease dance troupe; an Internet-based talent agency; and another restaurant in Orlando. He purchased a 16,000-square-foot home in Chaine du Lac, a tony neighborhood in Windermere, Florida, where his neighbor was Shaquille O'Neal. Major banks, including Bank of America, loaned him up to $130 million, which he used to keep his fraudulent schemes afloat. Roger Handberg continued: "He was the selling point behind most of these loans. 'You've heard of me. I'm Lou Pearlman. I'm basically the Brian Epstein . . . of 'N Sync and the Backstreet Boys.'" To further bolster his reputation, Big Poppa even commissioned a promotional videotape—*Lou Pearlman Livin' Large*.

Early in 2007, with the feds closing in, Pearlman fled the country, and was on the lam for several months. In his absence, the US government formally charged him with defrauding more than a thousand investors of $300 million. He was captured in Bali, where his celebrity proved to be his undoing. A German tourist spotted him at a Westin resort, and informed a reporter for the *St. Petersburg Times*, who in turn told the FBI. He was brought back to the United States in chains. In March 2008, Pearlman pleaded guilty to fraud and money laundering and was sentenced to twenty-five years in prison, although the judge offered to reduce his sentence by one month for every million he paid back to his investors.

Speaking from prison, Pearlman boasts that, were he free, he would "give One Direction a run for their money," mentioning the latest iteration of the boy-band template he perfected. "They don't really dance. We'd put together the dancing and choreography." But at present his only musical activities involve organizing the prison choir. "I put together a choir here in the prison, and it turned out pretty nice. It's a Christmas choir. I help with the selection of folks, choose the songs, help with the harmonies—that kind of thing. They sound really good. It's not profitable, but it's nice. And it shows me that I could do it again if I were given an opportunity."

PEARLMAN'S STEALING FROM 'N Sync indirectly allowed Clive Calder to poach the band from BMG. Even though he produced their rival, Backstreet Boys, Calder convinced the band that Jive's expertise would be uniquely valuable to 'N Sync. He signed them, and Jive took over the production of the band's next album. The title would be *No Strings Attached*, a reference to the band's entanglement with Pearlman. The first single, written and produced by Kristian Lundin, Jake Schulze, and Andreas Carlsson of Cheiron, was the megahit "Bye Bye Bye," another poke at Pearlman and Zelnick, which climbed to number four on the Hot 100. The second single, "It's Gonna Be Me," written by Max Martin with Andreas Carlsson and Rami Yacoub, went to number one. The album, released in March 2000, sold 2.4 million copies in its first week—shattering the mark Backstreet had set with *Millennium*, and becoming the first (and last) album ever to top 2 million in its opening week since the Nielsen SoundScan era began in 1991.

. . .

BY THE NEW MILLENNIUM, Stockholm seemed like the center of the pop world. In addition to Cheiron's incredible success with Backstreet Boys, Britney, 'N Sync, and the British boy bands Five and Westlife, Max Martin had a big hit with the anthemic "It's My Life," which revived Jon Bon Jovi's career. Meanwhile, Jörgen Elofsson had become British A&R man Simon Cowell's go-to songwriter for the show *Pop Idol*, the British precursor to *American Idol*, penning three UK number-one songs for Cowell's boy band, Westlife: "Evergreen," "Fool Again," and "My Love"; all three songs were produced by Per Magnusson. Kristian Lundin and Andreas Carlsson wrote and produced songs for Celine Dion, including the hit "That's the Way It Is." All while the Cheironites were still grieving for Denniz PoP. In 1999, ASCAP named Max Martin "Songwriter of the Year" (with Diane Warren), the first of many such honors. And in the spring of 2001, the normally press-averse Martin Sandberg actually appeared on the cover of *Time* magazine in Europe, with the headline "The Hit Man."

Thanks mainly to Cheiron's success, a Klondike mentality had developed in Stockholm, as A&R men from the United States as well as the UK came to Sweden prospecting for hits. If they were unable to interest Cheiron in working with their artists, they went searching for gold and platinum in the streets, which were now full of production studios. Even Tommy Mottola, the head of Sony Music, came to Stockholm. Andreas Carlsson wrote, "One rainy day in the fall, a man dressed in a mink coat showed up with his private chauffeur and umbrella. The man was Tommy Mottola. . . . He had taken his private jet to Stockholm to talk business in hope of taking part of the Cheiron phenomena. His arrival had not been taken seriously, so when he arrived there was nobody in the studio. People had gone to dinner or the movies. This didn't happen because we were rude, but more that we did not need the world around us, however the world around needed us."

At first, Denniz's death did nothing to diminish Cheiron's productivity. Max said, "We talked about all this before Denniz passed away. I felt like there was no way in hell I'd be able to go on my own . . . [b]ut he was firm in telling me that I couldn't give up." Soon, however, the stress began to undermine the magic. Carlsson wrote, "Our last year at Cheiron we had turned into more of a machine then the gang of young and happy guys working in the promised land of music." They also began to face copycatting, as all hit makers do. "Everything on the radio sounded like duplicates of our music, which made it hard for us to stay so far in the lead as we had before." In his book, Carlsson recalled a remark from Def Leppard's Phil Collen, who "explained the phenomena . . . in a very comprehensive way: 'Everybody else started becoming better at being Def Leppard than us.'"

Largely thanks to Cheiron, the music business enjoyed a banner year in 2000–2001. CD sales, which had brought so much treasure to the business, were at their apex. In 1999, in what would soon look like hubris, the industry's trade organization, the Recording Industry Association of America (RIAA), created a superplatinum award with which to honor the new megahits—the Diamond Award, bestowed on records that sell more than 10 million copies.

No one was having a better year than Jive in 2001. In fact, few record companies, major or independent, have ever had a year like Jive had in 2001. It owned the teen pop market, a remarkable transformation for a company that started out in the United States as a rap label. Over a two-year span Jive sold 60 million Backstreet albums, 30 million Britney Spears albums, and 14 million of 'N Sync's *No Strings Attached*. On the R&B front, the label had R. Kelly and the doomed seventeen-year-old R&B phenom Aaliyah. Calder's Christian-music unit was also going strong. It seemed he could do no wrong.

As Zomba creative director Eric Beall puts it, "Clive was probably the most strategic person I've ever met in the industry. Nothing was a random, one-off decision. Everything was part of a larger plan.

Sometimes at A&R meetings he would review the monthly schedule of Britney or Backstreet Boys, and on the fly would completely rework the thing in a way that he felt was more strategic and efficient. Amazing to watch how his mind worked. He truly was always three steps ahead of everyone else in the room."

But Jive's pop fortunes were built on shifting sands. It is an axiom in the music world that teen pop acts don't last, for the simple reason that teens grow up fast, and the next teen cohort will define itself against its predecessor's enthusiasms. Plus, the young stars themselves inevitably grow up, publicly, with all the pressures of celebrity weighing down on them. AJ McLean entered rehab in 2001, the first of three rehab spells over the next decade. Nick Carter also fought a long battle with drugs and alcohol, which he recounts in harrowing detail in his 2013 book, *Facing the Music and Living to Talk About It.* But neither would fall as far and as fast as Britney, who by mid-decade would find herself committed to a psychiatric hospital, attired in a straitjacket with a self-shaven head.

In 2001, Jive's and Zomba's revenues came to almost $900 million. That meant that Calder's put option with BMG, which gave him the right to sell BMG his company for three times the profits, was worth about $2.7 billion. When Calder started to show signs that he was thinking seriously of forcing BMG to buy Jive/Zomba, Thomas Middelhoff, the CEO of BMG (later, after leaving BMG, he was convicted of embezzlement) reportedly offered to make Calder the head of the company's music business instead, which would have put him at the levers of power at a major label. On the other hand, the music business as a whole was near a historic peak; there might never be a better time to sell. Napster had debuted in 1999, and it wasn't clear that the record men could put the free-music genie back in the bottle. If the game was to play for the highest stakes, then the winning move was to cash in now.

Steve Lunt says, "Actually, it was very sad. Clive didn't want to sell the company, but he felt he had to." There had always been a conflict between the music lover and the businessman in Calder, but people who had bet that Calder's heart lay with the music usually lived to regret it.

On June 11, 2002, Calder exercised his put option. He sold out to BMG for $2.7 billion, and disappeared from the music scene. He lives in seclusion in the Cayman Islands and is rarely seen in public. In a parting e-mail to the staff, Calder, ever prescient, pointed the way toward the future of pop music and articulated the record industry's guiding philosophy and way forward: *"HIT RECORDS ARE MADE IN THE RECORDING STUDIO."*

CHORUS
THE MONEY NOTE: THE BALLAD OF KELLY AND CLIVE

9 | My Ancestral Hit Parade

MY MOTHER GREW up playing the piano, as had her mother and my great-aunt, who everyone called Sister. They purchased the sheet music of the popular hits of the day and performed them for one another and for friends and family. When my mother died I inherited her sheet music, which I keep in a box in our basement in Brooklyn. It's my ancestral hit parade, beginning in 1889 with "What Would You Take Me For, Papa?," with words and music by Thomas Westendorf, and extending through "I Am Woman," by Helen Reddy and Ray Burton, 1975.

Here is "Hannah Won't You Open the Door" (1904) by Andrew B. Sterling and Harry Von Tilzer (who was also the song's publisher, with offices on West Twenty-Eighth Street in the heart of Tin Pan Alley.) And Al Jolson's "When the Grown Up Ladies Act Like Babies," and "My Pretty Little Indian Napanee" with words by Will S. Genaro and music by W. R. Williams. ("It 'Scalps' All Other Indian Songs," says the cheerfully racist jacket copy.) Many of the early sheets have illustrations of the subject of the song on the cover—dreamy damsels and happy white men enjoying the easy life back in Dixie. Photos of the Vaudeville singers who popularized the song often appear in insets; "Hannah Won't You Open the Door" sports a picture of a forgotten singer named Bonita.

By the 1910s, Irving Berlin has made an appearance in the box, with

"Alexander's Ragtime Band" (1911). (Like many of the sheets owned by my Midwestern maternal ancestors, this was purchased from F. W. Woolworth's Music Department on North Sixth Street in St Louis.) Then comes a spate of vogue-ish "stuttering songs" such as "Oh Helen!" by Chas. R. McCarron and Carey Morgan (1918), which, says the cover, "Can also be had for your phonograph or player piano," a sign of changes to come. There are songs from the *Ziegfeld Follies*, such as "Isle D'Amour" (1913), novelty songs such as "O'Brien Is Tryin' to Learn to Talk Hawaiian," by Al Dubin and Rennie Cormack (1914) (including tabs for the ukulele), and patriotic songs like "Dress Up Your Dollars in Khaki" (1918), by Lester Alwood and Richard Whiting.

The 1920s were glorious years for popular song. Both Al Jolson and Irving Berlin were hitting their stride. The Gershwins, Ira and George, make their first appearance in the box with their 1924 hit "Fascinating Rhythm," published by the proto–hit factory T.J. Harms. And, of course, "Yes! We Have No Bananas!" by Frank Silver and Irving Cohn, a novelty sensation in 1923 and an early example of melodic math that is, oddly, one of the best-remembered songs of the period. The decade closes with "Stardust" by Mitchell Parish and Hoagy Carmichael (1928).

In the 1930s, songs from musicals and Hollywood movies predominate. The music publishers have moved uptown to the Brill Building by now. Modern celebrity culture is taking shape in the photos of Ozzie Nelson and Rudy Vallée, and, above all, Bing Crosby, whose face, in gauzy soft focus, graces many a cover.

Then we're into my mother's music. I see her penciled notes above the treble line. I recognize songs she used to sing to me as a child, such as Cole Porter's "(You'd Be So) Easy to Love," and Irving Berlin's "I'm Putting All My Eggs in One Basket," both from 1936. There's lots of Rodgers and Hammerstein, and plenty of Jerome Kern, and here come the Andrews Sisters! At which point my mother's enthusiasm for new music evaporates. The box contains only a few items from the '50s, and even less from the '60s. Somehow "Didn't We" (1968) by Jimmy Webb made it into the box and, more improbably, "I Am Woman" the 1975 women's lib anthem by Helen Reddy. And with that final roar from Mom, my easy-play Neil Young guitar books take over, which she also saved.

It's striking how little the basic form of the popular song has changed. The delivery mechanism is in constant flux—from sheets to player piano rolls, to radio, vinyl, cassettes, CDs, MP3s, and now streams. But the emotional mechanics of songs have largely remained the same, whether they're embodied by Al Jolson's ivories or Slash's lead guitar. The verses build up the tension, and the choruses release it, letting the joy in. After two choruses, there's usually a bridge, also known as "the middle eight," which is a variation on the verse melody, followed by the final chorus and coda.

The fact that my ancestral hit parade concludes so abruptly tells of the massive changes that rock and R&B brought to popular song—changes my mother was not willing or able to absorb. But I did, gleefully; on the piano and, later, on the guitar, I picked up where my mother left off. Strange that these three-to-four-minute ditties should be the glue that connects us, even after she's gone. The music changes, but the song (as the song goes) remains the same.

10 | The Dragon's Teeth

JUST AS THE record business was nearing its historic peak, setting sales records that would never be broken, Napster disrupted the business model. It was the mother of all disruptions. In the last months of the twentieth century, music, which had been selling for $17 a CD, became free, thanks to the exploding popularity of Napster, the pioneering file-sharing service. Napster unleashed piracy on the record business, and began the cataclysm that caused worldwide revenues to decline from a peak of $27 billion in 1999 to $15 billion in 2014.

Napster was created by a nineteen-year-old Northeastern University freshman named Shawn Fanning. The software was a downloadable "client"—an app, basically—that allowed people who had it to scan one another's hard drives and download the music they wanted for free. In its early stages, Fanning told Sean Parker, a friend he knew over IRC, an early text-messaging network, about his idea, and they agreed to start a business together. Fanning was the coder and Parker was the pitch man who raised the money. The software spread rapidly across college campuses and beyond; the user base went from 30,000 to 20 million in about six months. Thanks in part to the dot-com boom, the company managed to score $70 million in venture capital. At its peak Napster had 60 million registered users.

The founders' fond hope was that the labels would take Napster over and make it their digital-music distribution service. But the labels weren't interested in joining forces with the devil. Instead, they put Napster to sleep, filing suit against the company for copyright infringement in December 1999.

"There was this unique opportunity in history," Parker says today. "We said, 'If you shut down Napster, it's going to splinter, and you're going to have a Whac-A-Mole problem on your hands, where you're fighting service after service and you're never going to get all those users back in one place.' And that's what happened." From the dragon's teeth sprang KaZaA, Grokster, Morpheus, and Limewire. Parker continues, "It was one of those things where it can be totally clear to you and everyone in your generation and you can explain it in the clearest of terms, not as a threat or a negotiating tactic—just, 'Look, you just have to see this'"—the Whac-A-Mole problem. "And they couldn't see it. This was the biggest existential threat to the music business, and they wouldn't listen."

AS THE RECORD INDUSTRY entered the twenty-first century, five global music groups controlled more than 70 percent of the market. The Universal Music Group, owned by Vivendi Universal, was the dominant player among the majors; it was run by Doug Morris. Then came the Warner Music Group, a division of AOL Time Warner, headed by Roger Ames. Warner had been the leading company in the record industry from the early '70s to the mid-'90s, but by the end of 2002, with a 16 percent share of the domestic market, Warner—"Warner's" is what you said if you were in the business, as if it were Jack Warner's corner record store—had fallen well behind Universal, which had a 29 percent share. Next came Sony Music Entertainment, led by Tommy Mottola, then the Bertelsmann Music Group (BMG), and lastly the EMI Group, which was perpetually on the verge of being gobbled up.

By the end the decade, BMG would be part of Sony and EMI would be bought by Universal, leaving only three.

The people who ran the groups were record men, who had made their bones before the labels consolidated. Some affected a gangster vibe—their enemies were "dead to them," and duplicitous managers or rival executives were going to "get their legs broken." In fact, the group heads were from nice homes in the suburbs, but record men have historically been tough guys, so they acted tough too. They sustained the paranoid style of the record business, that I'll-fuck-you-before-you-fuck-me mentality.

Their bosses were corporate managers, who worked for the global media companies that had bought into the record business. These suits knew little about making records. Universal Vivendi was run by Jean-René Fourtou, an ex-pharmaceuticals executive; and the head of Bertelsmann was Gunter Thielen, who previously ran the company's printing and industrial operations.

The groups were made up of dozens of formerly independent labels, which had been started by music-loving entrepreneurs in an earlier era—fanatics who had discovered creative ways to capitalize on their enthusiasms. The founders were men like Chris Blackwell, who launched Island Records in 1962 and brought reggae to the masses; and Ahmet Ertegün, who co-founded Atlantic Records in 1947, and Clive Calder. These were men of taste and musical discernment, business-minded aesthetes who cut a certain swath through the culture. But with the commercial success of rock in the '70s and '80s, driven by kids like me, and amplified by the introduction of the CD in the mid-'80s, many of the labels were bought by larger media companies. They kept the labels' names but little of their cool. The music business slowly changed from an art-house business run by men with ears into a corporate enterprise of quarterly earnings and timely results.

But corporate culture is not conducive to musical talent. Chris Blackwell says, "I don't think the music business lends itself very well to being a Wall Street business. You're always working with individuals, with creative people, and the people you are trying to reach, by and large, don't view music as a commodity but as a relationship with a band. It takes time to expand that relationship, but most people who work for the corporations have three-year contracts, some five, and most of them are expected to produce. What an artist really needs is a champion, not a numbers guy who in another year is going to leave."

And controversy, a pop star's wingman, is almost never good for the corporate image. In the mid-'90s, Warner was in a dominant position in the burgeoning rap market through its half ownership of Interscope. But bad publicity over lyrics and violence was hurting Time Warner's other businesses and straining the political connections that the corporation needed in Washington. In 1995, CEO Gerald Levin sold the company's half share of Interscope, jettisoning the troublesome hip-hop unit. Under Jimmy Iovine, a former engineer and producer turned mogul, the label eventually became part of Universal. Interscope went on to amass a remarkable string of hits, including records by Eminem and 50 Cent. The success of Interscope was the main reason Universal had eclipsed Warner in market share and become the industry leader.

FILE SHARING WAS A full-blown college-campus phenomenon by mid-2000, right around the time the Backstreet Boys and 'N Sync were setting records for sales. In that year, 70 percent of all college students had used Napster once in the previous month. For a whole generation of music fans (including a precocious fifteen-year-old programmer in Sweden named Daniel Ek, who would go on to create Spotify) Napster was the most amazing thing about the Internet. Music, which used to cost you seventeen bucks per CD in a store, was free! Plugging your new laptop—a high-school graduation gift from Mom and Dad—into the superfast university T1 line granted you access to the unguarded stockroom of the world's greatest music superstore. And feckless dithering by the label groups allowed Napster users to develop a sense of entitlement. It wasn't just that the music was free—it *should* be free. Anyone who said differently, like Don Henley of the Eagles, or Lars Ulrich of Metallica, or Dr. Dre, were greedy hypocrites.

Before 2000, not many of the leaders in the record industry could have told you what a MP3 was. Few were computer literate; some couldn't even type. That's what secretaries were for. Perversely, record men have always feared new technologies, which their business is founded on. Take away the technology to reproduce sound, and you're back in the parlor with my grandmother, listening to Sister play the piano. And yet, almost every time a new technology appears, the industry tries to stop it. Ninety years earlier, music publishers sued player-piano makers, fearing that people would stop buying sheet music. In the 1920s, the publishers sued radio broadcasters for copyright infringement. The CD, the main driver of the latest boom, was booed by record men in the audience when it was introduced by Philips in Miami in 1983.

The day after the 2000 Grammy Awards, Hilary Rosen, the head of the RIAA, convened the group heads in the Four Seasons Hotel in Beverly Hills, to explain what Napster meant for the industry, and why Shawn Fanning and Sean Parker had to be stopped. For many, this meeting was the first time they realized the full implications of file sharing: the business they had all profited from so handsomely was in dire trouble.

"So I set up a computer," Rosen recalled in the film *Downloaded*, "and I said, 'OK Tommy [Mottola], what's your latest single?' or 'Michelle [Anthony, a top executive under Mottola], what's your latest single?' Literally we played 'Stump the Napster.'" Every song the record men in the room could think of was available. In his 2003 book about Napster, *All the Rave*, Joseph Menn also described this meeting: "As the crowd grew increasingly uncomfortable, a Sony executive tried to cut the tension. 'Are you sure suing them is enough?' he asked. The capper came when someone suggested a hunt for the 'NSYNC song 'Bye Bye Bye.' The cut had been on the radio just three days, and the CD hadn't been released for sale yet. And there it was."

Napster was mostly shut down by mid-2001, but the users simply moved on to KaZaA, Limewire, and other file-sharing sites. (KaZaA was incorporated on the Pacific island nation of Vanuatu, where copyright laws didn't exist.) New music continued to be ripped from CDs and uploaded as soon as the records came out, and often before they came out, by studio technicians or by workers in CD production plants, who, thanks to industry consolidation, had a vast array of new music at their disposal, from many different labels, all in one CD factory. Touring acts were shocked to hear fans singing along to songs that hadn't been released yet.

By 2002, hit records were selling half the numbers they'd sold only a few years earlier. The eighteen-year-old Canadian singer Avril Lavigne was the biggest pop sensation of 2002; her debut album, *Let Go*, sold 4 million records in its first six months, whereas Alanis Morissette's debut album, *Jagged Little Pill* had sold 7 million when it was released in 1995. In 2002, the industry shipped 33.5 million copies of the year's ten bestselling albums, barely half the number it shipped in 2000. Don Henley of the Eagles said before Congress, "Whether we like it or not, Napster changed everything and the record companies are sadly behind the curve."

It was all over, and fifteen long years of piracy lay ahead. The studios where Clive Calder's hits were supposed to be made would go out of business. Few labels could afford them anymore. Record stores would all but disappear. A&R departments would shrink. But there was a glimmer of hope on the horizon, a lifeline flung to the drowning record men by Steve Jobs, in the form of the iTunes music store.

11 | The Doldrums

DURING THE YEARS he worked as a program director at Top 40 stations around the country, Guy Zapoleon observed that popular music fads seem to move in a three-part cycle. Over time, he formulated a set of laws that, he believes, drives the pop cycle. It starts in the middle, with "pure pop." This is the natural sweet spot for program directors, because it is the genre of music that draws in the largest number of listeners, boosting ratings. But pure pop eras inevitably give way to what Zapoleon calls "the doldrums," when Top 40 becomes bland and boring, and ratings decline. In response, program directors row away from pure pop, toward the more perilous waters Zapoleon calls "the extremes," in order to restore excitement to their stations. The extremes—alt-rock and hip-hop—attract younger listeners, always a desirable demographic for the advertisers (who, in a business sense, are a commercial station's real constituency), but repel older ones, and so program directors begin rowing back toward the pure-pop mainstream, and the cycle starts again.

Tom Poleman, who took over New York's Z-100 in the extremes of the mid-'90s, when grunge was polarizing listeners, endorses Zapoleon's cycle, although he isn't sure about who is at the wheel: program directors or the public. "I think sometimes cycles are caused by bad programming," he ventures. "We do things that overdose on one style, then the consumer gets sick of that and wants something completely different." However, he adds, "That's also the nature of pop culture: people tend to embrace one thing, then get tired of it and want something else. So both radio programmers and the consumer are chasing that next thing and influencing each other."

The musical movements of the '90s were a textbook illustration of Zapoleon's cycle. The decade had begun with New Kids on the Block, a pure-pop phenomenon if ever there was one. That phase led to the doldrums of '92, perhaps best represented by Michael Bolton's *Timeless: The Classics*, which topped the album charts that year. Grunge rock and gangsta rap combined to create an especially enticing extremes period, which lasted from 1993 until 1996. The Spice Girls' 1997 arrival in the United States led to the rebirth of pure pop, which lasted through the doldrums of 2001, when the public grew weary of boy bands. By 2001–2002, a new extremes period was under way.

As he had been in '92, Dr. Dre was on hand to drive the extremes part of the cycle, with his latest protégé, Eminem, whose 2000 song "The Real Slim Shady" managed to insult Britney Spears, boy bands, and the Grammys, all in one verse. The single was awarded Best Rap Solo Performance at the 2001 Grammys; the album also took home hardware. With three multiplatinum albums and a hit film, *8 Mile*, which mythologized his life story, Eminem was biggest artist in the world by 2002, and the latest bracing corrective to "manufactured" artists who didn't write their own material. He was angry, profane, and misogynistic—a mean voice for a dark time—and being white gave him a license no black rapper spitting comparable rhymes would have been granted, an inequity that made Eminem angrier still.

But Eminem was sui generis, and in spite of his insistence that

> *There's a million of us just like me . . .*
> *Who just don't give a fuck like me*

there was only one Eminem. His success redefined the rules about what you could say on the radio.

Eminem made Tom Poleman nervous. "We didn't want to go back to the extremes we'd come out of in '96," he says. "And Eminem was clearly an indicator of the extremes. Playing those hard, intense lyrics at midday was a concern. But P. Diddy was writing melodic music, and even 50 Cent's song 'In Da Club' with that hook 'It's your birthday,' managed to combine the exciting danger of Eminem with an appealing melodic presentation. It goes back to a safe place." Poleman adds, "I think people like to be surprised. They say, 'Oh, that's that cool music I've been hearing about. But it doesn't scare me because it seems really poppy and hooky.'"

AS PROGRAMMERS FLED THE doldrums for the extremes of Eminem and 50 Cent, the Klondike days in Stockholm came to an end. Swedish writers and producers had become identified with bland, artificial boy-band pop. Also, after 9/11, American artists and A&R men didn't want to travel to Stockholm; flying was too much of a hassle. Swedish writers and producers began a diaspora to Southern California, resulting in the large Swedish expat songwriting community that resides in L.A. today.

Cheiron Studios closed its doors toward the end of 2000, just as the doldrums began to set in. Max Martin, now the studio leader, had decided, "it's time to quit while we're ahead." As Kristian Lundin says of Cheiron's distinctive sonic tapestry: "When even our grandmothers said, 'Oh, you can hear that's a Cheiron song!' it was no longer inspiration, it was just copying ourselves."

Denniz PoP's disciples split into three different entities. Max Martin and Tom Talomaa, who had run Cheiron's business, formed Maratone Studio, which was named after one of Denniz's favorite computer games, Marathon. They brought in Rami Yacoub. Kristian Lundin and Andreas

Carlsson remained in the Cheiron building, but changed its name to The Location. And Per Magnusson and David Kreuger teamed up to form A Side Productions. Everyone struggled to come up with a new sound.

Even Britney, who wouldn't be a star without Cheiron, turned away from her Swedish song makers. Her 2003 album, *In the Zone*, featured not a single Cheiron alumnus on it (the sole Swedish contribution came from Cheiron's competitors, the songwriting duo who called themselves Bloodshy & Avant, and who later co-wrote one of the artist's best songs, "Toxic"). Instead, Britney used urban producers like Timbaland, Christopher "Tricky" Stewart, and the Neptunes to give an edgier sound to her music. The times were dark—racial profiling, enhanced interrogation techniques, and a push toward war with Iraq based on false intelligence. Swedish-made pop was an ill-fitting soundtrack.

As the most successful of all the Cheiron disciples, Max Martin had become synonymous with teen pop. 1999's "I Want It That Way," rightly seen as a classic when it appeared, became a leading example of the kind of pure pop that radio programmers in 2002 shunned. The Swede started to have trouble getting cuts on records. Hip-hop was where the red-hot center of pop music lay now, and Max Martin didn't have a clue about hip hop. Either he had to find a collaborator who could help him, or he needed to wait for the Zapoleonic wheel to turn again and bring pure pop back into vogue. But if the '90s were a reliable precedent, that might not happen until the 2010s.

In fact, a new force was about to disrupt the pop-music cycle. Weirdly, it came from TV. Zapoleon had met his "Waterloo."

12 | American Idol

LIKE THE IDEA of America itself, *American Idol* owes a lot to Great Britain. It is based on a British talent search show called *Pop Idol*, which in turn was adapted from a New Zealand and Australian show called *Popstars*. The main creator, Simon Fuller, had been the Spice Girls' manager, before they fired him. Fuller's partner was Simon Cowell, a successful British A&R man whose role as the "mean judge" on *Pop Idol* had made him famous.

The son of a music executive who grew up around show business, Cowell prides himself on his commercial tastes. He makes no pretense of caring about art in pop music, and sneers at those who do. He had his first big success with an album that featured songs sung by the Teletubbies, the children's-TV play pals; he'd followed this with a Mighty Morphin Power Rangers album, also a hit. During the teen-pop years, he made it big in boy bands; he signed Five, and the Irish group Westlife. Largely thanks to Cowell, Cheiron disciples such as Jörgen Elofsson, Per Magnusson, and Andreas Carlsson had plenty of work after 9/11, when the US market for Swedish-made pop songs dried up. Cowell's later group, Il Divo, was also a boon to Swedish songwriters.

Pop Idol contained all the raw materials of a hit factory—a large pool of versatile singers, a plentiful supply of professionally crafted tunes, and an experienced staff of talent coaches, image makers, and mentors to mold the kids into stars. Crucially, the show added the element of built-in promotion—the show's massive audience.

Pop Idol had not found any takers when it was first offered to US networks in the spring of 2001. After it became a hit in Britain, the producers were back in the States, pitching it again, to an equally tepid response. However, Rupert Murdoch's daughter Elizabeth, who was living in London and working for her father, knew and loved the show, and she told him about it. Murdoch called his number two at News Corporation, Peter Chernin.

"What's going on with this show *Pop Idol*, Peter?" he asked, according to Bill Carter's 2006 book *Desperate Networks*. "It's a big hit in England. I spoke to Liz and she says it's great."

"We're still looking at it," Chernin replied.

"Don't look at it," Murdoch shot back. "Buy it! Right now."

Fox bought it. The timing was right. In the post-9/11 era networks were looking for what Carter calls risk-free "comfort programming," and *Idol* seemed to fit the bill. Fox scheduled the show in the sleepy summer season of 2002, on Tuesday nights, right after *That '70s Show*.

The producers made one key change to the British show: they got rid of the word 'Pop' in the title. Although the show's musical fare was pop by any measure, "pop" still has a subtly negative connotation in America, more so than in the UK and Europe. In spite of the triumph of teen pop in the late '90s, the word still carries with it an element of guilty pleasure in the United States. The reasons for this are complicated (my book *NoBrow* is an attempt to explain them at length), but suffice it to say that Americans, lacking a class system within which to situate themselves, turn to culture to find their rank in society, and pop doesn't usually secure the status that more artistically prestigious fare offers. Only Michael Jackson could call himself the King of Pop and make the title sound like an honorific.

Apart from that, *American Idol* hewed closely to *Pop Idol*'s format

(Murdoch insisted on it). Fox even imported the British show's producers, Nigel Lythgoe and Ken Warwick, and most of its crew. The star was again Simon Cowell. Only the hosts, Ryan Seacrest and Brian Dunkleman, and the other two judges, Paula Abdul and Randy Jackson, were new.

At first, the record industry took a dim view of *American Idol*. The idea that the masses could spot talent as effectively as a trained A&R person was laughable. Record men went along with the show because it promised to deliver a mass audience, something sorely lacking in the fragmented world of popular music. But few thought *Idol* would sell records, and no one expected it to create lasting pop stars. (Clive Davis characterizes his colleagues' belief in the chances of a true star emerging from the show as "essentially unthinkable.") MTV videos were one thing (the industry had once been skeptical of those, too) but a live variety show, and a talent competition at that, was seen as very downmarket, and the "cheese factor," as Davis put it, was high.

Davis was nearly seventy when the *American Idol* gig came to him. Part of Cowell's deal with BMG stipulated that Arista make an album for US release with the winner. The show also needed a skilled song picker, someone who could put the artists together with flattering material, and Davis specialized in that. And Davis believed that variety TV could sell records. "I knew that with the weekly exposure of the personalities on TV," he says, "that if I treated the A&R as seriously as I treated what I had done for Whitney or Manilow, that we could have hits."

Europeans have grown accustomed to televised singing competitions thanks to decades of watching the Eurovision Song Contest, a monthslong pan-European tournament of song that had introduced ABBA to the world with "Waterloo," the winning entry in 1974, and that ends with the crowning of one country as champion, World Cup–style. Never mind that most of the songs are sung in English, and many are written by Swedes: eastern European countries such as Kazakhstan and Azerbaijan pay dearly for Swedish songs.

Talent shows tend to reward a facile ability to sing in different styles over deep artistry, and to favor singers who lean heavily on melisma—stretching a sung syllable out over several notes—because that's the way great vocal talents are supposed to sound. *Idol* might make good television, and it would probably bring quick but fleeting fame to the performers, but it wasn't going to create long-term careers.

Davis acknowledged that *American Idol* was not going to break "an artist as unique and individual as Alicia Keys" (presumably only Davis himself, who signed her, could do that). On the other hand, *American Idol* was a way to bring back the pop music Davis loved—not the dance-oriented stuff on the radio, but the classic ballad singing that he had built his career on. "I embraced *American Idol* because pop music was diminishing in impact," he says. "There was no new Barry Manilow, Barbra Streisand, or Celine Dion. Towering pop figures who had had so many hits were no longer part of the Top 40 genre. A Billy Joel. A Neil Diamond."

THE AUDITIONS FOR THE first season of *American Idol* began in April 2002, and carried over into May, in seven cities from coast to coast. Ads for the tryouts were broadcast on the Fox radio network; all together about ten thousand people turned up. It was a nationwide version of the boy-band-manufacturing process that Lou Pearlman and Maurice Starr had pioneered, and a measure of how industrialized the concept had become. The majority of the candidates were eliminated in the pre-screening rounds, before they even encountered the three judges.

In the very first auditions before the judges, which were taped for broadcast on the maiden episode of the show, no one knew what to expect from Simon Cowell. Few Americans had seen *Pop Idol* and were unaware of the Nasty Simon persona Cowell had cultivated. Even the hosts and Cowell's fellow panelists seemed taken aback when the judging started and the Kraken emerged from his cave.

Cowell's nastiness put hosts Dunkleman and Seacrest, who were supposed to comfort the kids before and after the auditions, in an awkward position. "It's one thing to watch it on television," Dunkleman later said in Richard Rushfield's book *American Idol: The Untold Story*, "but when you spend time with the kids and you have to look at them right in the eyes and then their mother is looking at you like, 'What just happened?'" And the kids are saying, "'You're telling me I suck? That I should never sing again?'" The show, which was supposed to be about finding talent, turned out to be about humiliating the talentless in front of a national audience. Somehow the contestants and their parents had missed that memo.

Justin Guarini, one of the singers who came to the New York auditions, and soon became a favorite, recalled waiting in the holding area to go before the judges, and seeing the other contestants coming back from their auditions in tears, one after another. "We're waiting and all of a sudden the doors grind open," he told Rushfield, "and it was this girl and she was bawling . . . It was shocking for us."

The Fox producers recognized immediately that Cowell was "the hook," as one put it, and featured his acerbic commentary in the footage from the auditions that they provided to the media. "The footage we gave the press," recalled Preston Beckman, who did publicity for the show, "was predominantly Cowell eviscerating people. . . . It was kind of like nasty . . . the way we were selling it." But there was no arguing with the ratings. Ten million people watched Simon reduce hopefuls to tears in that first episode, and the numbers only grew from there. The public loved it.

When all the auditions were complete, 121 wannabes received "golden tickets" to Hollywood. During Hollywood Week, these fortunate few were further winnowed to thirty by the judges. From that group, the audience got to choose their top nine contestants, and the judges added one wild card. Then the show began the process of elimination: two the first week, and one a week after that. Each week the contestants were required to perform pop songs from a different era, composer, or genre—Motown, '60s, '70s, Big Band, Bacharach, love songs, and so on. Through the summer of 2002, as Eminem threatened to move Top 40 radio toward the extremes, *Idol* kept the American public anchored in the pure pop center.

KELLY CLARKSON, THE YOUNGEST of three children, was a shy-seeming twenty-year-old, a sometime waitress from Burleson, Texas, who had entered the competition because her mother's friend had heard one of the Fox radio ads for the Dallas tryouts. Kelly's parents' marriage dissolved when she was six, and the family literally split apart, with her father taking her brother to California and her sister moving in with her aunt. Kelly and her mother, a first-grade teacher, remained in Burleson, where her mom eventually remarried.

The young Texan's musical influences were eclectic, which would serve her well on *Idol*. "My stepdad would wake me up at frickin' 6 a.m. playing Willie Nelson and Merle Haggard," she recalled in a 2012 interview with *Rolling Stone*, "and my mom was into Three Dog Night and Linda Ronstadt. But I loved Aretha and Otis and Bonnie Raitt—the heartfelt stuff." During a particularly unhappy period in her preteen years, her mother suggested she write in a journal as an outlet, and her journal entries came out in the form of song lyrics. Some of those lyrics later became the basis for Kelly's hit song about her father, "Because of You."

Clarkson knew she could sing. In her senior year in high school she won a vocal scholarship to Berklee College of Music, in Boston. But she passed it up with a breezy "you can go to college anytime," and lit out for California to seek her fortune. She found work in L.A. as a backup singer, and sung on demos for several producers, including Gerry Goffin, Carole King's former husband and writing partner. She also landed a few small parts on TV shows. But she never signed a record contract, and she did not have a manager, which were two of the prerequisites to be on *Idol*—the producers truly wanted neophytes. When the apartment building she lived in caught fire, she decided to go back home to Texas, where she was waitressing in a cocktail bar when her mom's friend told her about the show.

Kelly went to the Dallas auditions and sailed through the early screener rounds before meeting the judges. Like Guarini, she was stunned to see the kids in line ahead of her come out of the audition room in tears. "So I was like, 'Oh God, I'm going to go in there and he's just going to yell at me—OK, whatever,'" she said. When her audition was over, she was relieved. "I was just so happy because the British man didn't make me cry."

She performed two songs, a nervy pair—"At Last," made famous by Etta James, and Madonna's "Express Yourself." Even at this very early stage of the final competition, it was clear how good she is—her version of "At Last" was especially strong. But neither the judges nor the producers—whose greatest fear was that all of the contestants would be mediocre—realized what they had. Maybe it was because Kelly appeared toward the end of a long day, and Paula and Randy were deep into arguing with Simon about his viciousness. Still, for professionals who were in the business of spotting talent, it is striking that when they came face-to-face with that one-in-a-million singer who actually has the chops to be a great pop star, they didn't notice her. When Kelly finished, Randy mentioned that he had worked on "Express Yourself" with Madonna. This moved Simon to mock Randy for his boring industry-insider stories, which led to a charming bit of byplay between Clarkson and the judges, wherein Kelly took Randy's seat and Randy got up and sang a couple lines of R. Kelly's "I Believe I Can Fly" while Clarkson made jokes.

Clarkson did get a golden ticket, but her audition wasn't even deemed promising enough to show on the first broadcast. The next time she faced the judges, in Hollywood, Cowell, the great A&R man, couldn't remember who she was. "Did you not swap places with Randy?" he asked. "That's the only thing I can remember." You can hear him muttering to Abdul, "I just don't like this girl." What a pro!

Clarkson proceeded to sing the shit out of Aretha's "Respect," and that did force the judges to notice her. A superb belter, she could sing in her head voice with almost all the power of her chest voice. But incredibly, the judges continued to favor Justin Guarini, a tall, hunky rock singer with a halo of hair, and Tamyra Gray. The producers also shamelessly flogged their million-dollar human-interest story—Jim Verraros, whose parents were deaf; he sang to them in sign language.

Week after week, the judges kept giving Kelly progressively harder songs to sing, and she crushed all of them. After she sang "Walk on By," the Bacharach-David tune, Cowell finally saw the light. "We didn't pick up on you early in the show," he admitted, but now, "I truly, truly believe you are going to become a huge star at the end of this show." After Big Band week, when Clarkson sang "Stuff Like That There," which Bette Midler made famous, Randy said, "You're probably one of the most natural great singers I've heard in a long time." And after her shattering rendition of Badfinger's "Without You," during '60s week, there was a sense that she could actually win.

The finale, which took place on September 4, came down to Justin versus Kelly. By now the show was the ratings phenomenon of the summer: an astounding 23 million people watched the final broadcast. The demographic spread was Cronkitian; *American Idol* was the summer's highest-rated show for viewers aged eighteen to forty-nine. The two finalists looked like an adorable couple attending their high school prom. Even the odious Cowell, with his inimitable talent for making a compliment sound like a put-down, couldn't ruin the mood, though he tried, saying to Kelly, "If you don't win this competition, then we will have failed."

And then Clarkson went out and sang "A Moment Like This," a new song by Cheironite Jörgen Elofsson and John Reid, written specially for the show's finale. As the final chorus rolled around, you sensed that the song was building toward an emotional climax that people in the record business sometimes refer to as "the money note."

The money note is the moment in Whitney Houston's version of the Dolly Parton song "I Will Always Love You" at the beginning of the third rendition of the chorus: pause, drum beat, and then "*IIIIIEEEEEEEIIIIII* will always LOVE you." It is the moment in the Celine Dion song from *Titanic*, "My Heart Will Go On": the key change that begins the third verse, a note you can hear a hundred times and it still brings you up short in the supermarket and transports you from the price of milk to a world of grand romantic gesture—

You're here
There's nothing I fear.

David Foster, the producer of Whitney's version of "I Will Always Love You" and a contemporary master of the pop ballad, claims that he coined the phrase "the money note" during a session with Barbra Streisand. "Barbra had hit this high note," he says, "and she wanted to know how it sounded, because although you'd think Barbra was real confident, she's not. And I said, 'That sounds like money!' I don't mean money in the crass sense of 'That will make a lot of money!' although that's certainly part of it. I meant 'expensive.' It sounded expensive."

Kelly hit the money note in "A Moment Like This"—the key change in the final chorus—in full cry, a chill-making moment. And when she was crowned the following night, and Justin gave her a big hug, it was pure TV magic.

13 | "Since U Been Gone"

THE MP3 WAS the next format. By 2002, that much was clear to the label groups. Therefore, the record business needed a digital marketplace where MP3s could be purchased legally. But the groups couldn't agree on whose marketplace was better. Sony and Universal joined together to create a subscription service called Pressplay. AOL, BMG, and EMI teamed with RealNetworks to create MusicNet, a download service. Neither service would license to the other one, which crippled them both.

With the sense of urgency mounting, Steve Jobs, Apple's founder, stepped into the breach with a cool proposal—the iTunes music store. Roger Ames, head of Warner Music Group, saw Jobs's presentation as the future. "Yes, yes, that's exactly what we've been waiting for," he said. One by one, his fellow leaders signed on to Jobs's plan. Finally, Jobs went to see Doug Morris himself, and won the record man over with his charm. "When I met Steve, I thought he was our savior," Morris told writer Walter Isaacson in *Steve Jobs*. Morris called Jimmy Iovine at Interscope to get his impression. "You're right," Iovine said. "He's got a turnkey solution." So the deal was done, and iTunes opened its virtual doors on April 28, 2003, selling downloadable songs for 99 cents and albums for $9.99.

Jobs's digital record shop showed that some people were, in fact, still willing to pay for music—iTunes sold 1 million digital singles in its first six days, and 70 million in its first year. But iTunes didn't really solve the problem of piracy. And while the labels got to keep almost 70 percent of the money from each 99-cent sale, it wasn't like selling albums. Instead of the $10 to $12 of profit the companies had been enjoying on each CD, they got about 67 cents from a digital single. By shifting the standard unit of commerce from the album to the single, iTunes disemboweled the labels' profit margin. There was a 12 percent drop in revenues from 2000 to 2002 (the Napster era), but a 46 percent drop in revenues from 2002 to 2010 (the iTunes era).

The big money was in iPods, which the music helped to sell. Priced at $399 each, Apple had sold 200 million iPods by the end of 2008, and the music industry didn't get any of that money. And while the iTunes store gave people the option of paying for music, pirated MP3s worked on iPods as well.

IN PURSUIT OF A new sound and new collaborators, Max Martin started spending time in post-9/11 New York with Swedish colleagues and friends, going around to clubs. They needed a nightlife guide, a disco Virgil. An American demo singer who had sung background on some Cheiron productions had a boyfriend who was DJing in a couple cool clubs. His name was Lukasz Gottwald, but in the clubs and on his mix tapes he was called Dr. Luke.

Gottwald, twenty-eight, was also a guitar player; he had a regular gig with the house band for *Saturday Night Live*, a job he'd had for six years. He had an unusual range of musical skills. He had studied both rock and jazz, was a pretty good drummer, and he could sing, in a high voice. His job at *SNL* had acquainted him with a vast repertoire of American popular music, ranging over almost a century. As a producer, he knew his way around Pro Tools as well as anyone; he was as skilled at programming music as he was at playing his instrument.

Gottwald was ambitious for more. Like Denniz PoP before him, he wanted to expand his audience beyond the five thousand or so who could cram into a club to dance to his mixes. "I thought, Why not make records for millions of people?" he recalls. But he was unsure about how to do that.

He started paying attention to the songwriters of the big hits. "And I noticed the name 'Max Martin' on a lot of them," he says, "so I thought, Hmmm, maybe I should meet him." And so he did.

"I was DJing all the hot spots in New York at the time, so I knew everybody. I took them out one night and said, 'Hey, you need to go here.' They liked it, so when later they flew back in and wanted to go out again, they called me."

Gottwald was cocksure and arrogant—a completely different animal from Martin Sandberg. But he was also perceptive. He sensed he would spook the skittish Swede if he came on too strong.

"Everyone was trying to write with him," he says, "so I deliberately didn't do that. I'd play music sometimes so he was aware that I was good." He adds, "I made tracks. I was just starting to do melodies. One time, I was playing my tracks, and there was this one part where the singing came in and Max made a face."

Although Max was elusive, some of the other former Cheironites were more approachable. Gottwald began making regular trips over to Stockholm to hang, always angling for time with the master. Rami Yacoub, who had perhaps the most to lose from Max's subsequent partnership with Dr. Luke, was the most welcoming of all. Gottwald began spending all week in his new friends' Stockholm studios, making music, flying back to New York just to do his *SNL* gig and then heading back over to Stockholm again.

Sometimes Rami and Luke would go with Max to East, the sushi place that he frequented in Stureplan, Stockholm's Times Square, a high-end restaurant with beautiful tropical fish tanks that had been Denniz's hangout too (Tom Talomaa was a part owner). They talked about songs constantly, but still Max said nothing about working together, and Luke knew better than to ask.

Then, "One day I got a call from Max," Gottwald remembers, "and in a very Max way he asked me if he could rent my New York studio. I felt like it was a test. To see if I said, 'Sure, you could rent it,' or 'You could just use it.' And I said, 'Just come use it.' And once we started working together we really hit it off."

Right away Gottwald proved his mettle with guitar sounds—not the big metal sound that It's Alive had made, but a subtler, indie-rock sound. Gottwald is a Mutt Lange fan, and he had made a close study of Lange's work with the Cars, including the hit "You Might Think," which sounds like a template for Dr. Luke's later pop work.

Of the beginning of their songwriting partnership, Gottwald told *Billboard* in 2010, "We were listening to alternative and indie music and talking about some song." The song reportedly was "Maps" by the Yeah Yeah Yeahs. "I said, 'Ah, I love this song,' and Max was like, 'If they would just write a damn pop chorus on it!' It was driving him nuts, because that indie song was sort of on six, going to seven, going to eight," he said, describing the levels of intensity. Then, "the chorus comes—and it goes back down to five. It drove him crazy. And when Max said that about the chorus, it was like—light bulb! I said, 'Why don't we do that, but put a big chorus on it?' About two minutes into "Maps" comes a great hard-edged rock guitar riff, and Luke began trying to make a chorus out of that. Slowly, as they sat shoulder to shoulder in Gottwald's tiny West Twenty-First Street studio, "Since U Been Gone" began to take shape.

THE FIRST KELLY CLARKSON album, *Thankful*, had sold well, at least by 2003 standards, and produced a modest hit, "Miss Independent," which made it to number forty-four. The album's sales figures were one of the few bright spots in an otherwise dismal year, as the record industry's downward spiral continued. Sales for 2003 were 15 percent lower again than those of the disastrous previous year.

But Clive Davis knew that Clarkson's all-important sophomore album was the one by which she (and he) would be judged. The second album had to make her a global idol on her own merits. As he had with the first album, Davis put out a number of feelers to top-shelf songwriters he thought could write a rock-tinged pop song for Clarkson.

Clarkson had other ideas: she was going to write her second album herself. She had been willing to go along with Davis, who was almost fifty years her senior, in selecting songs for her first album, but she was damned if she was going to let him pick them again. People wanted to hear songs that came from a real twenty-three-year-old, not from some old man trying to imagine what young people wanted to hear. As Clarkson recalled later, "I just think it's funny that all these middle-aged guys told me, 'You don't know how a pop song needs to sound.' I'm a twenty-three-year-old girl! But I was fighting those battles alone." She added, "People can't fathom that someone who is vocally talented could have some kind of writing ability."

Davis understood where this was coming from. After all, Clarkson wasn't just some girl he'd found on the street. She was an *Idol* winner— millions of people had voted for her. "It's heady," Davis wrote in his 2013 memoir *The Soundtrack of My Life*. "And all that attention affects all *Idol* winners. But then suddenly you're in an entirely different world of making records in a studio, and you have to take direction. Kelly didn't like it." But Davis also knew that great vocal talents like Melissa Manchester and Taylor Dayne—both Arista artists—could have had much longer careers if they hadn't insisted on writing their own material.

Clarkson had written, with David Hodges and Ben Moody of the rock band Evanescence, a song called "Because of You." It was based on one of the teenage poems she had written about her father breaking up the family. Davis liked it but thought it was too downbeat. "I'm sorry I've inconvenienced you with my life," Clarkson later told him.

Davis asked Clarkson to record a song originally written for Avril Lavigne called "Breakaway," which Whitney Houston wanted to use in a Disney film she was co-producing, *The Princess Diaries 2*. Clarkson didn't want to record it, but she eventually agreed. She also allowed Kara DioGuardi to work on a number of songs for the album.

BY THE END OF 2003, the sophomore album was almost finished, but Davis was still looking for that elusive pop-rock song he had in mind for Clarkson. One day, Max Martin came to see him at his office. They'd become acquainted back in the Ace of Base days, and although the Swede had not penned any hits for Davis's other artists, he respected the record man's gifts as a song picker.

"Max had had this big run of hits with Backstreet Boys and 'N Sync," Davis recalls. "A huge, huge run that enabled Clive Calder to make almost three billion dollars. But he was trying to change his image after that run. He's grown very resentful of writing bubblegum-ish boy-band kind of songs. He kept saying, 'Look, I'm much more substantive. I don't want to be dismissed as a bubblegum writer.'"

After they had chatted for a while, Max played Davis a demo of the songs he and Dr. Luke had been working on, "Since U Been Gone" and "Behind These Hazel Eyes."

Max Martin had at first had Pink in mind for "Since U Been Gone," but she turned it down. And he didn't think Hilary Duff could sing the high parts. The Swede was hoping Davis would help "cast" the song with one of his rock-oriented artists, but Davis had someone else in mind: Kelly Clarkson.

"Are you crazy?" Max replied heatedly. "Didn't I tell you that I wanted this song to go to rock artists? That I didn't want to be typecast? Now you want to give it to an *American Idol* winner?"

"You don't understand," Davis told him. "Kelly's got a great voice, she's got real potential, and she likes edge. Look, you'll produce it. You'll get the right performance." It took several such conversations before Max finally agreed to give Clarkson the song.

Davis then presented the song to the artist. She didn't want to record it. "It didn't have any lyrics and the melody really wasn't finalized," she recalled. Also, "the track was done on a computer, there was no band on it," which offended her rock sensibility.

Nevertheless, Clarkson agreed to go to Stockholm, and she recorded the song with Max Martin at Maratone. She actually wrote the song's bridge, although she didn't get a writing credit. Dr. Luke was also around for the sessions, but he was still learning how vocal production worked and didn't contribute much. Clarkson did not enjoy working with Max Martin. He insisted that she sing "Since U Been Gone" exactly as he had sung the song on the demo—he didn't seem to have the least respect for her *Idol* status. Also, his obsessive "comping" of the vocals—comparing multiple takes of the vocal parts of a song to find the perfectly sung syllable in each take, and pasting all of them back together into a complete vocal—drove her mad. "Max is a very hands-on producer," Davis explained. "They clashed in the studio when she was doing her vocals." When the sessions ended and Clarkson was back home, she told Davis, "I'm never working with him again."

But in spite of the tension in the studio, the record they made of "Since U Been Gone" was magnificent. "I remember when we comped vocals for Kelly on 'Since U Been Gone,'" Max Martin said in a 2010 interview with *Billboard*. "We listened back to it and it started sounding like a record. I remember that was a big moment, like, 'Holy shit! I think we did it!' There was a lot of jumping around and laughing."

The song starts off sounding like a mashup of Cars hits: "Just What My Best Friend's Girl Needed." Eight measures of stripped-down rhythm are played by Gottwald, using his "bad guitar" technique, an intentionally amateurish-sounding thrashing of the bottom two guitar strings, fretted in a G chord. Then a punk-rock bass starts, along with electronic-sounding percussion. A subtle burst of squalling feedback, one of the song's signature guitar-rock sounds, leads into the distorted choral hook, a blast of pure melodic energy—

> *Since you been gone*
> *I can breathe for the first time*

carried along on Clarkson's powerful (and impeccably comped) vocal, for which she won a Grammy. Suddenly it's a great sing-and-jump-up-and-down power-pop song (if you listen closely you can hear Gottwald singing over Clarkson's voice), set to a rock 'n' roll backbeat made with crashing drums and cymbals. The song then reverts to indie rock in the next verse and bridge; we hear fingers squeaking on guitar strings, another indie trope. Everything is frosted with the electronic sheen produced by dynamic range compression, which pushes even the quiet sounds right into your face and gives the song a density that makes it stand out in loud public places.

The lyrics are in American vernacular, not Swenglish. On the chorus, Clarkson belts three octaves above the lowest notes in the song. The musical arrangements complement her voice beautifully.

Davis was thrilled. Luke's hard-edged rock guitar, combined with Max's soaring choral melody, was exactly the pop-rock sound he had been looking for. He played the song, together with the other Max/Luke collaboration, "Behind These Hazel Eyes," that Clarkson had recorded in Sweden, for the BMG international sales conference, which was attended by reps from all the territories worldwide where BMG sold records. They went nuts for both songs.

A few days after the sales conference, Clarkson came to see Davis in his office. According to Davis, she began the meeting by saying, "I want to be direct and to the point. I hate 'Since U Been Gone,' and I hate 'Behind These Hazel Eyes.' I didn't like working with Max Martin and Dr. Luke, and I don't like the end product. I really want both songs off my album."

Davis could not believe what he was hearing. Had winning *American Idol* addled this young woman's brains? He paused to compose himself.

"I'm heartsick," he said at last. "I just played these songs for the sales conference. You're too new to the industry to understand the value of this, but every country throughout the world is going to make you their number-one artist. If you had told me this before you recorded the songs, that would have been different. But I can't accede to your request now."

Hoping to make the pop idol see reason, Davis invoked his experience with Barry Manilow and Whitney Houston—how he had brought "I Write the Songs" to Barry, and how the artist had hated the song, swore up and down he wouldn't record it—and it became his signature tune. He brought "Why Does It Hurt So Bad" to Whitney; she kept it on hold for three years before she agreed to record it. Finally, after her divorce from the former New Edition star Bobby Brown, she said, "I'm ready to sing this song. I understand the song now." Davis also invoked the cautionary tale of Taylor Dayne. Ten straight hits Davis had chosen for her—ten!—and then she says she wants to write her own material.

"How do you keep a pop career going?" Davis asks rhetorically. "A continuity of hits"—his favorite phrase. "But in the case of Taylor, we had to wait two or three years while she wrote, and there were no hits. The public says, 'Why haven't I heard from Taylor Dayne?'" So many pop stars make that mistake—they want to be singer-songwriters, because in the United States that's who the critics respect. "And then you meet them twenty years later and they say, 'Why did you let me do it?'" Davis shrugs slowly, a signature gesture. "Because I let them."

In *The Soundtrack of My Life*, Davis described the momentous meeting with Clarkson over "Since U Been Gone." "It was a very tough conversation," he wrote, "and it didn't get any easier when Kelly burst into hysterical sobbing. We all just sat there as she cried for several minutes. No one knew what to say. Then she left to go to the ladies' room. When she came back the tension in the room was thick. Finally, I said . . . 'Since U Been Gone' is going to be the first single, and it's going to be a game-changer for you.' Kelly didn't say another word. She just looked at me with red, puffy eyes and a swollen face, and got up to leave. I truly felt awful. I've had differences of opinion with artists and my share of tough meetings, but I really had never been in a situation like that before."

Clarkson later disputed Davis's account on several points. "I just have to clear up his memory lapses and misinformation," she wrote in a post on her website, after Davis's memoir came out (the post later came down). She did not cry on that occasion, she said. "But, yes, I did cry in his office once. I cried after I played him a song I had written about my life called "Because of You." I cried because he hated it and told me verbatim that I was a 'sh*tty writer who should be grateful for the gifts that he bestows upon me.' He continued on about how the song didn't rhyme and how I should just shut up and sing. This was devastating coming from a man who I, as a young girl, considered a musical hero and was so honored to work with. But I continued to fight for the song and the label relented. And it became a worldwide hit. He didn't include that in the book."

But there could be no disputing that "Since U Been Gone" made Clarkson a superstar. The song did everything a hit can do for an artist. Thanks to "Since U Been Gone," and the second single, "Behind These Hazel Eyes" (which was also a big hit, peaking at number six), *Breakaway* sold 11 million copies worldwide—a huge post-Napster number—including 5.5 million abroad. Clarkson went on to win two Grammys, for her vocal performance on the album, and on "Since U Been Gone" in particular. The song also returned Max Martin to the upper echelon of the charts (the song peaked at number two), and it brought Dr. Luke to those lofty heights for the first time. The pair had discovered a special alchemy between them, a creative force that would shape pop for the next decade.

And yet, Davis wrote, for all Clarkson's subsequent worldwide success, "Was there ever any personal acknowledgment from her that I had been right?"

BY THE EARLY 2000S, record men routinely used advance testing to measure the hit potential of prospective singles. One of the leading testing services, Hit Predictor, was created by Guy Zapoleon, together with Rick Bisceglia and Doug Ford. Whether or not Hit Predictor really worked, it was accurate enough that some labels came to rely heavily on Zapoleon's method of testing songs. The labels' interest in Hit Predictor made the company so valuable that Clear Channel eventually bought it and began using Zapoleon's system in its own internal research as well.

The main difficulty Zapoleon had to overcome in creating Hit Predictor, he says, was that people don't know if they like a song unless they've already heard it. "There's an old adage that you can only do research on people who are already familiar with the song," he says. Zapoleon refers to this as the "rule of three"—you have to hear a new song at least three times before you know if you like it or not. Traditional call-out research, which radio stations do to test their playlists, is conducted on songs people have already heard. "They aren't taking a totally unfamiliar song and playing them that," he says.

Zapoleon's solution was to replicate the rule of three in a two-minute remix of the song. "We take the thirty-second meat of the song," he explains, "which is generally the chorus but sometimes it's not. And then comes a one-minute version that has the hook in it. And then we come back again to the thirty-second hook, what I call 'the filet mignon.'" Zapoleon's online respondents hear the essence of the song three times, all in the course of two minutes.

Hit Predictor was only one of a variety of different approaches to anticipating hits that became popular following the publication of

Michael Lewis's *Moneyball*, in 2003. The gut decisions record men were famous for making were subject to crippling psychological biases and hurt profits. A safer approach was, for example, Hit Song Science, a term trademarked by music entrepreneur Mike McCready. Hit Song Science was a computer-based method of hit prediction that purported to analyze the acoustic properties and underlying mathematical patterns in a new song, and compare them to those of past hits. In a 2006 *New Yorker* article, "The Formula," McCready told Malcolm Gladwell, "We take a new CD far in advance of its release date. We analyze all twelve tracks. Then we overlay them on top of the already existing hit clusters and what we can tell a record man is which of those songs conform to the mathematical pattern of past hits." Not only that, McCready's song machine could also tell a record man which aspects of the song needed to be remixed in order to make it a hit. It was all a question of giving the brain what it wanted from a song. "We think we've figured out how the brain works regarding music taste," McCready declared.

NOW THAT CLARKSON WAS a global idol, she took full control of song selection for her third album, *My December*. She and her collaborators wrote all the songs without Davis's involvement, and when the album was finished Clarkson's manager brought it to Davis as a fait accompli. He listened to the songs, and could hear only one minor hit among them. His staff, with ears of baser metal, agreed. Davis begged Clarkson to reconsider.

"'Number one, this material is not *Nebraska* by Bruce Springsteen,'" he recalls telling her condescendingly. "'It's not poetry. If you're saying you want to do an acoustic album of personal songs, if you've just given birth to a child and you want to do an album of lullabies, I wouldn't stop it. But these are pop songs that are not hits. So I have to point out the consequences. You just sold eleven million albums. As a businessman, and part of the team that got you these songs that sold eleven million albums, I do have the right to express my point of view. My advice is your sales will go down eighty-five percent if you do not have hits.'"

Clarkson didn't care, according to Davis.

"No argument. No yelling. She just didn't care."

Davis did manage to persuade the artist to let him test the songs with Guy Zapoleon, among others.

"They confirmed what the collective ears had stated," Davis goes on. "There's one top-ten record there."

"'I don't believe in testing,'" Davis says Clarkson replied. "'It's very important to me my album come out as-is.'"

Davis notes, "She had just broken off a relationship with a musician, and it was very important for her as a young girl that the irony and the bitterness be expressed, even though that irony and bitterness did not lead to hit songs." But in the end Davis agreed to release the album Clarkson wanted to release.

Davis was right. (In Davis's stories, he's always right.) Indeed, the results were even worse than the record man had feared. The album sold 1.1 million worldwide, a 90 percent drop-off from *Breakaway*. Clarkson fired her manager and had to cancel her world tour due to poor ticket sales.

In making her fourth album, *All I Ever Wanted*, and the final one that Davis executive produced, Clarkson obediently accepted the help of the pros. She even agreed to work with Max Martin and Dr. Luke again. The song they wrote for her, "My Life Would Suck Without You," which shamelessly returns to the melodic math of "Since U Been Gone" while inverting the lyrical message, became a number-one hit in February 2009. She also had a big hit with a song she co-wrote with Ryan Tedder, "Already Gone." And she had another number-one smash on her next album, a song co-written by Cheironite Jörgen Elofsson called "Stronger (What Doesn't Kill You)."

American Idol would go on to launch the careers of several more stars, including Clay Aiken, Jennifer Hudson, and Daughtry, and one other superstar, Carrie Underwood. (Cheironite Andreas Carlsson wrote Underwood's first number one, "Inside Your Heaven.") But since Clive Davis moved on from the show, in 2007, the number of lasting stars that *Idol* produced has notably declined. The doldrums of 2007 were perhaps partly to blame at the beginning, but the recent winners haven't come close to the stardom Clarkson and Underwood achieved (if only Davis had A&Red Adam Lambert's disappointing first album). The copycat talent shows that appeared on other networks—*The Voice*, *X Factor* (another Simon Cowell production), and *America's Got Talent*, among others—haven't produced a superstar either. Leading one to conclude that while a TV talent show can help get an artist noticed, it can't make a recording star. Only a record man can do that.

SECOND VERSE
FACTORY GIRLS: CULTURAL TECHNOLOGY AND THE MAKING OF K-POP

14 | "Gee"

TEENS HAVE HISTORICALLY provided hit factories with a ready market, but they also stamp the hit makers with an expiration date. Teens don't remain teens for long, and the next cohort is keen to differentiate themselves from their elders, particularly from their older brothers and sisters. Musical preferences work well for that: you hate the music your older sibling likes, simply because she likes it. In this way, the hit factories' successes have a built-in backlash; even Cheiron couldn't avoid it. The rock era greatly amplified this backlash, because it allowed the younger Beatles and Stones–loving teens not only to despise their older sibs' Brill Building records but also to feel morally superior in preferring "real" music sung by singer-songwriters to "manufactured" music sung by hired performers. In case the squares didn't get it, Dylan made the point explicitly in the spoken-word intro to his 1962 song "Bob Dylan's Blues": "Unlike most of the songs nowadays being written uptown in Tin Pan Alley . . . this was written somewhere down in the United States."

But what if the distinction between authentic and manufactured music—which is fraught with so many logical inconsistencies and built-in biases—didn't exist? What if factory-made products were perceived to be authentic? What would popular music be like then? American pop music seems to be heading in that direction, but in Korea it's already there. It's called K-pop.

LEE SOO-MAN, THE FOUNDER of SM Entertainment and the prime architect of the K-pop idol system, was born in Seoul in 1952, during the Korean War. He grew up listening to his mother play classical piano. At the time, the dominant Korean pop genre was trot (an abbreviation of "foxtrot"), pronounced "teuroteu." Trot borrowed from Western music and from Japanese popular songs, a legacy of the Japanese occupation, from 1910 to 1945. It blended these influences with a distinctively Korean singing style called *p'ansori*.

Lee, however, immersed himself in American folk and Korean rock music, which started on US Army bases and was popularized by the guitarist and singer Shin Joong-hyun, in the '60s. Long before K-pop came along, Korean musicians were masters at combining Western influences with traditional singing and dancing styles.

Lee made his name as a folk singer, and toward the end of the 1970s formed a short-lived hard-rock band called Lee Soo-man and the 365 Days. He also became a well-known DJ and the host of televised music and variety shows. But in the late '70s the Korean government cracked down on the music scene, arresting and imprisoning several prominent musicians on pot charges. When a military coup installed Chun Doo-hwan as president in 1980, Lee's radio and TV shows were canceled.

Lee moved to the United States, where he pursued a master's degree in computer engineering at California State University, in Northridge. He became fascinated with the newly launched MTV. If there is a single video from the '80s that captures many of the elements that later resurfaced in K-pop, it is Bobby Brown's 1988 hit "My Prerogative." Brown's dance moves—a swagger in the hips, combined with tight spins that are echoed by backing dancers—found their way into K-pop's DNA.

The fading career of producer Teddy Riley, who co-wrote the song, later found a second life at SM Entertainment—the company made him one of its go-to producers. Riley opened an office in Seoul, hired a staff, and started making hit records again.

In 1985, Lee received his degree, and, he told Mark Russell, the author of *Pop Goes Korea*, returned home determined to "replicate U.S. entertainment in Korea." Increasing prosperity, marked by the arrival of the 1988 Seoul Olympics, helped bring market-oriented democracy to the nation, and led to a general loosening of restrictions on the media. Around this time, Koreans coming back to Seoul from the United States brought the rhythms of rap and hip-hop, sung in Korean. The consonant nature of the language, with its abundance of *ka* and *ta* sounds, lent a hard-edged quality to the raps. In 1992, a three-member boy group called Seo Taiji and Boys performed a rap song on a Korean-TV talent competition, to the horror of the judges, who ranked them last, and to the delight of the kids watching at home (one of the boys was Yang Hyun-suk, the future founder of another important K-pop company, YG Entertainment). Korean music historians generally cite this performance as the big-bang moment in the origin of K-pop.

Lee founded SM in 1989. His first success was a Korean singer and hip-hop dancer named Hyun Jin-young, whose album came out in 1990. But just as Jin-young was on the verge of stardom, he was arrested for drugs. Russell wrote that Lee was "devastated" by this misfortune, and that the experience taught him the value of complete control over his artists: "He could not go through the endless promoting and developing a new artist only to have it crash and burn around him."

Henceforth his stars would be made, not born, using a sophisticated system of artistic development. Lee took Lou Pearlman's idea of putting together different personality types in a singing group and made a musical Samsung out of it, employing a method of cultural production Lee called "cultural technology." In a 2011 address at Stanford Business School, he explained, "I coined this term about fourteen years ago, when

SM decided to launch its artists and cultural content throughout Asia. The age of information technology had dominated most of the nineties, and I predicted that the age of cultural technology would come next." He went on, "SM Entertainment and I see culture as a type of technology. But cultural technology is much more exquisite and complex than information technology."

Lee had become aware of the Backstreet Boys in 1996 when they visited Seoul and near riots ensued. The passion of the fans impressed him, and that same year, SM debuted its first idol group: a five-member boy band called H.O.T. (short for High-Five of Teenagers). It was followed by SM's first girl group, S.E.S., after the given names of the three members (Sea, Eugene, and Shoo). Both groups were vastly popular in Korea, and inspired other groups. Soon K-pop was pushing both traditional trot and rock to the commercial margins of the Korean music scene.

In the mid- to late '90s, just as teen pop was sweeping over the US pop charts, the Korean Wave—a tsunami of South Korean culture—began flooding its Asian neighbors. In addition to K-pop, the Wave—*hallyu* in Korean—included Korean TV dramas and, to a lesser extent, Korean films. Korean TV producers established themselves during the Asian economic crisis of the late '90s by offering programming that was cheaper than the shows being made in Japan and Hong Kong and of higher quality than most other Asian countries could produce themselves. The biggest hit, *Winter Sonata*, a 2002 romantic drama, was huge throughout Asia. The series depicted young Korean actors in contemporary urban settings, but the stories embody traditional values of family, friendship, and romantic love.

In a classic example of "soft power," Korean cultural exports erased South Korea's regional reputation as an unsophisticated emerging industrial nation, and replaced it with images of prosperous, cosmopolitan life. Thanks to *Winter Sonata* middle-aged Japanese women now swoon over Korean men, while complaining about the "grass-eating"—that is, lacking in virility—males of Japan. Korean ancestry used to be a stigma in

Japan; now it's trendy. At home, K-drama's success has brought tourists from all over Asia to visit the sites depicted on the screen.

Lee led K-pop's expansion into the rest of Asia, where it became a staple in markets formerly dominated by Japan and Hong Kong. The Backstreet Boys had sung in French and Spanish, languages they didn't speak, to broaden their appeal in Europe; the Korean idol groups learned to sing in Japanese and Chinese, as well as English. But the synth-drenched sound and style of the music and the videos adhered to the principles that had made them popular in Korea.

Lee and his colleagues produced a manual of cultural technology that catalogued the steps necessary to popularize K-pop artists in different Asian countries. The manual, which all SM employees are instructed to learn, explains when to import foreign composers, producers, and choreographers; what chord progressions to use in particular countries; the precise color of eye shadow a performer should wear in different Asian regions, as well as the hand gestures he or she should make; and the camera angles to be used in the videos (a 360-degree group shot to open the video, followed by a montage of individual close-ups).

Cultural Technology (CT, Lee called it, for short) seemed to work. By the late nineties, H.O.T. was topping charts in China and Taiwan. Both H.O.T. and S.E.S. disbanded in the early 2000s, but Lee's follow-up acts proved to be even more popular. BoA, a solo female singer who made her debut in 2000, was a sensation in Japan. Super Junior, a boy group, debuted in 2005, and became even bigger throughout Asia than H.O.T. had been. And in 2007 came Girls' Generation, the nine-member group that represented cultural technology in its highest form, designed to conquer not only Asia but the West as well.

Lee retired as the agency's CEO in 2010, but he still has a hand in forming the trainees into idol groups, including EXO, a recent boy band. The group has twelve boys, six of them Korean speakers who live in Seoul (EXO-K) and six Mandarin speakers, who live in China (EXO-

M). The two "subgroups" release songs at the same time in their respective countries and languages, and promote them simultaneously, thereby achieving "perfect localization," as Lee calls it. "It may be a Chinese artist or a Chinese company, but what matters in the end is the fact that it was made by our cultural technology," he has said. "We are preparing for the next biggest market in the world, and the goal is to produce the biggest stars in the world."

THE SM WORLD TOUR III kicked off at the Honda Center in Anaheim, California, on a warm evening in May. It was still two hours until show time, but already thousands of K-pop fans were flooding the concrete plaza outside the arena. The night's performers were among the biggest pop groups in South Korea—SHINee, f(x), Super Junior, EXO, TVXQ!, and Girls' Generation. All were part of SM Entertainment, the largest of the so-called agencies that create the majority of Korean pop music, and the main sponsor of the tour.

For American K-pop fans, the Honda Center show was a rare chance to see the idols in the flesh. Outside the arena, clusters of fans were enacting "dance covers"—copies of their favorite idol groups' moves. People carried light sticks and bunches of balloons, whose colors signified allegiance to one or another idol group. The crowd was older than I'd expected, and the ambience felt more like a video-game convention than like a pop concert. About 3 out of 4 people were Asian American, but there were also Caucasians of all ages, and a number of black women.

Standing a little farther back was Jon Toth, a twenty-nine-year-old white dude, a computer scientist who had driven twelve hours straight from New Mexico. Toth is a fan of Girls' Generation. At the time he stumbled across the girls on YouTube, Toth was an alt-rock guy; he loved Weezer. "I was definitely not the kind of guy you'd expect to get into a nine-girl Asian group," he says. But before long Toth was studying

Korean in order to understand the lyrics and also Korean TV shows. Then he started cooking Korean food. Eventually, he traveled all the way to Seoul, where, for the first time, he was able to see the girls— Tiffany, Sooyoung, Jessica, Taeyeon, Sunny, Hyoyeon, Yuri, Yoona, and Seohyun—perform live. It was a life-changing experience.

"You think you love them, but then you see Tiffany point directly at you and wink, and everything else that exists in the world just disappears," Toth had written on Soshified, a Girls' Generation fan site. "You think you love them, but then you see Sooyoung look you dead in the eye and say in English, 'Thank you for coming.'" Toth concluded, "I might not know how much I love these girls."

Outside the Honda Center, he tells me, "They take the love the fans feel for them, and they return it to the fans. . . . When you see them onstage, it's like they've come to see you."

IN SEOUL, K-POP IS all around you. You feel the constant presence of the idols on billboards and in display ads. Life-size cutouts of idols greet you at the entrances of the big department stores. On the streets and in the subways you see echoes of the idols' faces. (On one occasion, in a hotel lobby, I strode up to what I thought was a cutout of a K-pop idol only to find that it was a real woman, who frowned and moved away.) In Gangnam, the ritzy shopping district on the south side of the Han River, the architecture was as showy as the idols themselves.

Three music agencies dominate the K-pop industry. All are headquartered in Seoul: SM Entertainment is the largest, followed by JYP Entertainment and YG Entertainment. They have the kind of control over the idols' careers that American hit makers can only dream of. The agencies act as manager, agent, and promoter, controlling every aspect of an idol's career: record sales, concerts, publishing, endorsements, and TV appearances. SM and JYP are headquartered in Gangnam, and there are always groups of young girls, many of them Japanese, in the streets outside, hoping for a glimpse of an idol or two (the idols generally move anonymously through the city, in minivans with tinted windows). Both sets of offices are surprisingly shabby inside, with cramped studios and worn-looking decor. YG, across the river, has much more lavish facilities, including around a dozen state-of-the-art recording studios and a staff of sixteen in-house producers, among them Teddy Park, who wrote the smash hit "Fantastic Baby" for BIGBANG, and most of the music for 2NE1, YG's two most popular groups

At JYP, I briefly met the founder, Park Jin-young, a tall, athletic forty-year-old who was educated in the United States. He had been in the agency's training facility. Dressed in workout clothes, he was in the middle of a session with some of the trainees, and he couldn't stop to talk; he disappeared into a dance studio, outside of which there was a pile of kids' shoes. However, I was able to chat with the five Wonder Girls, the agency's most successful girl group. In their video "Nobody," they wear shimmering dresses and bouffant hairdos—Korea's answer to the Supremes. Out of costume and without makeup, they are almost unrecognizable. They sit at a conference table, with lead singer Sohee, who looks very tired, in the middle. We talk a lot about jet lag. Sunye, sitting on Sohee's left, looks at the clock on the wall, which reads 5:00 p.m. "This time of day is the worst!" she declares.

The agencies recruit twelve-to-nineteen-year-olds from around the world, through both open auditions and a network of scouts (Big Poppa Pearlman never got that far). Girls' Generation, the dominant girl group in recent years, includes two members, Tiffany and Jessica, who were born and reared in California. (Native English- or Chinese-speaking boys and girls, usually of Korean origin, are highly prized.) Tiffany, who was born in San Francisco and grew up in Los Angeles, was recruited at fifteen while auditioning for a talent show, and brought to Seoul, where she trained in the idol-making system. Jessica, who was born in the same hospital as Tiffany, was discovered in Seoul at twelve. "I didn't really audition," she says. "I went to Korea to meet my dad's side of the family, and I was shopping, and one of the agents saw me, and picked me and my sister together." Her sister, Krystal, was seven at the time; now she is a member of the group f(x). In Seoul, both Tiffany and Jessica attended an international school by day; after school, they reported to SM, where they trained until ten, and then they had to do homework. Jessica's training lasted for seven years.

Idols receive extensive media coaching and are readied for the intense scrutiny they receive on the Internet from the "netizens" of Korea, the most wired country on Earth. ("Netizens Love Seohyun's Aegyo Mark" declared a typical headline from the K-pop website Soompi, regarding the small beauty dot to the left of the singer's eye.) Public drunkenness, brawling, and serial misbehavior can enhance an artist's reputation in the American pop scene; in Korea, a rumored sex tape or a positive test for marijuana can derail a career. Training lasts years before a boy or girl is assigned to a group. Only one in ten trainees makes it all the way to a debut.

The groups are generally put together by the heads of the agencies, according to an alchemy of individual and collective qualities. "The members of a group shouldn't be completely alike and indistinguishable," says Melody Kim, a community manager at Soompi, "but they should be complementary enough so that together they form a really great, cohesive whole." Groups debut on one of the many musical variety shows that play on Korean TV almost nightly. I attended a taping of one, for the Mnet musical program *M! Countdown*, where new and established groups perform their latest songs and the audience votes for its favorites; I was reminded of the days when MTV actually featured music. If idols are successful, they are often expected to churn out a full album every eighteen months or so and a five-song mini album each year. The charts change rapidly, and, because youth and novelty are at such a premium, established groups usually don't last long: five years is the average shelf life of an idol. (Some idols extend their careers by acting in K-dramas and K-musicals.) New groups appear regularly; in 2013, about sixty groups made debuts, an unprecedented number. Only a fraction is likely to last; most fade away after a couple of songs.

Good looks are a K-pop artist's stock-in-trade. Although some of the idols are musicians, K-pop artists rarely play instruments onstage. Where K-pop stars excel is in sheer physical beauty. Their faces, chiseled, sculpted, and tapering to a sharp point at the chin, look strikingly different from the round faces of most Koreans. Some are born with this bone structure, no doubt, but many can look this way only with the help of plastic surgery. Korea is by far the world leader in procedures per capita, according to *The Economist*. Double-fold-eyelid surgery, which makes eyes look more Western, is a popular reward for children who get good marks on school exams. The popularity of the K-pop idols has brought hordes of Chinese, Japanese, and Singaporean "medical tourists" to Seoul to have their faces altered to look more like the Korean stars. Some hotels have partnered with hospitals so that guests can have in-house procedures. The Ritz-Carlton Seoul offers an $88,000 "anti-aging beauty package." Women come to have their cheekbones shaved down and undergo "double jaw surgery," in which the upper and lower jawbones are cracked apart and repositioned, to give the whole skull a more tapered look.

THE MEET-THE-IDOLS press briefing before the Anaheim show took place in a long, narrow room on the third floor of the Honda Center. Two idols from each of the six groups who were performing filed in and sat on high stools on a small raised platform. Each was wearing one of the many different costumes that he or she would sport in the course of the four-hour show. The boys' faces were as pancaked and painted as the girls', and their hair was even more elaborately moussed, gelled, and dyed, in blond and butterscotch hues. Some guys wore high-waisted jackets with loose harem pants or jodhpurs, circus-ringmaster style; others wore white cutaways with high, stiff collars and black ties, like dream prom dates. They were more androgynous than the girls, who wore gold hot pants or short skirts, sparkly tops, and lace-up leather boots. Everyone looked very serious.

Once the idols were seated, a woman appeared with a stack of white gym towels. She gave one to each of the female idols, who arranged it atop her exposed thighs, as a makeshift modesty panel. I sat opposite Sooyoung, of Girls' Generation, a willowy brunette. She seemed distant and frosty, like a figurine in a glass case.

SM had prepared questions for the idols. An SM company man ran the proceedings and read the questions out loud, in English and Korean. The first question, for the two members of Girls' Generation, was: "Every time you visit the States it seems like you receive crazy love and support. Can you feel it? Can you explain the wonderful reception your fans have given you?"

The same question was put, in slightly different forms, to all the groups. The two representatives of Super Junior, a twelve-member boy group, were asked, "How do you always manage to have an explosive reaction from your fans worldwide? What's your secret?"

One of the members hazarded a guess: "Maybe it is because of our great good looks?"

NEIL JACOBSON, AN EXECUTIVE in the A&R department at Interscope Records, has large eyes. He has a habit of standing close and training his orbs on you, encouraging you to ponder the mind-boggling import of the point he is making. A rising star, Jacobson has a large corner office at Interscope's headquarters in Santa Monica, where, along with his other responsibilities, he was A&Ring Girls' Generation's debut American album. He had met Chairman Lee in Hong Kong, and they had attended a Girls' Generation show together. "It blew my mind how conceptual he is!" Jacobson exclaims. "Every little thing is thought out.

Every song is like a mini epic! And the fans—oh, my God!" He pauses, slightly staggered by the memory.

The group's size posed problems. "Obviously, there are nine of them," Neil Jacobson says of Girls' Generation. "Getting Americans to accept nine girls isn't going to be easy."

Jacobson also had to put together an album that highlighted the Girls' Korean-ness—the distinctive sweetness and purity that sets them apart from other pop acts—while making the music urban-sounding enough to get on the radio and be embraced by, say, Nicki Minaj or Rihanna, who could introduce the K-pop sound and style to their fans. The rapper and producer Swizz Beatz wanted to pair Chris Brown with YG's BIGBANG, a five-member boy group, and Nicki Minaj with 2NE1, the fashion-forward four-member girl group. "Bridging the gaps with collaborations can be the start of a global phenomenon," Swizz told *The Fader*, a music magazine.

But so far only one artist had come close to bridging the East–West pop-culture divide: the rapper PSY. His video "Gangnam Style," featuring the pudgy Korean artist doing his now world-famous horse-riding dance, while beautiful women, including the K-pop star Hunya, glide around him, was the first video in the history of YouTube to be seen 1 billion times (as of this writing, views have eclipsed 2 billion). It remains to be seen whether his success will be a one-time novelty, like that of the other Asian star to reach the top of the US charts, the Japanese crooner Kyu Sakamoto, whose song "Sukiyaki" topped the Billboard Hot 100 in 1963.

The directive to make a Girls' Generation album for the US market had come from on high. Max Hole, an executive at Universal's international division, says, "I keep close tabs on what's happening in Japan, so of course I was aware that Girls' Generation had become monstrously huge there, and they do these amazing synchronized dances—a very visual act—and I thought the songs were great. So, at one of our meetings which the heads of all the North American divisions attended, I played Girls' Generation for them. And Jimmy Iovine said, 'These are really good records.' And the decision was made that we should try Girls' Generation in America."

Like everyone else in the record industry, Hole wants to do business in China, which one day will be the world's biggest market for pop music. The question is when, and what kind of pop music the Chinese will prefer. "China is obviously a huge opportunity for us in five to ten years' time," he says. "Right now, the market is so small, but we make money on endorsements and touring." Collaborating with SM on a US record for Girls' Generation could lead to other collaborations in China, where SM is better connected than Universal.

Touring, which the label was counting on the Girls to do, could also be a problem. In Korea, record promotion is built almost entirely around television appearances. In Seoul you see members of Girls' Generation on TV every night. In the U.S., with the exception of awards shows, which are infrequent, there are few prime-time TV formats for promoting pop music; artists must rely on radio and concert tours to build a mass following.

"The usual rule for English-speaking acts is that they are ten months touring here and in Europe and one month in Asia," Jacobson says. "But these girls are ten months in Asia."

Product endorsements represent a significant portion of their income—the GG girls have more than forty endorsement deals in Asia, from cell phones to roast chicken. An extended sojourn in the West would incur significant "opportunity costs," as an agent at YG put it to me, in the form of lost advertising revenue, and, worse still, in being absent from TV. The Wonder Girls, who used to be the biggest girl group in K-pop, spent two years in New York trying, unsuccessfully, to break into the American market, and they were eclipsed at home by Girls' Generation.

"And I wouldn't want them to just do New York, Chicago, L.A.," Jacobson goes on, pacing around his office. "I'd want them to go to

Alabama and Missouri and Kansas. We need them to eat, breathe, and sleep this stuff. So that's going to be an interesting negotiation."

Ultimately, Jacobson faces the same conundrum as Lee Soo-man: how do you come up with music that appeals to both the East and the West without alienating the fans of either? Jacobson was commissioning hundreds of songs from a broad range of songwriters—Asian, American, and European—as more and more Western writers become aware of K-pop's potential. "I don't want to lose the Asian flavor. I want songs that speak to Girls' Generation's brand and also speak to the sound in America right now."

HALF AN HOUR BEFORE the Anaheim show, I am backstage, on my way to meet Tiffany and Jessica, the two members of Girls' Generation born and brought up in the States. An SM man is guiding me through the labyrinth of dressing rooms, where various idols, mainly guys, are having their hair fussed over and their outfits adjusted. There is a lot of nervous bowing. My handler hustles me along, telling me which questions on the list that I had submitted for preapproval I should *not* ask the girls. "'Was it sad to say goodbye to your friends who didn't make it?'" he says, reading from the list. "'Do you have a boyfriend?'" He pauses. "Look. This is all going to Korea, and it's a little different there. So if we could stay away from the personal questions like boyfriends."

I meet the idols in an anteroom. They sit down on folding chairs as the handler hovers. Tiffany is lovely. Jessica seems like she doesn't really want to be there. In fact, Jessica's days with Girls' Generation were numbered. She would fall afoul of management by starting her own fashion line, Blanc, and by deciding to get married against the agency's wishes. In October 2014, SM released the shocking news that Jessica was leaving the group.

What challenges had they faced, coming from California to Seoul and having to adapt to Korean culture?

"I thought I would be able to adjust, because my parents spoke Korean at home," Tiffany says, widening her eyes and making a charming How-could-I-have-been-so-silly! expression. "But I didn't even imagine how different it would be. American culture is so open compared to Korean culture, which is really conservative. So I would be, like, 'Hi!' and they were, like, 'You don't say "Hi!" You bow!'"

And what were their living circumstances like now? Tiffany replies, "Six of us live together, and the other three live, like, a minute away. So we're always going back and forth to each other's houses."

Do netizens chronicle their movements on the Internet?

"Yeah, that's true," Jessica says listlessly. "I'll be at a restaurant and it will be on Twitter in, like, ten minutes."

What's that like?

"I think we've been brought up to be really careful and to take responsibility in our actions, in order to be in this position," Tiffany says sincerely. She adds, "We always stay at home."

I ask if it was true that the girls try to disguise themselves in the streets of Seoul, but that their limbs alone—the shape of their arms and legs—give them away.

"It is," Tiffany says, shooting an accusatory glance at her arm. "It's just so . . ." she pauses, searching for the right thing to say. "Freakishly cool!"

From out in the arena comes a long, low wailing sound—the screams of the fans, dying for the idols to appear.

"OK, we have to go," the SM man says.

I have an unscripted question for Tiffany: "Your 'eye smile': did you learn that, or is it natural?"

"No," Tiffany replies, giggling. "My dad smiles this way." She eye-smiles me from three feet away: a jolt of pure cultural technology.

As I was heading back toward the stage entrance, I came upon a circle of idols tightly bunched around a small man in a dark-blue suit. He was quietly giving some sort of exhortation; occasionally he paused and the group would send up a shout. Moving a little closer, I recognized Lee Soo-man himself. I was struck by the rapt attentiveness with which his "family" hung on his every word. He was directing his remarks at EXO, his new Chinese-Korean group; all twelve members were present. With each shout, the twelve EXO boys bowed deeply from the waist.

NOT EVERYONE IN THE SM family is as close to Chairman Lee. Several family members have sued the company over abusive treatment and so-called slave contracts. Perhaps the most notorious case was that of Han Geng, a Chinese-born, Mandarin-speaking dancer. SM discovered him in Beijing in 2001, and he debuted as a member of Super Junior in 2005. In 2009, he accused the company of, among other things, forcing him to sign a thirteen-year contract when he was eighteen; paying him only a fraction of the profits earned; fining him when he refused to do things the company asked him to do; and making him work for two years straight without a single day off, which Han claimed caused him to develop gastritis and kidney disease. The Korean courts ruled in Han's favor, but shortly after the ruling he withdrew the suit, and eventually left the group.

SM initially defended its long-term contracts by pointing to the costs of housing, feeding, and training recruits for five years or more, which can run into the millions of dollars. But the furor over "slave contracts" damaged SM's reputation among netizens, and in recent years its contracts have become more equitable. Girls' Generation's members are rumored to have signed up with SM for seven years each, and are paid salaries of $1 million a year, which can hardly be called exploitative.

Other agencies employing an SM-style factory system are less progressive. In February 2011, three members of KARA, a hugely popular girl group with DSP, one of the smaller agencies, filed a lawsuit claiming that, even though the group earned the agency hundreds of thousands of dollars, each member was paid only $140 a month. The agency disputed that figure, and eventually the two sides settled. The onerous restrictions that some agencies place on idols have been widely publicized in Korea. Another small agency, Alpha Entertainment, forbids its female trainees to have boyfriends and bars any food or water after seven p.m., according to the *Straits Times*, Singapore's English-language newspaper. They are not allowed to go anywhere without supervision. When the paper asked the mother of Ferlyn, one of the Alpha trainees, how she felt about her daughter's regimen, she replied, "What the girls have gone through so far has been quite reasonable. The company has invested a lot in them, so they need to work hard for the company. I am not worried about Ferlyn. I want her to follow her dreams and make it big."

THE FIRST GROUP TO take the stage in Anaheim was SHINee, a boy band. The boys were fun to watch—heavily made-up and moussed, doing strenuous rhythmic dances. Then Girls' Generation came out, in blue jeans and white T-shirts, to perform "Gee." The whole place shouted the hook: "*Geegeegeegeebabybaby.*" It is the ultimate K-pop song, because the sound of the "Gee" is at once familiar and foreign. When the song ended, the girls deployed around the stage. Sooyoung came to where I was standing and began frantically winking and waving her way through the crowd, wearing a blissful smile and shaking her glossy hair. She was no longer the cold idol in the pressroom but a super cheerleader. Jon Toth had said it would be thus: Girls' Generation had come to see us.

But after the girls left the stage the concert flagged a bit, and I found myself wondering why overproduced, derivative pop music, performed by second-tier singers, would appeal to a mass American audience, who can hear better performers doing more original material right here at home? Girls' Generation's strenuous efforts notwithstanding, the mythical mélange of East and West remained elusive.

Interscope had reserved a box on the premium level. The woman running the elevator told me that she couldn't remember hearing screaming this loud at a show. She had put in earplugs.

The box held Interscope people from the marketing and A&R departments. There were drinks and food—anything you want, Jacobson says, putting an arm around my shoulders and guiding me down to a seat in the front row of the box.

"Now, I am here purely as an observer," he says, settling into the seat beside mine. "I just want to open my eyes and take all this in."

Jacobson gestured around the arena. "OK, notice no one is sitting down. No one. Even up in the rafters. So, obviously, there's a connection there." Connection, he explained, was the essence of pop music, according to his boss, Jimmy Iovine: "Jimmy always says it's all about the connection between the artist and the fans," he says. "This whole business, it's just about that connection. And, clearly, people feel that connection with the girls."

There were some covers: Jessica and her sister Krystal did Katy Perry's "California Gurls," and Amber, the tomboy from f(x); Kris, from EXO-M; and Key, from SHINee, covered Far East Movement's "Like a G6." Acts came on and went off, changed costumes, and came back on again. In between, we were treated to messages from the SM family. At one point, the crowd watched a slightly creepy video with cartoonish illustrations about the love that the SM family members feel for one another. Occasionally, the concert seemed like a giant pep rally. But at its best it elicited primal pop emotions that only a few of the greatest pop artists—the Beach Boys, the early Beatles, Phil Spector's girl groups—can evoke: the feeling of pure love.

When Girls' Generation came out again, Jacobson observed them closely. "OK, it's all about humility," he says, making submissive gestures with his hands. "Look how they bow to their fans. That's a big part of it." He starts ticking off the group's qualities on his fingers. "First, beauty. Second, graciousness and humility. Third, dancing. And fourth, vocal. Also, brevity. Nothing lasts more than three and a half minutes. Let's time it."

THANKS IN NO SMALL part to Chairman Lee, K-pop has become a fixture on pop charts not only in Korea but throughout Asia, including Japan—the world's second-biggest music market, after the United States. Taiwan, Singapore, the Philippines, Hong Kong, Thailand, Vietnam, and Malaysia are major K-pop consumers. South Korea, a country of fewer than 50 million, has somehow figured out how to make pop hits for more than a billion and a half other Asians, contributing $2 billion a year to Korea's economy, according to the BBC. K-pop concerts in Hong Kong and on mainland China are already lucrative, and no country is better positioned to sell recorded music in China, a potentially enormous market.

The K-pop idol factory may be the most elaborate hit-making operation on Earth. And yet, for all the money that the agencies have invested in idol making, the first Korean pop star to break through in the States came from outside the idol factory system. PSY was with the YG agency when the "Gangnam Style" video broke. But he has never been idol material. His first album, *PSY from the PSYcho World!*, was condemned in South Korea for "inappropriate content," and his second, *Ssa 2*, was banned for anyone under nineteen. In 2001, he was arrested and fined for smoking pot, and during his mandatory military service, he was alleged to have neglected his duties, and had to serve again. He's a Korean pop star, but he's not K-pop, and by satirizing standard K-pop tropes in "Gangnam Style," PSY may have subverted K-pop's chances of making it big in the West. At the very least, that a pudgy guy with a goofy horse-riding dance could succeed where the most brilliantly engineered idol groups have not suggests that cultural technology can only get you so far. In the end, as Denniz PoP used to say, sometimes you have to let art win.

CHORUS
RIHANNA:
TRACK-AND-HOOK

15 | "Umbrella"

EVAN ROGERS GREW UP loving Stevie Wonder; his friends liked Elton John. Raised in Storrs, Connecticut, a university town, Rogers was always the white guy in R&B bands. As a teenager he hooked up with a local soul outfit called Too Much Too Soon; they modeled themselves on Earth, Wind & Fire, the '70s post-funk group. The band played all over New England—high school and college dances, and at clubs that played Top 40; sometimes they had six gigs a week. Among their go-to numbers was "I Wanna Be Your Lover" by Prince; "September" by Earth, Wind & Fire; "Ain't No Stopping Us Now," by McFadden & Whitehead; and "Brick House" by the Commodores. Rogers was having such a good time that he decided to put off college, upsetting his parents, both Cornell graduates; his two sisters had gone to Middlebury. Finally, he convinced his parents to let him take one year off from a real career path to give the music a try. "And I'm still going," he says, forty years later.

Another white guy, Carl Sturken, joined the band. Sturken was a skilled guitar player who had graduated summa cum laude from Wesleyan. They wrote a few tunes together—some early Sturken & Rogers originals. The band traveled farther out once in while, and on a road trip to Barbados in the mid-'80s, both Rogers and Sturken met

Bajan women who would become their wives and, in a roundabout way, would determine the direction of urban pop. But not for another thirty years.

The band broke up, and Sturken and Rogers moved to New York and focused on songwriting. Rogers handled lyrics and melody while Sturken did rhythm and chords, although they exchanged ideas about both. Their first cut was a song called "Heartbreaker" on Evelyn "Champagne" King's 1984 album *So Romantic*. But then Rogers got signed as a solo artist by RCA, and in 1985 he released an album called *Love Games*, featuring Evan on vocals and Carl on guitar, doing their own songs. The album stiffed, and RCA dropped Rogers, but Capitol picked him up and put out a second album, *Faces of Love*, in 1989, which didn't sell either.

Their writing and production career was blossoming, however. Sturken & Rogers had had a cut on the soundtrack of *Beat Street*, the influential 1984 film about early hip-hop culture in the Bronx, and that gave them some cred in the urban community, and led to writing and production work with Cheryl Lynn, Stephanie Mills, and Jennifer Holiday.

In 1989, the pair embraced their pop side, writing and producing half the tracks on Donny Osmond's comeback album, including the hit single "Soldier of Love," which Rogers had originally written for himself. Donny Osmond had been a teen pop star back in the heyday of bubblegum music. His cover of "Puppy Love," the song Paul Anka wrote for Annette Funicello, came out when I was thirteen, and it helped mold my teenage music preferences: whatever this song stood for, I was for the opposite. Seventeen years later, the label was so unsure about how to market a thirty-two-year old former teen star whose career was at a standstill that "Soldier of Love" was promoted to radio programmers as the work of an anonymous "mystery artist."

Set to a New Jack Swing beat, the song got as high as number two, one rung higher than "Puppy Love" (although not as high as Osmond's 1971 chart-topper "Go Away Little Girl," a Goffin-King tune from the

Brill Building era). "Soldier of Love" showed that teen pop stars could survive beyond their teens. The song also showed that Sturken & Rogers could write pop hits.

Just like Lou Pearlman, Rogers and Sturken took notice of New Kids on the Block's enormous commercial success in the early '90s. They decided to start a grown-man boy band with some other former members of Too Much Too Soon, and call it Rythm [sic] Syndicate. The five guys played instruments onstage like a rock group, but also did synchronized dancing like a boy band, and they had boy-band haircuts. It is not something they are particularly proud of, looking back. "The problem was that we weren't boys," Rogers notes. Sturken was pushing thirty-five by that point. Nevertheless they managed to have another big hit with their song P.A.S.S.I.O.N; it reached number two in 1991. The band released two albums, and toured internationally, but broke up in 1993 as grunge took over. Rythm Syndicate, in its high cheesiness, probably helped push the Zapoleonic pendulum away from pure-pop doldrums toward the grungy extremes.

But teen pop predictably followed grunge again in the second half of the '90s, and Sturken and Rogers's R&B-inflected pop sound, the legacy of Too Much Too Soon, turned out to be perfect for white boy bands. The pair wrote and produced four songs for Boyzone's 1998 album *Where We Belong*, which was five times platinum in the UK (Denniz PoP also worked on the album). One of their songs, "All That I Need," was number one in the UK. They also wrote 'N Sync's 1999 single "(God Must Have Spent) A Little More Time on You," which got to number eight. Also in 1999, they had two cuts on Christina Aguilera's self-titled debut album, and that opened the door for Sturken and Rogers to work with an exultation of teen pop artists, including Jessica Simpson, Alsou, Mandy Moore, Christina Milian, and former Spice Girl Emma Bunton. And, as the 1990s came to a close and the teen-pop fad cloyed and curdled, Clive Davis brought the pair in to work on Kelly Clarkson's debut album, *Thankful*. The song they wrote, "The Trouble with Love Is," was a modest hit, and, thanks to Davis's string pulling, wound up as a featured song in the film *Love Actually*.

In the early 2000s, the partners began to expand their business. Instead of just writing songs, they started looking for artists. "We felt like we'd built up all this knowledge over the course of our careers," Sturken says, "both as artists and as songwriters, about what it takes to be a star, and we might as well put it to good use." The plan was to sign an artist to a production deal, develop his or her sound, and attempt to broker them to a major label.

They had an artist called Javier they were excited about, but things didn't work out (eight years later, Javier won the first season of *The Voice*). In the wake of that debacle, they changed directions again, deciding they should sign writers, not artists, and share in the publishing—the old Clive Calder approach. "No artists" became their watchword.

FOR CHRISTMAS OF 2003, Rogers and his Bajan wife, Jackie, went to Barbados for the holidays, as had been their custom for years, to visit family and friends. They stayed in a villa at the Accra Beach Hotel.

As often happened when they went to Barbados, Rogers heard about some singers. "There's always someone who wants to audition, because people know we're writers and producers," he says. "I'll be down at the beach and somebody will come up to me and start singing—it's like that."

As it turned out, a good friend of Jackie's had a fifteen-year-old daughter named Kleanna Browne, who was in a girl group called Contrast with two other teenagers, Jose Blackman and Robyn Fenty. All three were students at the Combermere School, a well-known secondary school for striving West Indian parents. The group had never actually performed in public, but they had worked up a version of "Emotion," Destiny's Child's cover of the Bee Gees song; and "Killing Me Softly," the Lauryn Hill version; and "Dangerously in Love," Beyoncé's song. The friend said they sounded really good.

Rogers arranged to meet the girls at the hotel. They were late, because one of them, the Fenty girl, took so long changing out of her school uniform and fixing her hair and makeup. "The others were saying, 'Where the hell is she?'" Rogers recalls.

"And then she walked in," Rogers remembers, "and I said to myself, 'If that girl can sing, then—holy shit! Because she had such a presence! Her makeup was perfect, and she had these capri pants and matching sneakers, with her green eyes and her long supermodel neck." But of course, Rogers immediately thought, "She probably can't sing, because usually it's the pretty one who can't."

But Fenty could. Rogers had the three of them sing together, and each sing separately.

"And the whole time I'm thinking, 'OK I have to have a follow-up meeting with *this* one.'"

The following day, Fenty, her mother, and her mom's boyfriend came back to Rogers's villa. The girl was quiet, listening intently. Rogers wanted to hear her voice again, just to be sure, so he taught her the song he had written for Kelly Clarkson, "The Trouble with Love Is."

"I'd sing a line," he says, "and she'd sing it back to me, and I was going, 'I think this girl's got something.' She was rough around the edges, but had a very distinctive sound to her voice. She also had a charming girl-next-door quality, Rogers thought.

He called Carl.

Sturken: "When Evan called me from Barbados the first thing he said was, 'I know we said no more artists. . . .'"

Rogers: "But man, this girl is special."

Sturken: "Go for it."

Rogers explained to Robyn and her mother that he'd like to bring her to the New York area, to work in their studio in Bronxville, which was called the Loft, located next to the Metro North train station. She would live with Evan and Jackie in their home in Stamford, Connecticut.

"Her mom was hilarious because she was so low-key about her," Rogers recalls. "She didn't really get that her daughter had anything special. She was like, 'Well, if you see something. I just want her schoolwork to be done. Education is very important.'" Fenty's mother wanted to wait until summer vacation, so that Robyn wouldn't miss any school.

Rogers then turned to the girl. "I said, 'Look, if we're going to do this, you should know this business is brutal. Are you sure you love it that much that you're willing to go through all this?'

"And without any hesitation at all, she said, 'It's all I've ever wanted to do.'

"And I was like, 'That's the right answer!'"

So Rogers signed her to their production company, Syndicated Rhythm Productions.

In a photo taken that day at Rogers's villa, Fenty is wearing a short-sleeved white shirt, part of her Combermere uniform. Her hair is primly pinned up on her head and she is smiling guardedly at the camera. Her life is about to change, and somehow it is clear that she knows it.

LIKE BRITNEY SPEARS AND Kelly Clarkson, Robyn Rihanna Fenty experienced a childhood fraught with parental discord, a violent domestic nightmare from which fame seemed to offer safe harbor. Her father, Ronald, was descended from the seventeenth-century Irish who had been "Barbadosed" by Oliver Cromwell's troops and sold to British planters on the island as indentured servants. He was an alcoholic and a drug abuser. Fenty later recalled in a 2011 *Rolling Stone* interview, "Fridays would be scary because he would come home drunk. He'd get paid, and half of it would go toward alcohol. He'd walk in the door, and it was all eyes on him." On more than one occasion he struck Fenty's mother,

Monica, an accountant who was originally from Guyana, once breaking her nose in front of Robyn.

Eventually her father lost his job as a supervisor in a garment warehouse, and hung around their home in Bridgetown, getting high. Robyn learned to be wary whenever she saw unwrapped packets of tinfoil in the ashtray at home; it meant Dad had scored some coke. Once, when she was nine, peering through a doorway, she saw her father with his lips around a crack pipe, and when Robyn told her mother what she had seen, Monica made her husband leave the house. Throughout her childhood, Robyn suffered badly from recurring headaches. Doctors feared she had a brain tumor, but CT scans showed nothing. The headaches disappeared shortly after her parents' divorce, which occurred around the time she met Evan Rogers.

Fenty didn't write songs, or play an instrument; she had never had any formal training in either voice or dance before meeting Rogers. Her main qualification as a singer was that she wanted to be one so badly. Rogers sensed that ambition ran deep—"I saw it in her eyes," he says. But what was "it," exactly? No mere girlish desire for fame; it was more likely a much more urgent need to escape from the anxieties of a violent home life into the illusion of security and boundless love that a life onstage seemed to offer. That desire, more than any inborn talent, is what fans will connect to, and that is what record men look for in a new artist. It's the one thing they can't manufacture.

In the summer of 2004, Robyn and her mother traveled to Connecticut to work with Rogers and Sturken on demos. The songwriters wanted to record four songs that would give A&R departments a sense of their options with the artist. She could be a power diva, in the classic R&B tradition ("Hero") or she could be more of a ballad singer (as in Whitney Houston's version of the Isley Brothers' "For the Love of You," which she also recorded). In addition to covers, Fenty recorded an original pop-soul song Sturken and Rogers wrote for her, "Last Time." They also changed her professional name to Rihanna, Fenty's middle name.

Robyn didn't feel like a Rihanna. She remained Robyn to her friends and family (to this day, she says, she sometimes doesn't realize people are addressing her when they call out "Rihanna!"). But the Swedish Robyn was well known throughout the world, largely thanks to Cheiron, and two pop artists with the same name would complicate the branding.

In the fall, Fenty went back to school in Barbados, while Sturken and Rogers continued to search for the right song for her—a song with the right amount of rhythmic edge to make it cool and danceable, accompanied by a pop melody that would sound good on the radio.

Several months later, a producer named Vada Nobles sent the partners a rough demo of a song called "Pon de Replay," a Caribbean-flavored dancehall tune. The demo had drums and some half-sung lyrics, and a sketch of a melody. Sturken and Rogers finished the song, and then called Barbados and said Robyn needed to come back and record it, because this was the song they felt could get her a deal.

They played the song for her over the phone, and she thought it sounded like "a nursery rhyme." But she agreed to fly up to New York, and they recorded her vocal just before Christmas 2004.

Then Fenty went back home again. Rogers and Sturken started sending their package of four demos, along with some photographs of the singer, to major labels. Record execs generally take long Christmas breaks, filtering back into their offices the second week of January. By the end of January several labels were interested.

In late January, Sturken and Rogers's lawyer, Scott Felcher, played "Pon de Replay" for Jay Brown, the head of A&R at Def Jam. Brown loved it, and when Felcher passed him a snapshot the guys had taken of Fenty in the Loft, he wanted to meet her.

He went to find his boss, Jay-Z, the president of the label.

"I played it for Jay," Brown recalled in the *Rolling Stone* article, "and Jay was like, 'That's a big song.'" For Jay-Z, Brown explained, "you've got to be bigger than the song, otherwise the song dictates to you." Jay-Z wasn't sure this girl was that big, but she was certainly pretty, and they decided to invite her to audition for them in the office, to see if she had anything more than talent and good looks.

The phone call came to the Loft. "Jay Brown called us up and said, 'Where is she?'" Rogers recalls. "I said, 'She went back to Barbados but we can bring her back in a couple of weeks.'"

"Why do I have to wait a couple of weeks?" Brown asked. "I want to meet her now." They scheduled a meeting for the following Monday afternoon.

That was on Thursday. Fenty got up to New York by Friday afternoon, and they had the weekend to prepare for the audition.

"At that point we didn't know her as a performer at all," Sturken says. "I thought we were going to have months to work on her presentation. Instead we had two days."

The rehearsals did not go particularly well. Fenty sounded "pitchy"—out of tune.

"When a person sings a cappella, like they do on *American Idol*, you can't quite tell if they're on pitch," Sturken says. "But when you sing [along] to an instrument, you can tell right away. And she was pitchy."

They also had no idea how Fenty would respond to the pressure of an audition. "I mean it's one thing to be in front of Clive Davis, who she's never heard of," Rogers says. "It's another thing to be in front of her idol, Jay-Z. She could go all to pieces."

DEF JAM WAS STARTED by Rick Rubin in his dorm room at NYU in 1983, after Rubin produced Jazzy Jay's album *It's Yours*. Thanks mainly to the A&R work of Russell Simmons, with whom Rubin soon joined forces, and some deft MTV dealings, Def Jam brought hip-hop into the commercial mainstream. They broke seminal acts like LL Cool J and the Beastie Boys, and signed Run-D.M.C. ("Run" Simmons was Russell's brother, Joseph) and Public Enemy. The label was bought by PolyGram in 1994 and became part of the Universal Music Group in 1998, which paid Simmons $100 million for his stake, bade him farewell, and merged Def Jam with Island Records, the Jamaica-based label started by Chris Blackwell.

Since 1988, Def Jam had been run by Lyor Cohen, a well-known industry player, who like Simmons had begun as a promoter of hip-hop shows. He is tall and broad-shouldered and somewhat fearsome-looking, and presents himself like some kind of white gangster. His physique adds to his bad-guy-in-a-Bond-film vibe, plus the fact that he travels with bodyguards, several real beefalos—those football linemen types who protect rap stars. His rise to the top, which began when he forced out Rick Rubin, has been replete with cold-blooded corporate executions. He exudes a menacing calm.

Cohen mostly kept Def Jam close to its rap roots—its biggest artists were DMX, Ja Rule, Foxy Brown, and Jay-Z himself, whose label, Roc-A-Fella Records, Def Jam distributed. But Cohen did not succeed in making this new generation of hip-hop stars bigger than their predecessors. Hip-hop's success was partially due to its aggressive and dangerous-seeming blackness, but that quality also limited its appeal to white soccer moms. The genre also defined itself by a lot of things it was not. It was not pop. It was not sung. And rappers rarely danced, except to swagger suggestively around the stage. With the usual paths to dominant chart success blocked, it seemed there were barriers to how big hip-hop was going to get.

Cohen also signed Mariah Carey in 2002, and created a new label just for her. But Carey's career languished, and over the course of the next eighteen months Def Jam stopped producing homegrown hits on the hip-hop side too. In January 2004, Cohen departed for Warner. He was replaced by L. A. Reid, whose background was not in hip-hop at all, but rather in pop-inflected R&B, going back to the Atlanta-based LaFace Records, which he co-founded with Babyface Edmonds in 1989, and which signed Toni Braxton, TLC, and Usher, helping put Atlanta on the map as an important center of urban music production.

Reid had a sure hand when it came to dealing with R&B singers like Carey, whose career he helped revive, but he was confident in the hip-hop world. Def Jam's artists worried that Reid would soften the label's hard edge. Partly to counter those fears, Reid persuaded Jay-Z to assume the title of president of Def Jam. He also arranged for Universal to buy Roc-A-Fella, the label that Jay-Z and his friends Damon Dash and Kareem Burke founded in 1996, back when they were still street hustlers. Jay-Z started his corporate gig in the late fall of 2004, not long before Rogers and Sturken sent out their Rihanna demos.

For Jay-Z, whose real name was Shawn Carter, the Def Jam job was the culmination of a hip-hop Horatio Alger story. Raised in the Marcy Projects, a lower-income housing development in Brooklyn, Jay-Z had lived the "hard knock life" he later rapped about, working as a small-time drug dealer in a criminal gang. In his 2010 memoir, *Decoded*, he hauntingly describes his time as a drug dealer, where he and his crew sold "work"—crack and cocaine—to desperate addicts on the streets. He writes that he was saved by his love of words, which led him to writing rhymes.

After appearing on several established rappers' records, most notably Big Daddy Kane's, Jay tried to get his own record deal, but the labels he approached, including Def Jam, turned him down. So he and his boys started their own label. They didn't have a distribution deal; they sold their music out of the back of people's cars in Brooklyn. His first album, *Reasonable Doubt*, told stories of the hustling life; and the single, "Ain't No Nigga," featuring Foxy Brown, got to number fifty on the Hot 100. He followed that with a new album each year, each stronger than the last, up through *The Black Album* (2003), establishing himself as the preeminent rap lyricist of his generation. Roc-A-Fella also signed other artists—notably Kanye West, who, like some of label's other signees, began as a beat maker for Jay-Z himself.

But the knock on Jay-Z as a label head was that he cared more about his own records than those of his artists. Some said he sabotaged his artists if they threatened his top-dog status. That kind of criticism was partly why Jay had announced his retirement as a rapper after *The Black Album*—in order to focus on his responsibilities as a record man: discovering and developing talent. To assist him, Jay-Z brought in Jay Brown, who had worked for Quincy Jones's publishing company, and put him in charge of A&R.

BEFORE GOING TO DEF JAM on Monday afternoon, Sturken and Rogers took Fenty to a morning meeting at J Records, Clive Davis's label. They were well known at J because of their work with *American Idol*. "So we walked in," Rogers says, "and we are sitting there waiting for our meeting with Steve Ferrera," the well-respected head of A&R for Davis, who died in 2014. Rihanna said she had to go to the bathroom. No sooner had she gone than the elevator doors opened and out came Clive Davis himself, returning from the weekend, trundling a suitcase behind him.

"Hello, guys, what are you doing here!" Davis exclaimed.

They explained about their artist Rihanna, who was with them, only she happened to be in the bathroom right at that moment; perhaps he could wait until she came out. Sturken was saying to himself, *Rihanna, get out of the bathroom!* After several minutes Davis said, "Well, I got to go," and went into his office, never seeing the girl.

Might Davis's antennae have picked up the bat squeak of incipient stardom emitted by the young singer? Maybe; however, his lieutenant, the late Steve Ferrera, did not. Rihanna sang, "For the Love of You" for him, accompanied by Sturken on acoustic guitar. Ferrera was unimpressed. He suggested she try "Pon de Replay," in front of the marketing team, who happened to be meeting in a nearby conference room. When she finished that song they applauded politely; an excruciating fifteen seconds of silence followed. Sturken and Rogers thanked everyone and beat a retreat to the sidewalk with their artist.

"We were all a little shaken by that," Rogers says. "We went to lunch around the corner and we were saying, 'This is going to be tougher than we thought.'"

After lunch, they went to Def Jam, located on the twenty-eighth floor of the Worldwide Plaza building at Eighth Avenue and Fifty-First Street. Fenty was very nervous. She had stayed up almost all night trying on outfits, finally choosing white jeans with a pale-green blouse and white high-heeled boots. It was the dead of winter in New York, and she looked like she was ready for the beach.

"We got off the elevator," Rogers says, "and when she saw Jay-Z for the first time, down the hall, she began to hyperventilate."

"That's when I really got nervous," Fenty said in a 2007 interview with the *Observer*. "I was like: 'Oh God, he's right there, I can't look, I can't look, I can't look!'"

She was somewhat calmed by the fact that Jay-Z was casually dressed in jeans and a polo shirt. He brought her into his office, where an enlarged version of Rihanna's head shot had been affixed to a wall. They all talked for a while. Also present was Marc Jordan, who would become Rihanna's manager.

"I was very shy," Fenty said. "I was cold the entire time. I had butterflies. I'm sitting across from Jay-Z. Like, Jay-Z."

Jay Brown joined them, as did Tracy Waples, the head of marketing at Def Jam. Tyran "Ty Ty" (pronounced "Ta Ta") Smith, a friend of Jay's from the old days who consulted on all A&R decisions, was also in the room.

Jay-Z had a thick shag carpet in his office. Sturken, who had seen it before, had counseled Fenty to remove her boots before she started performing, but when the moment came she forgot. "And I just went, 'Oh no,'" Sturken says, "because I imagined her catching a heel and flying across the room."

Finally Fenty was ready to begin. The moment that would change her life, and Sturken's and Rogers's, was at hand.

She sang "The Last Time" first. "And she did it the best she'd ever done it!" Sturken says. That was when he realized he needn't have worried about this girl: she was a killer. "I was like, 'Wow, she brings it when she has to.'"

"She was obviously nervous," Jay-Z later told *Rolling Stone*. "Now she has a big personality, but I didn't get that in the meeting. What I did get was her eyes, this determination. She was fierce—like Kobe Bryant." He added, "I knew she was a star."

After the first song, Rihanna sang along with and danced to a recording of "Pon de Replay."

When she was finished, Jay looked at Rogers and Sturken and said, "So what do I have to do to get you guys to cancel all your other meetings?"

Jay called L.A. Reid in, and Rihanna performed again for him. Reid recalled, "We see pretty all the time. Pretty's a dime a dozen. But those eyes said, 'I'm going to make it. You're gonna be on board or not. But this train is leaving the station.'"

Def Jam offered Fenty a record contract on the spot. The offer was an intuitive, gut-based decision, rather than a data-driven one, but it had a certain logic to it. A pressure-cooker situation allows labels to leverage their enormous power, bargaining that the artist's ambition and desire for stardom will work against their best interests. The artist takes the bird in hand even though it is a decoy that conceals a snare, denying themselves the leverage that other offers would provide.

Sturken and Rogers got a piece of Rihanna's record sales for her first five albums (their deal was later extended to seven albums), and a percentage of her management fees. Plus, they got to write and produce most of the songs on the first album. Finally, as the "furnishing company," Syndicated Rhythm Productions secured the right to sign off on every penny Def Jam spent on Rihanna's career.

Jay-Z wouldn't let Fenty leave the building until she signed, fearing that another label that had also received her demo might swoop in and steal her away. They were all there until three in the morning while the lawyers worked out the details. Fenty later recalled Jay-Z saying, 'There's only two ways out. Out the door'"—if she signed the contract—"'or through this window'" if she didn't. Was that a threat? "It was very flattering." She left through the door.

RIHANNA'S FIRST ALBUM, *Music of the Sun*, was completed in a speedy three months. Sturken and Rogers wrote or co-wrote all but three of the thirteen songs on the album, and they produced all of the tracks, with a notable assist on "Let Me" from a Norwegian production duo called Stargate, who had recently arrived in the United States and who would soon figure largely in Rihanna's career. For added chutzpah, the producers had Rihanna cover Dawn Penn's marvelous reggae song "You Don't Love Me (No, No, No)," produced by Wycliffe Johnson and Cleveland Browne (Steely & Clevie), which the sixteen-year-old proved barely capable of handling. In the imaging for the album, Rogers mostly stuck to his girl-next-door notion of Robyn Fenty, presenting her as a doe-eyed innocent in hoodies and sweats.

With Rihanna, Jay-Z seemed determined to prove himself as a record man, and show that he could guide another artist's career as deftly as he'd handled his own. The singer became his special project. Fenty worked hard to justify his faith in her, putting in long days of vocal and choreography training. Though she lacked Britney's Mouseketeer grounding as a preteen star, Rihanna learned fast. She continued living with the Rogerses in Connecticut as they oversaw the production of her debut album.

"Pon de Replay," the first single from the album, was released in May 2005. It became a summer hit, getting as high as number two on the Hot 100 (Mariah Carey's "We Belong Together" couldn't be dislodged from the top spot). Def Jam had thought it was an R&B song, but pop stations played it. The single also performed well in the relatively new realm of digital sales, a harbinger of digital dominance to come.

But the second single, "If It's Lovin' that You Want," didn't do well, nor did the album, which came out at the end of August. Worse, the album failed to make it clear what kind of artist Rihanna was—was she island, R&B, hip-hop, or pop? That summer, Jay-Z summoned her and Rogers and Sturken to his suite at the Four Seasons Hotel and told Rihanna she had to step up her game. He reminded her that the artist needed to be bigger than the song. "You could be done," he warned her.

In October, L.A. Reid heard a Europop-sounding dance song called "SOS," a homage to early '80s British synth pop (and, of course, ABBA); the song samples the synth riff from "Tainted Love," made famous by Soft Cell. Reid had originally offered the song, by "J.R." Rotem, Evan Bogart, and Ed Cobb, to Christina Milian, but she thought it was too pop. So he took it to Rihanna. "SOS" wasn't the kind of song that the other men steering her career had in mind for her—it wasn't urban enough, they thought—but Reid said, "Forget all that. She's Madonna. She's an international pop star. Let's make people dance." The song earned Rihanna her first Billboard number one.

The second single from the album was a sophisticated ballad called "Unfaithful." Once again, the Norwegian duo Stargate co-wrote and produced the track, which was distinguished by a lovely melody and lyrics from Shaffer Smith, an up-and-coming R&B writer and artist who called himself Ne-Yo. The song also performed well in the charts. The album, *A Girl Like Me* did not do that well—album sales would never be Rihanna's strength. But as album sales declined across the board, thanks mainly to the singles-based pricing model of iTunes, they came to matter less to an artist's success. Rihanna would emerge as the consummate singles artist, always ready with a new product for the market regardless of whether it was attached to an album. Lacking an overriding artistic vision for her music, she is well supplied with a diverse and expanding clutch of vocal personalities, which adds variety and allows her to make a strong impression in the three or four minutes a song lasts.

But that eclecticism also worked against her. Two albums into her career, it still wasn't clear who Rihanna was. To her detractors, and there were many, she was just another wannabe-yoncé who sang through her nose and couldn't really dance. To prove them wrong, she needed a song that would define her as an artist.

LIKE MANY AN ARTIST'S signature song, Rihanna's breakout, "Umbrella," was actually written for someone else.

The song was the work of three men: Tricky Stewart, a producer; Terius Nash, a singer-songwriter who called himself "The-Dream"; and Kuk Harrell, a vocal producer. Together they make up the songwriting team at RedZone Entertainment, a music production company and publishing firm based in Atlanta.

Tricky Stewart comes from a musical family. His uncle Butch was a successful commercial jingle writer in Chicago, and owned an advertising company with his father, Phillip. His mother, Mary Ann, and her sisters, Vivian and Kitty Haywood, put out two records as "Kitty and the Haywoods," and also sang on the jingles as needed. The Stewarts created jingles for Coke, McDonald's, and Anheuser-Busch, among many other top brands. Their children Laney and Mark, joined by cousin Kuk Harrell, and Kuk's sister Cynthia, sang on the jingles too. "They were always looking for kids to sing on a spot," Mark remembers. "So that was our exposure to the process and to paying attention [to] making records. We were studio rats." Tricky, born Christopher Alan, the baby of the family, was a musical prodigy. As a drummer he had started playing on records when he was thirteen, and planned to be a session musician. But Mary Ann convinced her son to learn music production, because the horizons were higher. (Good call, Mom—producers would put session drummers out of business.)

In the 1980s, the younger generation started their own jingle house, but their real ambition was to make records. First Laney got a publishing deal at Sony. "And because Laney got in the door," says Mark, "he got a joint venture that pulled the rest of us in the door too." In the mid-'90s, with an investment from L.A. Reid's LaFace Records, the Stewarts established RedZone in Atlanta. Tricky, later joined by Kuk and Dream, handled the songwriting and production work; brother Mark managed them; Laney ran the publishing, and Mark's wife, Judi, handled administration.

According to Kuk Harrell, the secret of their success is that they approach songs like they are jingles. "We all learned from an early age to approach music as a business," he explains. "As opposed to some other guys who may do it for fun or whatever. We were trained to do exactly what the client wants you to do, and do it when they want it. So if they have to have it by Monday, then you give it to them on Monday. It has to be precise." He adds, "See, with a lot of guys, you're getting someone who is a track guy, but he's not an experienced producer—he just makes beats. And when you put him in a pressure situation where Rihanna is sitting there and the label is sitting there, and they want the song and you got to perform right then, they can't do it. That's what we learned in writing jingles; you don't feel the pressure. You're like an athlete—like, what pressure? You are there to perform."

RedZone was set up as a mini-Motown, but the hits were slow to come. Tricky had a minor hit, his first, with "Who Dat" for JT Money, a rapper from Miami. In 2000 the song reached number one on Billboard's rap chart. When Tricky did "Me Against the Music" (2003) for Britney Spears, the lead single from her 2004 album, *In the Zone*, he seemed poised to enjoy the mainstream chart success that Timbaland and the Neptunes were then enjoying. But for the next five years, until "Umbrella" came along, RedZone had only minor hits.

Harrell describes how the song came to be. "I was fooling around with Logic," he says, "trying to learn it, and I had gone into the samples and found this high-hat loop, which I put on a beat. *Cha chick cha bun tha smoth*," he mouths, making the percussion sounds with his breath and lips.

"Then Tricky comes in and says, 'What's that?'" Stewart sat down at a keyboard and started playing chords into the box, over the looped high hat and snare sound. Then he programmed a bass line. At that point Dream came into the studio, listened to the track, and the word "umbrella" popped into his head. He went into the vocal booth and got on the mike, singing "Under my umbrella." And then, inspired, added the all-important echoes—"ella ella ella eh eh eh"—that became the song's signature hook.

"Umbrella" is basically a four-chord vamp built around that central riff played on the high hat and snare, and underpinned by a heavy, hip-hop bass line. A fifth chord, the B, comes in on the bridge. The wonderful title hook is deployed with almost classical restraint, not coming until the refrain at the end of the first chorus. In the studio, the songwriters worked out a bridge for the song—most urban songs of that period did not have one. In about two hours, the song was finished. The brilliant trace vocal that The-Dream recorded on the demo has all the song's signature elements, from the Caribbean flava in the "ellas," to the lovely concluding hook, "Come into me."

"We knew it was special," Harrell says, once it was finished. "We didn't know it was a hit. Nobody knows that."

Tricky Stewart had known hits. He had not known smashes. What's the difference? "A hit is just a hit," as he puts it: "a smash is a life changer." How? Brother Mark says, "Nothing has been the same since we created that record. We had experience in record making but not hit making. All of a sudden you have major artists blowing up your phone. And we knew exactly how to service them; we reverted back to that jingle mentality— we were prepared for that pressure. So whether it was Beyoncé calling or Bieber calling, we knew how to operate."

But in order for "Umbrella" to be a smash, the Stewarts first needed to get it into the hands of a top artist. The biggest artist they knew personally was Britney Spears. Tricky had co-written and produced "Me Against the Music" for her.

But by the time "Umbrella" came along, Spears was working on her fifth album, the aptly titled *Blackout*. Mike Stewart sent a copy of the demo to Larry Rudolph, her manager, who passed it along to Jive, her label. Jive rejected the song, saying *Blackout* had enough material already. It is unclear whether Britney ever even heard the demo. Just as her career was launched by ". . . Baby One More Time," a song meant for TLC, so now, at a point when she could have desperately used a comeback hit, a song meant for her slipped through her fingers. "Gimme More," the highest-charting single from the *Blackout* album, was a hit but hardly a smash, although it did introduce the line "It's Britney, bitch," which became a trademark.

In trying to fathom how Britney could have rejected "Umbrella," Tricky notes drily that "her personal life was . . . a little out of control" at the time. Britney, the first of the modern teen pop divas, who rose the highest and fell the furthest, was hitting her nadir when "Umbrella" was offered to Jive. She was monumentally innocent, and when that innocence was taken, she broke. In December 2006, paparazzi were on hand to capture an unflattering view as she got out of a low-slung sports car without any underwear on. The following February, Spears checked herself out of Eric Clapton's Crossroads Centre, a drug rehab clinic in Antigua (after staying for one day), flew back to L.A., and walked into Esther's Hair Salon in Tarzana complaining that her hair extensions were too tight, demanding that Esther Tognozzi, the owner, shave her head. When Tognozzi refused, Britney took the electric shaver and did the job herself as a pap snapped pictures through a window. The strands of hair Spears left on the salon floor were later auctioned for exorbitant sums on eBay. (It was rumored, but not confirmed, that she had cut her hair to remove traces of methamphetamines, which would have undermined her struggle to keep custody of her children.) Now bald, Spears drove to Body & Soul, a body-art parlor in Sherman Oaks, where she got a tattoo of a cross on her hip, and another of red lips on her wrist. She told the artist who did them, "I don't want anyone touching me. I'm tired of everybody touching me."

In early 2008, after a drugged-seeming performance of "Gimme More" at the MTV Video Music Awards, Spears barricaded herself inside her home, refusing to comply with a court order to surrender custody of her two children to her estranged husband, Kevin Federline. The police broke down the door and took her away. Not long after that, Spears was committed to the psychiatric ward at the UCLA Medical Center.

After Jive passed on "Umbrella" for Britney, Stewart sent L.A. Reid the demo, and Reid gave it to Rihanna. She recalled, "When the demo first started playing, I was like, 'This is interesting, this is weird.' But the song kept getting better. I listened to it over and over." She told Reid, "I need this record. I want to record it tomorrow."

But the Stewarts were reluctant to give the song to Rihanna, because she wasn't an established star. "They had to talk us into it," Mike says. "I remember Grammy weekend I was being hounded by every label executive to get that record. At parties people were running up on us everywhere. But L.A. Reid and everyone associated with Rihanna—they were the most passionate. Jay Brown put me on the phone with Rihanna, and I said no at the time, and to this day when she sees me she says, 'Oh you're the one who tried to take my record away.' And she's so wrong—I didn't try to take her record away! I was just evaluating what was the best situation." After all, it was still their song.

Finally, after weeks of daily calls from both L.A. and Jay-Z, the Stewarts agreed to give "Umbrella" to Rihanna. She recorded the vocals, with production by Kuk Harrell, in Westlake Recording Studios in Los Angeles. Now it was her song. Ten rhythmic syllables, "umbrella-ella-ella-eh-eh-eh," did what the two previous albums together had not done: they defined Rihanna as an artist. She was chilly and warm at the same time, caring and not caring. She had swag, with a dash of island flava, but she also had a heart; the song is remarkably tender, considering that men wrote it for a woman. And, as a commenter on the website Rap Genius wrote of the hook, "These syllables made more money than you will ever dream of."

"When she recorded the 'ellas,'" Tricky says, "you knew your life was about to change."

Just before the single was released, a remix came in from Jay-Z, which shook up the song's middle-of-the-road vibe. His rapped intro has prescient allusive verses about the coming financial crisis, finished off with the thrilling envoi:

> *Little Miss Sunshine*
> *Rihanna where you at?*

Jay's verse injected a little bit of the extremes into an otherwise pure pop song, which made it seem edgier than it actually was: the perfect blend for hits radio.

"UMBRELLA" WAS RELEASED to 133 CHR stations on March 24, 2007—basically all the Top 40 stations in large and mid-sized markets across the United States. Twenty two percent of them put it into rotation on the first day. What was the reason for this remarkable uniformity? There were three possible explanations. It could be that the song itself was just that good. It could be the result of radio consolidation—some Clear Channel chief programmer e-mailed a single playlist to all its programming directors. Or, it could be the label.

In his book, *Climbing the Charts*, UCLA sociology professor Gabriel Rossman examines this question. He concludes that while Clear Channel provides the corporate structure that makes concentration possible, individual PDs and DJs don't act in lockstep. He explains, "If stations were playing songs because they are taking orders from corporate headquarters, we would expect to see stations within a company behave the

same as each other, but differently from stations owned by other companies. In fact, stations in a given format all act the same, regardless
of ownership, and there is no special tendency for stations in the same
company to behave similarly." Therefore the forces behind the ubiquity
of "Umbrella" on the radio, he suggests—and by extension, other radio
hits—must be coming from the label.

Big Radio is still the best way—some would argue, the only way—to
create hits. If the song seems to be playing everywhere at the same time,
all at once, so that Zapoleon's Rule of Three is fulfilled in a day or so, it
is perceived to be a hit, and becomes one. To make that happen, a radio
promotion team—either on staff at the label, or working for an independent promoter—needs to visit every PD in every important market in the
country and make sure they know about that song, and follow up with
a steady stream of phone calls and e-mails. Only a major label has the
resources for that kind of campaign. According to an NPR investigation,
it can easily cost more than a million dollars to promote a single song.

One former program director at a commercial radio station explains
how it works. "If you look at a typical record on FM radio," he says,
"the major labels say, 'We want to add this single on such and such a
date. Don't play this till September thirtieth, because we can get forty
other stations to add it on that date.' And then the label can say to other
stations, 'Look forty other stations just added it, maybe you should too.'
And then the chart game starts from there." The label works the record,
orchestrating enthusiasm, employing a specialized language of "spins,"
"power ups" and "heavies" that you see in the ads labels take out for
records in radio trade publications. "The label says, 'Hey, I think we're
seeing something, can you give us medium rotation?' And then: 'We're
shooting for heavies now, can you give us heavy rotation?' 'Yeah, we can
give you heavies now!' Then the label says, 'We're going for number one
now. Can we power up to number one?' And this is how it works at FM
radio. And it's not necessarily illegal, per se. They just all kind of work
together on it."

Radio is integral to the survival of the old hit-making mentality. Clive Davis would spend a fortune to promote songs to radio. In the '70s, Davis was fired from Columbia for allegedly engaging in payola—a charge he always denied. These days song promotion is mostly above board. The label doesn't pay for individual songs; it pays the radio station for access to its program directors, so a promotions person can personally pitch the music. Labels also send stars to Clear Channel's big Jingle Ball Christmas concerts on both coasts and cities in between from which the radio conglomerate profits handsomely in ticket sales (a practice sometimes called "showola").

Although the labels have lost much since the appearance of Napster, they still have one thing no one else has: their control of radio. The record and radio industries have been engaged in a mutually profitable, though at times adversarial, marriage for more than eighty years, and the old folks still love each other. Radio needs music that's compelling enough to keep people listening through the ads, and the record companies need radio to sell records. Both need hits.

"UMBRELLA" WAS NUMBER ONE for seven weeks, and helped make Rihanna's third album, *Good Girl Gone Bad*, her most successful to date, although once again her fans seemed to prefer to cherry-pick the singles. The video of "Umbrella" received four nominations for MTV's 2007 Video Music Awards, and won for Video of the Year. Rihanna performed "Umbrella" at the 2008 Grammys, and later that night she and Jay-Z took the stage together to claim the award for best sung collaboration—a moment of triumph for them both.

"Umbrella" marked the arrival of something new in pop: a digital icon. In the rock era, when the album was the standard unit of recorded music, listeners had ten or twelve songs to get to know the artist, but in the singles-oriented world of today, the artist has only three or four minutes to put their personality across, and at that Rihanna would prove to be without peer. She seems to release a new single each month, often recording the latest while she is on an eighty-city world tour promoting the previous ones. To keep her supplied with songs, her label and her manager periodically convene "writer camps"—weeklong conclaves, generally held in Los Angeles, where dozens of top producers and writers from around the world are brought in and shuffled and reshuffled in pairs over multiple-day writing sessions, in the hope of striking gold.

Last but not least, "Umbrella" was the song that earned Rihanna a prime spot at Clive Davis's Grammy party the following year, on February 8, 2009—the night her life would change again.

16 | "Ester Dean: On the Hook"

ONE SEASONABLE NIGHT in the spring of 2005, three years before the smash that changed their lives, Tricky and Mark Stewart attended an outdoor concert given by the Gap Band, a funk ensemble made up of the three Wilson Brothers, from Tulsa, Oklahoma. Like many producers in Atlanta's vibrant hip-hop scene who had come out to see the group, the Stewarts had been sampling the Gap Band for years. The slap-happy bass lines of '70s funk that Denniz PoP loved—James Brown, of course, but also other less well-known funk bands that rose to fame with Brown's success—were part of hip-hop's musical backbone. Many of the Gap Band's songs, such as "Humpin'," "Outstanding," and "Yearning for Your Love," had been sampled by Jay-Z, Kanye, and Missy, among many other leading hip-hop artists.

The Wilson brothers were nearing the end of a long career as grand funk masters, and they still put on a good show. Dressed in their trademark white tailcoats, backed by a smoking brass section, they combined old-school funk with '80s arena rock flourishes. The crowd loved it.

Standing on the side of the stage, Tricky was trying to listen to the group's main singer, Charlie Wilson, but he was distracted by a voice in the crowd—an inspired fan was singing along perfectly. "I heard this

singing coming from somewhere around me," he recalls, "and my producer's ear started listening to it. And I'm thinking, 'Wow, that is not
natural.' Charlie Wilson is a damn good singer, but this other voice is
keeping right up, executing all the tricky little runs perfectly. Finally,
I just had to find out who that was singing like that." He followed the
sound through the crowd, and it led him to Ester Dean.

Dean, twenty-four, was also from Oklahoma, and she was counting
on the Gap Band to remind her of happier days. She was born in Musk-
ogee: her great-grandmother on her mother's side was a full-blooded
Cherokee, according to Dean. Her father drank, and after her parents
split up she moved with her mother and five siblings, of whom Ester was
the youngest, to Tulsa, and then later to Omaha. Dean left school after
tenth grade, and, guided by a sense of her own destiny, and her kooky
but unshakeable conviction that life had something special in store for
her, took off for Atlanta by herself.

She had lots of dreams. Sometimes she saw herself as a professional
chef, the owner of a restaurant called À La Esta. Other times she envisioned running a children's day-care center that would double as a home
for senior citizens. "Because that way the old people could look after the
kids, and keep themselves young too!" she explains with great enthusiasm. But at the time, and for the last eighteen months, Dean had been
working as a nurse's aide, making $10 an hour in an Atlanta hospital.
She was in Section 8 government housing, and her mother, sister, and
nephew were all living at her place; she was sleeping on the couch. She
had even been tempted by the easy money offered by the city's sex trade,
but a brief stint as a stripper changed her mind.

A ticket to the Gap Band show—ten bucks—was a significant
splurge, but Dean decided her happiness was worth it. She was in "a bad
place."

Dean knew many of the Gap Band's songs by heart, and, standing
there in the crowd, she was belting them out along with Charlie Wilson,
putting body and soul into classics like "Oops Upside Your Head." She

had that bullfrog croak of funk in her throat. It emerged from her body in an echoey rumble, exuding a profane joy, like a musky perfume.

Tricky introduced himself, and complimented Dean on her singing. "Do you have any musical training?" he recalls asking her.

Dean had never been to a music class, or learned an instrument: music education had not been an option at the schools she attended. She sang beautifully in church—everyone told her so—but she had never studied music.

"Well, a person who can sing like you has a gift," Stewart said.

He left her with his card, suggesting she stop by RedZone one day and try singing on the mike. "I just wanted to put her in a room with some other talented musicians to see what she could do," Stewart says.

SEVERAL DAYS LATER, Dean drove out to Buckhead, a prosperous commercial district in the northern part of Atlanta, where RedZone is located. There she met the rest of the team. They all talked for a while. Whatever she might be capable of doing on the mike, it was quickly clear to the others that Ester possessed a rare gift for swagger. In a voice that combined a Betty Boop–ish exuberance with a low-down raspy growl, she talked and talked, mixing her nutty quicksilver thoughts with profanity so rich that it blued the air. The men, no strangers to cussing themselves, were taken aback to hear a woman curse so profligately (especially Kuk Harrell, who had been a worship leader back in Chicago). "I'll get around guys and I'll cuss so fuckin' much and I'm like, 'Yeah this bitch did this,'" she explains, "that they'll stop talking and just look at me, like I'm supposed to say, 'Oh! I'm so sorry for shocking you!'"

But just because she came on with that dirty, sexy swagger didn't mean Esta wanted to be your girlfriend—a point that led to considerable misunderstanding. That was partly why she dressed conservatively—to offset her mouth. "I'm going to come and wear the baggiest pants and no makeup and I'm not going to do my hair in any kind of sexual way," she goes on, "because I don't want you grabbin' on my ass and I don't want you doin' none of that shit. I'd rather you think I'm a fuckin' dyke than I wanna be your girlfriend. I'd rather be motherly, and I do that—'You need something to eat honey?'—and make 'em comfortable that way, than to try to get these breasts up and get some tight pants on this ass. I'm like, 'That shit is tiring!'"

Tricky invited Dean to sing, and it was obvious to the pros at Red-Zone that she had the vocal chops to be a demo singer and make the vocal trace patterns that producers give to the artists to follow.

Tricky also asked Dean to try some writing, because, he said, "I truly believe if you can sing you can write songs." He played her snippets of some tracks he had devised, which had no melodies yet—just beats, chord progressions, and instrumentation. He told her that when she heard one she liked, she could go into the vocal booth and freestyle, to see what came out. Ester tried it, and within a minute or so of making subvocal grunts, a very credible hook had fallen out of her profane mouth. She tried another track, and it happened again.

Ester Dean turned out to be a hook-spitting savant. Somehow she could absorb the beat and the sound of a track and distill its melodic essence. Her hooks were more like vocalized beats than like lyrics, and they didn't communicate meaning so much as feeling and attitude—they nudged you closer to the ecstasy promised by the rhythm and the "lift" as the track built to a climax. Later, she tries to explain her gift, saying, "I just go into the booth and I scream and I sing and I yell, and sometimes it's words but most time it's not, and I when I get this little chill, right here"—she touches her arm, just below the shoulder—"I'm like, 'Yeah, that's it. That's the hook.'"

Before she left RedZone that day, Ester Dean had herself a publishing deal. She got an advance, which she would pay back by giving Red-Zone 50 percent of the royalties she might earn in the future. She was now one of the studio's stable of "topliners," whose job was to come up with the melodies to place on top of the producers' tracks. She could also earn extra money for singing on demos. Clearly she had a melodic gift, but whether she could tailor it for a specific artist in her style remained to be seen. The only way to find out was to "put her in a room," Tricky says, and see what she could do.

BY THE MID-2000S the track-and-hook approach to songwriting—in which a track maker/producer, who is responsible for the beats, the chord progression, and the instrumentation, collaborates with a hook writer/topliner, who writes the melodies—had become the standard method by which popular songs are written. The method was invented by reggae producers in Jamaica, who made one "riddim" (rhythm) track and invited ten or more aspiring singers to record a song over it. From Jamaica the technique spread to New York and was employed in early hip-hop. The Swedes at Cheiron industrialized it. Today, track-and-hook has become the pillar and post of popular song. It has largely replaced the melody-and-lyrics approach to songwriting that was the working method in the Brill Building and Tin Pan Alley eras, wherein one writer sits at the piano, trying chords and singing possible melodies, while the other sketches the story and the rhymes. In country music, the melody-and-lyrics method is still the standard method of writing songs. (Nashville is in some respects the Brill Building's spiritual home.) But in mainstream pop and R&B songwriting, track-and-hook has taken over, for several reasons.

For one thing, track-and-hook is more conducive to factory-style song production. Producers can create batches of tracks all at one time, and then e-mail the MP3s around to different topliners. It is common practice for a producer to send the same track to multiple topliners—in extreme cases, as many as fifty—and choose the best melody from among the submissions. Track-and-hook also allows for specialization, which makes songwriting more of an assembly-line process. Different parts of the song can be farmed out to different specialists—verse writers, hook smiths, bridge makers, lyricists—which is another precedent established by Cheiron. It's more like writing a TV show than writing a song. A single melody is often the work of multiple writers, who add on bits as the song develops.

It is also worth noting who *isn't* in the room when track-and-hook songs are made. Large-bellied men with their beer cans perched precariously on the lip of music stands—session musicians, to paint them in stereotype—are nowhere to be seen. Where are they? The two or three at the very top of their game might be working somewhere, but most of them are unemployed, trying to make ends meet by giving guitar lessons. They have been superannuated by the song machines that do their work more cheaply and efficiently than they can, and don't require beer.

In the melody-and-lyrics approach to songwriting, a song generally begins with a melody, or with lyrics, and a rough sketch of the song is worked out by the composers before the production is done. In track-and-hook, the production comes first, and then melody and words are added. Often producers are not looking for a single melody to carry the song, but rather just enough melody to flesh out the production. That's why producers generally speak of a song's "melodies" rather than its melody.

As a working method, track-and-hook tends to make songs sound the same. Dance music producers have always borrowed liberally from others' grooves. There's no reason not to: beats and chord progressions can't be protected under the existing copyright laws, which recognize only the melody and lyrics. As dance beats have become the backing tracks to a growing number of pop songs, similar-sounding records have proliferated. The melodies themselves are still supposed to be unique, but because of the way the way producers work with multiple topliners, tracks and melodies tend to blur together.

In 2009, for example, both Beyoncé and Kelly Clarkson had hits from tracks written by the superproducer Ryan Tedder. One was Beyoncé's "Halo," which peaked at number five in May, and the other was

Clarkson's "Already Gone," which got as high as number thirteen in August. Clarkson wrote her own top line, while Beyoncé shared a credit with Evan Bogart. When Clarkson heard "Halo," she thought it sounded too much like "Already Gone," and feared the public would think she had copied Beyoncé's song. (Tedder later said that Clarkson's allegations were "hurtful and absurd.") But nobody cared, or perhaps even noticed; both songs were hits.

In a track-and-hook song, the hook comes as soon as possible. Then the song "vamps"—progresses in three- or four-chord patterns with little or no variation. Because it is repetitive, the vamp requires more hooks: intro, verse, pre-chorus, chorus, and outro hooks. "It's not enough to have one hook anymore," Jay Brown explains. "You've got to have a hook in the intro, a hook in the pre, a hook in the chorus, and a hook in the bridge, too." The reason, he went on, is that "people on average give a song seven seconds on the radio before they change the channel, and you got to hook them."

Hook writing tends to encourage a "first thought, best thought" approach to songwriting. Inspiration, not perspiration, is the order of the day. Since producers generally have a batch of tracks already prepared, like doughnuts ready for the honey glaze, topliners needn't labor over any one track for long. If inspiration doesn't strike quickly, move on to the next track and begin anew. It might require twenty tracks to yield one recordable song, but that is an acceptable percentage for most songwriting teams. Whether or not this method makes for better songs, it certainly yields more of them, and allows the creators to enjoy a (possibly illusory) sense of accomplishment at the end of the day.

The track-and-hook method makes the producer the undisputed king of the song-making process. As the producer Timbaland put it in *Billboard* in 2004, "My producing style is this, 'I am the music.'" The topliner works for the producer, in the sense that the producer books and pays for the studio—generally out of up-front money that labels pay him—and he runs the session, often charging a daily rate. The producer almost always gets a big piece of the publishing, which was not the case in the old days. A lot of pioneering hip-hop producers were ripped off because they didn't understand the value of the publishing, and sold the rights cheap. Modern producers are wise to that scam. That's why hip-hop hits often have half a dozen or more songwriters and producers listed as authors.

In the hip-hop world, the producers are as celebrated as the artists. Dr. Dre is bigger than any of his rappers. At Aftermath Records, Dre's hip-hop hit factory in L.A., dozens of young beat makers and topliners put in long hours. The Canadian rapper Drake worked there for a while, before he was famous. "It was some of the most strenuous militant shit I've ever done," he says. "But no useable songs came out of it. When I think of how he worked us, it's no wonder he didn't get anything out of it. It was just writers in a room churning out product all day long."

Producers are known for their signature sounds. Timbaland (Timothy Mosley) has his funky Eastern strings; Dr. Dre his wheedling Parliament-Funkadelic-inspired gangsta beat. For Cheiron, it was the wet kick drum/dry snare combo. Those sounds are their brands, and they tell music fans who's in charge of the record. But eventually every producer's sound gets dated. A producer is vulnerable to changing fashions in pop music in a way the topliners are not. A great melody is timeless.

Timbaland was hot in the first half of the 2000s. He produced the first three Missy Elliott albums, as well as several tracks on Rihanna's breakthrough album, *Good Girl Gone Bad*. Jay-Z regularly shouted him out in his raps. But Timbaland was virtually absent from the radio by 2010. His sound abruptly got stale. The Neptunes, the producing and songwriting duo of Pharrell Williams and Chad Hugo, were also much in demand early in the 2000s and largely out of favor by the end of the decade, though Pharrell would be back in a big way.

The track-and-hook producers are almost always men (less than 5 percent of music producers and engineers are women, according to most estimates, and no woman has ever won a Grammy for Producer of the

Year). The topliners are often women (because their clients are likely to be women too), but male artists like Ne-Yo also topline for other artists. Most topliners want to be artists themselves, performing their own songs. But they are in the same predicament as Edmond Rostand's Cyrano de Bergerac. They have the music in them, but they lack the star quality necessary to put the songs across and make them hits. Very occasionally a male topliner does cross over and become a star—Pharrell Williams would do it, and Ne-Yo had managed it to a certain extent—and those rare instances give every other topliner hope. But for most, it is false hope. (Women almost never cross over—Skylar Grey is a rare exception but hardly a major star—although the topliner Kara DioGuardi did manage to achieve fame as an *American Idol* judge.)

Most important, the producers and labels that hire topliners aren't inclined to unplug them from the assembly line of song creation and help them become stars. That would mean denying already established artists the benefit of potential hits. Powerful interests are invested in keeping the topliners where they are—in the studio rather than onstage.

ESTER DEAN GOT HER first cut in 2006, a demo single for an artist called Bayje that didn't lead to an album deal. In 2007, she got another cut with an R&B trio called Dear Jayne, and another with a female trio, Girl Called Jane (no relation)—a good song called "He's Alive" that didn't get noticed. Also in 2007, Dean had a song on an album by Mya, who had burst onto the scene as one of the singers in the hit cover version of "Lady Marmalade" in 2002, which won Video of the Year at the MTV Awards. But Mya's career was on the wane by 2007, and the album was never released in the United States.

Ester was likable—a valuable trait in a topliner. She was a force of nature, with a quick wit, a knack for out-of-left-field associations, and a bawdy, raucous laugh. Women liked her because she was warm and chatty; guys liked her because she was dirty and could curse as fluently as any man. The studio got pretty stale after a while, as the producer spent day and night working up his onanistic sound tapestries. A topliner like Dean, who could walk in and splash color and magic around the room, was a valued partner.

And yet she began to see how the deck was stacked against the topliners. In theory, the producer and the topliner split the publishing proceeds from a song 50-50. But the producers are usually paid for their time in the studio, regardless of whether it results in any hits, whereas the topliner only gets paid if the song is recorded and put on sale, which very likely it would not be. Leading producers can also negotiate percentage points of the record sales; topliners almost never get points. The producer, in sending his track out to dozens of topliners, maximizes his chances that it will result in a salable song, maybe even a hit record, but all those writers whose toplines aren't chosen have squandered a melody on nothing.

On a more basic level, Dean came to feel that "anybody can be a producer, but not anybody can be a writer. Hell, you can buy beats and tracks online! But the melody gotta come from in here!" She taps her skull. "I don't care how good the track is, the track don't make the song."

Nor does Dean appreciate the sexist aspects of the songwriting world. When a gal spends long hours in confined spaces with guys, singing about love and sex, and shaking her butt to the beat, professional boundaries can get crossed. "Yeah they gonna come to you any kind of way. Because music doesn't have a union, or sex discrimination laws—it's got nothing that keeps everyone in check."

Meanwhile, Dean watched as The-Dream lived out every topliner's fantasy with "Umbrella," earning millions from the song. She was close enough to see how transformative a smash could be, but too far away to enjoy the benefits of one.

Dean's luck began to change over Super Bowl weekend in 2008, when she saw a movie called *The Secret*. The secret itself is "the law of attraction," a supposedly ancient principle long suppressed by nefarious powers. It holds that if you want something badly enough, and if you "manifest" your dreams clearly in your mind and remove any doubts you harbor about attaining them, they actually *can* come true. (Who knew?) This power scares the shit out of the people who benefit from keeping us from our dreams, so they try to keep it quiet. That's *The Secret*. It's like a religion based on a conspiracy theory. The idea started out as a film, then the bestselling book, by Rhonda Byrne, followed, offering a manual for people who wished to discover the secret for themselves. Ester Dean was one of those people.

The film advocates making a "vision board": a poster with taped-up pictures of people, achievements, and things you admire, aspire to, or covet. After watching it, Dean took the plastic cover off a storage container in her apartment and taped to it a picture of an artist, Ciara, a house, a car, and an American Express card.

In short order, Dean wrote her first two charting hits: "Like Me" by Girlicious, which got to number seventy, and "Remember Me," for T.I., which got to number twenty-nine. She also wrote "Never Ever" for Ciara, the first Ester Dean topline to show flashes of her signature style. But the song went nowhere. Dean believed she could have made "Never Ever" a hit if she'd been allowed to record it herself. Deep in her heart she cherished the notion that she was an artist—she had a vision board for that, too.

After three years, Dean had paid back her publishing advance to RedZone, and she decided to move on, signing another publishing deal with a well-known producer, Polow da Don, whose real name is Jamal Fincher Jones. Though she signed on as a topliner, Polow told Ester he believed in her as an artist, and to that end he also signed her to his label, Zone 4, brought her to Los Angeles, and introduced her to Jimmy Iovine, the former sound engineer turned producer and music mogul, who was the chairman of Interscope Records. Iovine told Dean he thought she was an artist too, and made vague plans to bring out an Ester Dean EP at some point in the next year or two. Polow also introduced Dean to Stargate, with whom she would have her first Billboard number one.

Ester had written and demoed a song for Ciara called "'Drop It Low." But the artist had been lukewarm about it. "She didn't come get the song," Dean says. "And then Britney wanted it." But by then Dean had decided she would keep the tune for herself. Her trace vocal for the demo seemed to her like the definitive version of the song. Polow encouraged her in this belief. "During the demo Polow kept telling me, 'You gotta believe it' as I was singing it," Dean recalls. "A week later he asked if I wanted to hear my new single"—"Drop It Low."

The Secret—Ester the artist—was about to be revealed.

17 | Stargate: Those Lanky Norwegian Dudes

NE-YO WAS BOOKED into Sony Music Studios on Tenth Avenue in New York City, trying to finish his debut album for Def Jam, *In My Own Words*. He had a song in his head, but he couldn't seem to get it out.

Then twenty-three years old, Ne-Yo had been signed as an artist by Columbia in 2000, and recorded an album, but the label dropped him before it was released. One of the songs he wrote for the album, "That Girl," was rerecorded by Marques Houston, and it became a modest hit. That led to work as topliner and lyricist; Ne-Yo could do both the tune and the words. That's why he's called Ne-Yo—he can see music around him in the way that Neo sees the Matrix.

In 2003, Ne-Yo toplined "Let Me Love You," a number-one hit by the R&B singer Mario. (Sia, a future hit maker, also worked on the song.) As a result of that triumph, he was invited to Jay-Z's office on the twenty-ninth floor of Worldwide Plaza, where he auditioned. Def Jam signed him as an artist, and Ne-Yo was in the process of finishing up his album. If only he could find this one last song.

Walking the halls at Sony, Ne-Yo ran into a manager he knew, Tim Blacksmith, a charming British bloke whose laddish South London accent conceals a quick, probing mind. Tim explained that he was in town for a week with his clients, two Norwegian producers, Tor Hermansen and Mikkel Eriksen, who called themselves Stargate. They were trying to get work in the United States. They had taken a room at Sony Studios for a week and were looking for topliners to collaborate with. Would Ne-Yo *please* come visit?

"They do pop, they can do R&B—they can do it all!" Blacksmith declared.

"They can do R&B?" Ne-Yo asked skeptically.

"Oh yeah, they do R&B," Blacksmith assured him.

Ne-Yo didn't believe him, but promised that he'd stop by.

GROWING UP IN TRONDHEIM, a small seaside city in Norway, Mikkel Eriksen was nuts for American R&B and hip-hop, but there was no Norwegian urban-music scene. He made hip-hop drum loops on his Commodore 64 computer, and he kept all his electronic gear under the bed—keyboard, tape machine, sequencer. "That was my whole life," he says, "buying gear, and playing in cover bands to make money to buy more gear." He also DJed at parties and clubs, but being the focus of attention at a live performance wasn't Eriksen's thing; he was too shy and introverted to enjoy being onstage. Eriksen had also briefly worked at Mega, the Danish label that signed Ace of Base, and he knew Denniz PoP's work well.

One day in 1998, a friend said to him, "'You should meet this guy Tor Hermansen—you are the only two guys who listen to urban music in Norway.'"

Hermansen's parents divorced when he was five, and he lived with his father, who drove a backhoe for work. He wasn't around when Tor came home from school, so Tor listened to lots of music, to pass the time. "I got hooked on American culture from movies—Steven Spielberg, *Grease*, and *Beat Street*," he says. "I was obsessed with the South Bronx, from songs like 'The Message,' without even knowing where it was." He started writing stories and taking pictures for local newspapers when he was thirteen. He wrote frequently about music, and eventually got a job at Warner Bros. in Oslo, where he worked his way up to head of A&R for the Norwegian office.

Eriksen made an appointment with Hermansen and took along a demo of an artist he was working with. Hermansen didn't like the artist, but he liked the backing track. "He said, 'Did you make this music? It's good,'" Eriksen recalls. Before long, Hermansen had quit his job and joined forces with the other half of Norway's urban-music fan base.

Although they were fellow Scandinavians, the Norwegian duo's musical background was very different from most of the Swedes at Cheiron. Whereas Max Martin grew up with glam rock and Europop, Mikkel Eriksen and Tor Hermansen were steeped in American R&B and early hip-hop. They actually *could* write urban songs, whereas Max Martin could only try in vain.

They complemented each other well. Eriksen was happy to remain inside the studio, programming and working the synths, while Hermansen, who was more of an extravert, met artists and drummed up work. Their big break came when Tim Blacksmith and Danny D, an energetic and resourceful British management duo, started bringing them to London to remix American urban hits for the European market. Their job was to add Europop sweetness to the city grit. "The idea at the time was that urban music needed to have more sparkly, brighter choruses, and more of a lift, to work in Europe," Eriksen says. He adds, "Our experience with remixing really has helped us in the way we work today, because we know that if we have a good vocal we can strip out the music and replace it with other music."

Their dream was to be on the radio in the United States. "We had tried a few times with labels in the US, without success," Eriksen says; "it wasn't our time." From around 2000 to 2003, hip-hop was dominated by big beats, created by producers like Timbaland and the Neptunes. "We loved it, but we couldn't make that kind of music," Eriksen says. Hermansen adds, "As much as we wanted to do the typical stripped-down hip-hop record, we were better at the melodic stuff."

In 2004, things suddenly slowed down for Stargate in the UK. "People got fed up with Stargate's sound—things change fast in the music business—and there was no work," Eriksen says. It can happen overnight: the moment you are perceived to be not quite as hot as you used to be, the A-list projects go to other producers, and you get stuck with lesser talents. "We were sitting back in Norway wondering, What do we do now? Should we shut it down and do something else? Our manager, Tim, said, 'Let's just go to New York, book a studio, and give it a shot there.' My wife told me, 'I know you guys can make it in the US.' I was up for it, but Tor was skeptical." They decided to go to New York. "We didn't have much money left, but we paid for the trip."

In the spring of 2005, Stargate came to New York and spent $20,000 to rent a studio for a week in Sony Studios on Tenth Avenue. "No one knew who we were," Eriksen says. "We didn't have any top-ten hits. We were there for a week, sitting there with our beats, and no one came," Eriksen goes on. "Our goal was to sell one song, and we did, we sold one, so we came back for one more week of sessions, and then we were going to call it quits."

Back in New York for a second time, they booked a studio at Sony again, and it was there that Tim Blacksmith encountered Ne-Yo in the hall.

NE-YO CAME BY STARGATE'S studio later that afternoon. "So I walk into the room," he remembered in an onstage interview at the 2013 ASCAP Expo in L.A., "and I see two tall lanky Norwegian guys, and clearly I was a little skeptical." Tor and Mikkel actually looked like characters from the Matrix—tall, skinny ectomorphs with pale shaved heads. They didn't look like R&B producers. But when they started playing tracks for Ne-Yo, he was immediately captivated. The beats were up-to-the-minute, but there was also a lovely choral feeling in Mikkel's synth playing/programming.

"When the track started," Ne-Yo recalled, "I teared up. . . . It's a story I've had in here"—he pointed to his head—"and here"—he pointed to his heart—"for a really long time. And the second the track started, it was like, 'This *is* that story.'" Ne-Yo sat down and in twenty minutes wrote the song "So Sick," which became the lead single off his album.

> *'Cause I'm so sick of love songs . . .*
> *So done with wishing she was still here*

By that evening, word had gotten back to Def Jam that Ne-Yo and the lanky Norwegian dudes had come up with something special. A&R people stopped by; an informal listening party ensued. "We were just jumping up and down, buzzing," Eriksen says. He couldn't believe it. That morning they were contemplating the end of their careers. By evening they were hosting a listening party in their studio that included Ty Ty fucking Smith, Jay-Z's homeboy and trusted A&R consigliere. Ty Ty liked "So Sick," and talked to the Norwegians about doing something for a new Def Jam artist called Rihanna.

"So Sick" came out in January of 2006, and went to number one. And just like that, Stargate was bigger than ever. "We thought we'd have to adapt to the beat-driven music here, but it turned out that it was our more choral, melodic music that people gravitated toward," Hermansen says. "When we first got here, American pop music was linear and minimalistic, with few chord changes, and no big lift in the chorus. If you listen to radio today, there are big breakdowns, buildups, instrumental parts, and more tempo."

By 2007, when "Umbrella" came out, Stargate had written several modest hits for Rihanna, and they collaborated with Ne-Yo again to create "Irreplaceable," which they gave to Beyoncé, who was soon to be Jay-Z's wife. It spent ten weeks at the top of the US singles chart—a bona-fide smash. As far as Jay-Z was concerned, Tor and Mikkel were made men.

AT THE END OF his four-year term as president of Def Jam, Jay-Z decided not to renew his contract, in order to pursue a joint venture with Live Nation, the concert promoter, to be called Roc Nation. The new company would take in all the major kinds of revenue from a song—sales, concert revenues, merch, and, down the road a bit, streams. Plunging record sales had made alternative sources of revenue crucial to the record companies' survival. These kinds of 360-degree deals allowed the label to get in on the rest of the action. Roc Nation was a label, a management company (Jay Brown came from Def Jam to run it), a music publisher, and an in-house studio that was called Roc-the-Mic, where material for Roc Nation artists would be created—a hip-hop hit factory. Stargate was the obvious choice to be the in-house producers, and they moved into the studio, on the fourth floor of a commercial building on West Twenty-Seventh Street, toward the end of 2008. Rihanna remained at Def Jam for the time being, but in 2010 she dropped her manager, Marc Jordan (thus ending Sturken and Rogers's involvement in her management), and became Jay Brown's client, keeping her within Jay-Z's orbit. Later she would join Jay's label, too.

The first room you see at Roc-the-Mic is the lounge, which has a pool table covered in taupe-colored felt, with hangout areas around it. Two sets of soundproofed doors lead to the control room, a windowless cockpit that looks like a model for the flight deck of the starship *Enterprise*. A state-of-the-art mixing board takes up one side of the room—a big hunk of high-tech hardware that was already redundant by the time it was built. Pro Tools is all the producers really needed.

With their managers, Tim Blacksmith and Danny D, orchestrating demand, Stargate would become one of a very few writer-producer teams that labels approach when they absolutely have to have a hit single—a "bullet," as Hermansen calls it—that they can take to radio as the first single. Often, panicked label execs approach them in the final weeks, or even days, before an album is mastered, because Stargate has a reputation for speed. "You can have two or three hot singles on an album, or no singles," Hermansen explains, "and that's the difference between selling five million copies worldwide and launching an eighty-date sold-out world tour, and selling two hundred thousand copies and having no tour. That's, like, a twenty-million-dollar difference."

If you hang around Roc-the-Mic long enough, you see just about all of the premier topliners pass through. A-list artists, on the other hand, rarely appear in the studio. The steady decline of record sales since Napster means that artists have to spend most of their time on the road, singing the songs they used to sell recordings of. Top-tier artists tour for most of the year, generally recording new material in between shows, in mobile recording studios and hotel rooms, working with demos that producers and topline writers make for them to use as vocal trace patterns. For example, the production notes for a Stargate-produced Rihanna single called "Talk That Talk" say that her vocal was recorded on "the Bus" in Birmingham, Alabama; in Room 538 of the Sofitel Paris Le Faubourg; and in Room 526 of the Savoy, in London. Hermansen, asked about this peripatetic recording method, says, "It's music as aspirational travel."

If the Stargate guys want to work in the same room with Rihanna, they have to travel to wherever she is, which they do not enjoy. Nor are the artists happy with this working arrangement, as it often means recording vocals late at night in mobile studios parked in trash-filled empty stadium parking lots that reek of urine after a show. But because the money is in ticket sales, not record sales, nonstop touring is the norm, and record making has to be fit into breaks in the grueling schedule.

I WAS AT ROC-THE-MIC one day when Ne-Yo came through. He was wearing a knit wool cap and a preppy wool sweater. An enigmatic singer, shy, his eyes hidden behind dark glasses, Ne-Yo tended to swallow his words in conversation. He said he was collecting songs for a new album, and hoped to work the old magic once again with Stargate. In spite of his success with "So Sick," Ne-Yo still hadn't quite distinguished himself from Usher, who was an obvious influence.

In the control room, Eriksen and Hermansen played Ne-Yo a track they had prepared for him. He listened with a yellow legal pad and pencil in his left hand, at the ready. Before the track was even halfway through he was scribbling notes and by the time it ended, he said, "Fuckin' love it."

"That's what we like to hear!" Hermansen exclaimed.

Eriksen said, "So the bridge just goes back to the second verse."

"Got it," said Ne-Yo, still scribbling. "I'm already halfway through." The Norwegians left him there and went to their office, which was opposite the control room, and closed the door.

Hermansen says to me, "If it takes him more than hour to do, we know it's not going to be that good."

After about twenty minutes there was a whistle at the door, and it was Ne-Yo, holding his pad—he was finished. Hermansen and Eriksen got up and went back into the control room. Ne-Yo seated himself at the control panel, his back to the others, and as the music played he sung his lyrics, which were built around the days of the week. It went something like: Monday put me down, Tuesday and Wednesday messed me around, Thursday had me on the ground, and Friday can't do it all. I need Saturday, which was the chorus.

"I love the buildup," Hermansen said, "but is Saturday enough? Why is Saturday so amazing?"

Ne-Yo said, "It's about release. It's like, 'Saturday, come save me.'"

"Oh, right," said Eriksen, somewhat dubiously.

"Got it," said Hermansen. "Let's hear it again. I love the space in it."

Ne-Yo sang it again, and when he finished, there was silence.

"It's about being revived," Ne-Yo said. "That's the concept of the record."

Hermansen said, "Maybe it could be a little more personal."

"I was trying not to be personal." Ne-Yo sounded hurt. "It's universal. Because everybody knows what Saturday means."

Hermansen gently asked him if he would mind writing another lyric. Ne-Yo looked crestfallen but said he would try. The Norwegians went back into their office to wait.

Eriksen: "He seemed a little disappointed."

Hermansen: "It's hard to explain why an idea isn't good. I know it when it *is* good. But it's hard to say why it's not."

Soon Ne-Yo's whistle was heard again at the door. He had written an entirely different song to the same track. This one was about a guy and his girl who were breaking up and saying goodbye. He sees her look back through the window of the taxi as she's pulling away, and he realizes she wanted him to fight for her. The hook was, "I made a mistake." Ne-Yo sang the words and melody, and when it was over Hermansen said, "Now that's a story! That's more like Ne-Yo."

"Grabs you by the balls!" Eriksen said.

Hermansen said, "Love the melody right there, it's crazy with the chords. That line is sick— 'to fight for you.' Maybe you can get that 'fight for you' line in twice."

"Let's do it," Eriksen said, and Ne-Yo went into the vocal booth, where he took off his sweater; the booth was warm.

Hermansen tells me, "You want to see a master at work, listen to him cut his vocals."

Ne-Yo laid down the main vocal, then sang harmonies against it on the playback. They had the basic vocal finished in ten minutes. However, as with almost all the songs they recorded on any given day, this song would never see the light of day. It wasn't "The One." They had produced a song with their process, and it was pretty good. But they were quick to discard it because it wasn't amazing enough. It was better to toss it and start again rather than try to fix it.

．　．　．

THE MAGIC REALLY HAPPENS at Roc-the-Mic when Ester Dean comes to town. She stays for three or four days, and they knock out six songs or more. The cockeyed Okie and the Norwegian ectomorphs make a hilarious combination. They order in some sushi, say, and the soft-spoken Eriksen murmurs, "I have a hard time putting weight on." Dean, hearing that, begins whooping. "Oh my gawd! I want to manifest that! 'I have a hard time putting weight on!' Motherfucker, I have a hard time putting weight on too! See this ass? The pounds just *fly* off this ass! Oh. My. Gawd!" So it goes, sometimes for hours.

Before going up to Roc-the-Mic this time, Dean picked up an iced coffee at the Starbucks on the corner. Aubry Delaine, her vocal engineer, whom she called Big Juice, accompanied her. Hermansen and Eriksen were waiting for her in the control room. Dean reached up to give them big hugs, which was how she greets almost everyone, including strangers. Candles burned low in the corners of the room, a universal mood enhancer that one sees in studios everywhere.

In advance of Dean's coming to Roc-the-Mic, Stargate had prepared several dozen tracks. They create most of them by jamming together on keyboards until they come up with an idea—generally a central chord progression or a riff—around which they quickly build up a track, using the vast array of preprogrammed sounds and beats at their disposal. Hermansen likens their tracks to new flavors awaiting the right soft-drink or potato-chip maker to come along and incorporate them into a product. Though they work on everything together, they have different strengths. Eriksen's impulses are more melodic; Hermansen's more track-based, though it's hard to generalize. Hermansen has musical chops too: he came up with the chords for Rihanna's number-one hits "What's My Name" and "Only Girl (In the World)." In the studio, Eriksen tends to sit at a synth keyboard, which is within easy reach of his computer. He'll play chords, then switch back to the computer. Hermansen sits at his desk or on the couches at the back and listens to sounds, making suggestions about other rhythms and sounds.

With Dean they try to do one or two songs a day. Most will be relegated to the "good but not good enough" file. Around Roc-the-Mic, writing songs for any reason other than making hits is a waste of time.

Eriksen said, "Ready to work?"

"That's what I'm here for," said Dean. She went into the booth.

Eriksen then spoke to her through a microphone.

Eriksen: "You ready?"

Dean: "Let's do it."

Eriksen: "Give us that attitude."

Several of the tracks that Stargate had prepared for Dean were "cray-zee," one of Hermansen and Eriksen's three go-to superlatives around the studio; "dope" and "sick" are the others. But since they had days of sessions ahead, and Dean often requires time to get into her zone, there's no point in squandering the best tracks right away. So they warmed up with a throwaway number, which all parties knew immediately was not "The One."

Their second attempt was more promising. Dean was dimly visible through the soundproofed glass window, bathed in greenish light. She took out her phone, and as the track began to play she surfed through lists of phrases she copies from magazines and television programs: "life in the fast lane," "crying shame," "high and mighty," "mirrors don't lie," "don't let them see you cry." Some phrases are categorized under headings like "Sex and the City," "Interjections," and "British Slang."

The first sounds Dean uttered were subvocal—*na-na-na* and *ba-ba-ba*. Then came disjointed words, culled from her phone—"taking control . . . never die tonight . . . I can't live a lie"—in her low-down, growly singing voice, so different from her coquettish speaking voice. Had she been "writing" in a conventional sense—trying to come up with clever, meaningful lyrics—the words wouldn't have fit the beat as snugly. Grabbing random words out of her phone also seems to set Dean's melodic gift free; a well-turned phrase would restrain it. There was no verse or chorus in the singing, just different melodic and rhythmic parts. Her voice as we heard it in the control room had been Auto-Tuned, so that Dean could focus on making her vocal as expressive as possible and not worry about hitting all the notes.

After several minutes of nonsense singing, the song began to coalesce. Almost imperceptibly, the right words rooted themselves in the rhythm while melodies and harmonies emerged in Dean's voice. Her voice wasn't hip-hop or rock or country or gospel or soul, exactly, but it could be any one of those. "I'll come alive tonight," she sang. Dancing now, Dean raised one arm in the air. After a few more minutes, the producers told her she could come back into the control room.

"See, I just go in there and scream and they fix it," she tells me, emerging from the booth, looking elated, almost glowing. She touches the back of her arm, feeling for that million-dollar chill.

Stargate then went to work putting Dean's wailings into traditional song structure. Eriksen worked the box, using Pro Tools, while Hermansen critiqued the playbacks. On Eriksen's Apple Cinema Display screen, small colored rectangles, representing bits of Dean's vocal, glowed green, and he briskly chopped and rearranged them, his fingers flying over the keys, frequently punching the space bar to listen to a playback, then slicing and dicing some more. The studio's sixty-four-channel mixing board, with its vast array of knobs and lights, remained idle, a relic of another age.

Within twenty minutes, Dean's rhythmic utterances had been organized into an intro, a verse, a pre-chorus (the pre), a chorus, and an outro; all that was missing was a bridge. (The final day of the sessions was reserved for making bridges.) Big Juice sat down at the computer and began tweaking the pitch of Dean's vocal. Dean went back into the booth and added more words: "Give me life . . . touch me and I'll come alive . . . I'll come alive tonight . . ."

Hermansen listened, his shaved head bobbing to the beat. "You don't want 'I'll come alive at night,'" he said, over the booth's intercom. "That's too zombie."

"I'll come a-LI-I-IVE," Dean tried, drawing out the syllables.

In a little less than two hours, they had a finished demo. Was it "The One"? Hermansen wasn't sure; they would listen to it again tomorrow. (And, in fact, when they listened to it again the next day it was tabled: not good enough.)

Big Juice seemed to like it, though. After hearing the playback, he spoke for the first time.

"That's dope," he said softly.

18 | "Rude Boy"

CLIVE DAVIS'S ANNUAL pre-Grammy party, held at the Beverly Hilton in Los Angeles on the night before the awards, is a ritual unlike any other in show business. It is both a dinner and a floorshow, like the Golden Globes and the Grammys combined. No awards are given; the award is getting invited. The event features the year's biggest musical stars, performing not for their fans but for their peers. In Davis's view, "There is not a more powerful or prestigious audience they will ever appear in front of."

The stars share the stage with a promising new talent or two, along with one of two heritage acts Davis invites, to show the kids what real talent is like. He recalls asking Johnny Mathis to perform one year for that reason. "I wanted these young guys to see what Johnny Mathis was about," he says. "I'd say to the young artists, 'You've had some success, but think about this. His greatest-hits album was in the top one hundred for ten consecutive years! And there's a reason for that—because people danced to it, got married to it, made love to it, whether it's 'Chances Are' or 'It's Not for Me to Say' or 'Wonderful! Wonderful!' And I would say, 'You, Kelly Rowland!,' and 'You, Beyoncé! Listen to the phrasing! Listen to the magic!'".

Davis emcees the event himself, affecting a stentorian broadcasting voice that sounds a little like Ed Sullivan—a CBS Tiffany network accent that brings a sense of discernment and gravitas to the business of entertainment. "Ladies and gentlemen of the audience, please give it up for so-and-so," he'll say, and for a moment Clive's guests really do seem like ladies and gentlemen, and not the demon-driven strivers they actually are.

But if Davis's patrician air seems to summon one's higher nature, the seating arrangement at the party makes brutally clear your importance in his world. It really is all about a continuity of hits. If you are having hits, you are at one of the power tables close to the dais, dining with stars. But the very next year, with no hits, you find yourself seated on the outer rim, along with the press and some luckier guy's wife and kids. "Other people might think, Oh, he just had a bad year, let him keep his spot at the good table, he'll be back on his feet soon enough," a down-on-his-luck artist manager tells me at the 2014 party, sitting forlornly in the back. "But Clive isn't sentimental about this stuff. He lets you know right away where you stand." The man smiles ruefully.

At the 2009 party, you were indeed at the top of your game if you were at the table "anchored" by Rihanna and Chris Brown, who were among the biggest stars there and certainly the best-looking couple. Their presence shed fairy dust over the soiree. Davis singled them out in his remarks from the podium, noting that both were scheduled to perform at the Grammys the next day. Rihanna, radiant in a floor-length Gucci gown, rose to acknowledge the industry crowd's warm applause, while Brown, handsome as sin in a black leather jacket and tie, beamed up at the beautiful face he was about to beat to a pulp.

Chris Brown was a good singer and an exceptional dancer who had taught himself by watching Michael Jackson on TV. Some called him the next MJ because of his triple-threat musical gifts (he can sing, dance, and write). Temperamentally, he may be closer to Marvin Gaye. He was born in a small town in Virginia, where his parents listened to soul music and Stevie Wonder. They divorced when Brown was seven, and his mother married again. Brown later said his stepfather hit his mother, usually at night when Chris was supposed to be asleep. She hid the marks with makeup in the morning, but Chris could see the bruises and the swelling. When he was eleven, he told her, "I want you to know I love you, but I am going to take a baseball bat one day when you are at work and kill him."

Brown had signed with Jive because the label had Britney Spears and Justin Timberlake on it. Tina Davis, a former Def Jam A&R executive, was his manager. The first single he put out as an artist, "Run It!," in June 2005, was a number-one hit. He pulled off an unforgettable performance at the 2007 MTV Video Music Awards, where he followed Britney's robotic "comeback." He had a second number one with "Kiss Kiss," two years later, and it received a Grammy nomination in the "Best Rap/Sung Collaboration" category, losing out to Rihanna and Jay-Z for "Umbrella."

"Forever" had an unusual provenance, which gave new meaning to the concept of bubblegum music. The song was actually commissioned by Wrigley's, the chewing gum company, as a jingle for Doublemint, and the lyrics include the brand's well-known tag line—"Double your pleasure, double your fun." Brown wrote the jingle first, and during the recording session, which was overseen by Polow da Don, they worked out a full-length version of the tune, which became "Forever." A classic four-chord vamp, with lots of squishy-sounding synths and heavy Auto-Tune on Brown's voice, the song is an urban take on a Euro-disco sound—the opposite of what the Swedes at Cheiron had been trying to achieve in writing for urban artists.

SHORTLY AFTER MIDNIGHT, Davis's gala broke up and the beautiful young couple left the Beverly Hilton in Brown's Lamborghini. They hadn't gone far before Fenty confronted Brown about a long text message from another woman she had discovered on his phone. Shouting, she slammed both hands down on the dashboard in anger. Brown stopped the car in the neighborhood of Hancock Park and leaned across Fenty to open her door, trying to push her out. But Fenty had her seat belt on. Her door swung closed and Brown pushed her up against it, punching her in the left eye and in the mouth. He started to drive again, steering the car with his left hand while he continued to hit her with his right.

When the beating temporarily stopped, Fenty sat up and looked at her left eye in the mirror. It was starting to swell, and her mouth was filling with blood. "I'm going to beat the shit out of you when we get home," Brown reportedly said. "You wait and see."

Fenty called her assistant and got voicemail, but pretended she was talking to her. "I am on my way home," she said. "Make sure the cops are there when I get there."

"You just did the stupidest thing ever!" Brown cried. "Now I'm really going to kill you!" He started punching her again. At this, according to the police report, Fenty "interlocked her fingers behind her head and brought her elbows forward to protect her face." His blows thwarted, Brown got Fenty in a headlock. She couldn't breathe and began to lose consciousness. She gouged at his eyes, and Brown bit her left ring and middle fingers, and then released her.

Brown stopped the car and got out while Fenty screamed for help. A resident called 911. When the cops arrived they found a "very upset and crying" Fenty seated in the driver's seat of the parked vehicle, with Brown nowhere to be seen. He didn't reappear until seven that evening, when he turned himself in to the LAPD and was booked on assault charges, as the Grammys were going on at the Staples Center. Needless to say, the couple did not perform at the show after all.

Fenty suffered two black eyes, with large contusions under both caused by Brown's ring, a split lip, and bite marks on her hands and body. More damaging to her image were the pictures of her swollen and battered face that two female L.A. police officers leaked to TMZ, the gossip site, several weeks after the incident. For Robyn Rihanna Fenty, the pain of the beating itself was augmented by the humiliation of the whole world seeing her as the victim of an angry lover, just like her own mother and Brown's. She was forced to confront in the most public possible way the psychic memento mori of domestic violence that lay underneath the enamel of glamour. In the end, fame couldn't save little Robyn from the horror of her parents' marriage, as she had dreamed it might.

AS WITH MANY OF Rihanna's albums, *Rated R*, her fourth, began with a writer camp. There was a real danger that the artist's career could be seriously damaged by the beating, especially among her younger fans, many of whom seemed to be willing to forgive Brown because, as it was said by astoundingly vicious YouTube haters, "the bitch hit him first." A lot of people had invested a huge amount of time, energy, and money in building up the Rihanna brand, and with "Umbrella" it was poised to become very, very profitable. But in a moment her image had changed. She wasn't the haughty ice princess of the fashion mags. She was a victim. She bleeds.

L.A. Reid, who was still running Def Jam in the wake of Jay-Z's departure, was determined not to lose all they had invested in the young star. He put on the mother of all song camps. A-list producers and topliners were summoned to Los Angeles for two weeks and installed in studios around the city, their hotel and food all paid for. It was the kind of immensely expensive undertaking that only a major label can afford to arrange.

Nowhere are the production efficiencies of the track-and-hook method of writing better realized than in writer camp. A camp is like a pop-up hit factory. Labels and superstar artists convene them, and they generally last three or four days. The usual format is to invite dozens or more track makers and topliners, who are mixed and matched in different combinations through the course of the camp, until every possible combination has been tried. Typically, a producer-topliner pair spends the morning working on a song, which they are supposed to finish by the lunch break. In the afternoon new pairs are formed by the camp counselors, and another song is written by dinner. If the artist happens to be present, the artist circulates among the different sessions, throwing out concepts, checking on the works in progress, picking up musical pollen in one session and shedding it on others. At the end of each morning and afternoon session, the campers come together and listen to one another's songs. The peer pressure is such that virtually every session produces a song, which means twelve or more songs a day, or sixty a week, depending on the size of the camp.

The Rihanna writer camp was an elite affair. Ne-Yo was there, as was Stargate, and Ester Dean. Jay Brown played counselor to the campers, under the aegis of Def Jam management.

For Dean, writing for Rihanna was liberating. In spite of her earthy vocabulary and her 'hood style, Dean was a prude at heart, and her inner Baptist minister regretted her transgressions. But writing for Rihanna set her bad girl free. She became the woman she imagined Rihanna was, a woman Rihanna herself, tall and slim and sexy, would never aspire to be with such urgency: a swaggering vixen. In Dean's demos for her Rihanna hits, which can be heard on YouTube, it's hard to tell whether she is channeling Rihanna or Rihanna is copying Dean. "People put comments on my YouTube demos saying stuff like, 'This cover sucks,'" she says indignantly. "I ain't never covered a song in my life!"

"Rude Boy" was the work of five different songwriters, including Makeba Riddick, who helped Fenty write the bridge, and Rob Swire, who contributed to Stargate's production work. (Hermansen wrote and played the chord progression on this song too.) The hooks were pure Ester Dean. The first hook comes right away in the song, a sort of rhythmic pre-chorus, followed by the main hook, which will become the refrain of the song. Then a third hook, "take it, take it"—is the full Esta. And then there's a fourth hook—"what I want want want"—another straight-from-the-mouth classic—which brings us back to the title hook again. The track-and-hook method of songwriting reaches its apotheosis with "Rude Boy"; the song is virtually all hooks.

"Rude Boy" is a concise illustration of Stargate's gift to urban music. The beats are crisp and hard, but the crystalline synth chords lift the song from its crude lyrical context—challenging a rude boy about his manhood—and makes it sound like a love song. Musically, a Scandinavian snowfall filters down over a sweaty Caribbean drum circle. The stuttering sound that the chords make, created with a software module known as an arpeggiator, would become perhaps the signature Stargate sound.

Stargate had achieved with "Rude Boy" what the Swedes, for all their melodic gifts, were never able to pull off: a perfect hybrid of Nordic and urban. It marked the start of a hot streak that would bring the duo such smashes as "Firework," "Only Girl (In the World,)" and "S&M"—all collaborations with Ester Dean. In 2010, ASCAP named them songwriters of the year. In 2011 Rihanna's "Only Girl (In the World)" won them their first Grammy, for Best Dance Recording.

Most important of all, at least from L.A. Reid's perspective, "Rude Boy" in particular, and *Rated R* in general, erased any lingering impression of Rihanna as a victim. The gentle island girl-next-door Evan Rogers signed in Barbados is gone, and a steel-plated Valkyrie is firmly, and coldly, in control. From the Ellen von Unwerth cover photo of the unsmiling artist in mesh and black leather, palm cupped over one of her previously blackened eyes as though it still ached, to the lyrics of the lead single, "Russian Roulette," and the second single, "Hard," and the song "Cold Case," the whole album obliquely refers to the beating; "Stupid in Love" explicitly so, with its line about blood on your hands. Timbaland was on the album, as well as Will.i.am, Justin Timberlake, and many other top producers and songwriters—even Slash, the former Guns N' Roses guitarist, makes an appearance. A notable exception was Sturken and Rogers. *Rated R* is the first Rihanna album without a single cut from them on it.

. . .

ROGERS AND STURKEN'S SONGS for Rihanna began to wane with *Good Girl Gone Bad*. "After *Good Girl Gone Bad* she really grew up and became an adult," Rogers says, with a note of acceptance in his voice. "She wanted to work with younger, cutting-edge producers. I get that." Still, letting go wasn't easy. "There was a bit of a struggle, but we didn't want to be the guys who were trying to force songs on her."

The darker and more explicitly sexual turn her work had taken wasn't easy for them either. As Sturken notes, "It was hard for us to write sexual lyrics for Rihanna, being who we were to her." But they are philosophical about their situation. "We signed and discovered one of the biggest stars on the planet," Rogers says, "so after we got over our being mad, we got busy working with other artists."

Sitting in their studio in Bronxville, they can recall the first time she came there like it was yesterday. "She was sitting right there, right where you're sitting!" Sturken cries. He digs up some old video of the frantic two days of rehearsals they put Rihanna through at Rogers's house in Stamford, before her audition with Jay-Z. Up comes the image of Robyn Fenty, in her jeans and T-shirt, singing her Whitney cover in Rogers' spare bedroom while an NFL game plays on the muted TV behind her. The longtime partners watch the video in silence. They seem moved. When it ends, Sturken says, "This is a gut-wrenching change for everybody, as she grows up and her career moves on. It is earth-shattering. What do we want to be to her?" A long pause. "We talk all the time. And she thanked us at the American Music Awards."

"RUDE BOY" WAS THE SMASH that changed Ester Dean's life. It established her as one of the most sought-after topliners in the music business. The next year would bring "S&M," her second number one with Stargate.

'Cause I may be bad
But I'm perfectly good at it . . .

Dean says the lyrics came to her on a Sunday, adding, "Father, forgive me."

She also wrote the hooks for Rihanna's "What's My Name" ("Oh, na-na-na, what's my name?"), and for two Nicki Minaj smashes, "Super Bass"

Boom, badoom, boom, boom, badoom, boom bass
Yeah, that's the super bass

and "Turn Me On"

Make me come alive
Come on and turn me on.

Her vocals on the demos of the Nicki Minaj songs provide more than just trace patterns; on "Super Bass" in particular her voice serves as an (unaccredited) second vocal, used to augment Minaj's less-than-stellar singing voice. The voice that Tricky Stewart had heard coming from somewhere in the crowd at the Gap Band show that night in Atlanta was heard all around the world. Jay Brown himself would take Dean on as a client, putting the resources of Roc Nation behind her.

Everything Dean manifested on her vision board would become a reality, except for the most important vision: "Esta the artist." And the surer her Midas touch with other artists became, the farther her most cherished desire receded from her grasp. Her new manager, Jay Brown, wouldn't have it any other way; Dean was too valuable as a hit maker to turn her into a star. But Jay Brown wouldn't be her manager for much longer.

Dean is grateful for her success. (In addition to her talents as a hit maker, she has a thriving second career as an actress, appearing in the

Pitch Perfect movies and voicing characters in major animated films.) "It's a lot better than working at McDonald's," she has to admit. But she is weary of the way that producers now expect a hit from her every time she walks into a studio. "Everyone is so hit-minded. They're always looking at you, going, 'Didja get it? Didja get it? Is that the hit?' And I don't know what I'm going to give them. I never try to tap and find out what it is; I just do what I do."

That's why she stopped going to other producers' studios, with the exception of Stargate's, preferring to work with Big Juice in her own studio in L.A.'s Brentwood section that her success bought for her. Later, she moved into a still swanker studio in Santa Monica.

The EP that Jimmy Iovine had promised never materialized. A remix of the song Polow da Don had allowed her to record, "Drop It Low," featuring Chris Brown, did not make much of an impression on the charts, getting only as high as number thirty-eight. But Dean wasn't worried. Her destiny was to be the artistic reincarnation of Missy Elliott, she would tell you. Beyoncé was Diana Ross, Lady Gaga was Madonna, Usher was R. Kelly, and Dean herself was Missy. Thus, her success as an artist was only a matter of time. She had the title for her debut album already: *UnderEstaMated*.

STARGATE AGREED TO A week of sessions with Dean, ostensibly to create songs for her own album. But if a potential hit came out of the sessions, all bets were off. Why waste a hit on an unknown artist like Dean, even if she did write it—who cares? Especially when you could give it to Rihanna.

What does Eriksen think of Dean's prospects as an artist? "A lot of writers want to be artists," he replies cautiously. "Most of them can sing, and a lot of them can sing really well. But to be an artist, that's another story. To be able to perform, to be the person everyone looks at when you walk into the room, with all the publicity and touring, and then to be able to get that sound on the record—that's not easy. You can be a great singer, but when you hear the record it's missing something."

What is that something?

Eriksen thinks for a while. "It's a fat sound," he says, "and there's a sparkle around the edges of the words."

It was a cold winter day in the city, but inside the windowless studio, weather doesn't exist. Dean picked up her usual, an iced coffee at Starbucks, and took the elevator up to Roc-the-Mic. She wore a floppy knit hat, leather jacket, jeans, and boots—her usual casual-but-fly style. Again, Big Juice accompanied her.

Stargate began the session by playing one of their cray-zee-est tracks. It started with a snare drum layered with hand claps, joined by an evil-sounding, guitarlike synth moving in and out of the foreground. Dean listened to the track for about twenty seconds, until she began humming a melody softly. "OK, got it," she said. "Let's do it."

She went into the booth, got out her phone, and, as the music started, she began to vocalize. "How do I get it . . . walkin' in the cold to get it . . . you gotta, I'm-a wanna." About a minute in, she hit on the main hook, "How you love it," in which the words played a syncopated rhythm with the beat. It was classic Dean, freestyle and suggestive-sounding. This was followed by a secondary hook: "Do you do it like this, do you do it like that/If you do it like this can I do it right back."

In the control room, Hermansen and Eriksen sensed something special was happening, and they worked quickly to capture it in song structure.

"Let's loop the first half."

"Do the synth chords and then use the arpeggiator to set the rise."

"I love the straightness of the beginning. Put a couple more notes in the pre."

In the booth, Dean touched her shoulder, feeling the telltale chill. Then she put her hands in the air and did a snaky dance, testing the hook on her hips.

Back in the control room, Dean wrote a verse, which Eriksen looped. He double-tracked the vocals to create a choral effect.

They had half of a great song, but Hermansen thought "it runs out of ammo in the middle." Then Eriksen remembered a rap that Nicki Minaj had written for another Dean-Stargate song that hadn't made it onto Minaj's debut album. He stripped out Minaj's vocal and added it to their new track. "Let's see if it fits," he said. It fit perfectly. Another playback. The song sounded sensational.

"It's a smash!" Hermansen declared.

Everyone was giddy, like children on Christmas morning. Stargate's managers, Blacksmith and Danny D, came into the control room and listened to the playback, whooping raucously at the choruses, perhaps the very first of countless revelers who would bounce to the song. Dean danced. Aubry Delaine declared it dope. When it was over, everyone cheered.

Then Danny D said, "Let me just interject one word. You know who's looking? Pink."

"I'm keeping that one for myself," Dean said firmly.

"I know. I'm just saying. Pink's looking for an urban song with a contemporary beat."

"No!"

"Kelly Clarkson's supposedly looking. And Christina!"

BRIDGE
DR. LUKE: TEENAGE DREAM

19 | Speed Chess

DR. LUKE WAS TURNING FORTY. He liked to say that he loves the songs he makes because he has the musical sensibility of a twelve-year-old girl. But how long could his golden preteen taste endure? Hit making is a young man's game. At some point, even if you're Paul McCartney, you stop writing hits. And when the hits go away, they almost never come back.

But Dr. Luke didn't seem too concerned about losing his edge. Or at least the prospect made him no more paranoid than he already was. He did allow, forebodingly, that "all your instincts that make you successful, at some point in anyone's life, those instincts will be wrong." But did he really believe that would happen to him? His manic energy was devoted to making sure it did not.

In the summer of his fortieth year, Dr. Luke was living and working at his beach house in L.A.; his mansion in the Hollywood Hills was being renovated. He'd bought the beach house from Ozzy Osbourne, the Black Sabbath front man, several years earlier, and set up his studio on the second floor, in the formal, wood-paneled room that used to be Ozzy's library. That's where he spent his workday, which began around noon and ended at three or four in the morning. There's a window, which was open slightly, and the ocean could be heard faintly outside.

Dr. Luke is a born hustler, and he always will be, no matter how much money and power he accumulates. He has investments in real estate, in a high-end water brand called Core Natural, and in Summit Series, a company that organizes business conferences. Of course, he has his own label, Kemosabe Records, backed by Sony to the tune of some $60 million. He had also made a lucrative deal with Doug Morris, the head of Sony Music, to serve for five years as an exclusive in-house hit maker to the superstar artists on Sony's major labels—Epic, RCA Records, and Columbia—who include Kelly Clarkson, Pink, Miley Cyrus, and Britney Spears.

His publishing company, Prescription Songs, consists of some fifty songwriters and producers, with Cheiron-like specialized overlapping skills. At this stage, the writers were still dispersed in studios across Los Angeles, from Venice to Hancock Park, but the plan was to create a physical factory—Dr. Luke was in the process of renovating a building in Brentwood for that purpose, with twelve studios for Prescription writers. Dr. Luke describes his songwriting roster as "a combination of artists, producers, topliners, beat makers, melody people, vibe people, and just lyric people." Vibe people, he adds, "know how to make a song happen, understand energy, and where music is going, even if they can't play a chord or sing a note."

Dr. Luke's ultimate ambition is moguldom—Clive Davis and Doug Morris–sized success. But could Dr. Luke continue to do what he does best as a writer-producer, which is to create a hit song for the artist, while also running the label the artist is signed to? Clive Davis succeeded by bringing the artist the best possible song, regardless of who wrote it; Dr. Luke had succeeded because of his songs. A label chief has to at least pretend that the artist has creative input into the music. Pretending wasn't one of Dr. Luke's strengths. And his relationship with Kemosabe's biggest star, Kesha, was in trouble, and the trouble was about to get much worse.

. . .

DR. LUKE SAT IN AN AERON CHAIR, at an array of computers. Dressed in T-shirt and jeans, no shoes, slightly silvered with Hollywood stubble, he stared into his Pro Tools rig. He got up, paced, and stretched his arches, yoga-style. (His girlfriend, with whom he has two children, is a yoga instructor.) He is zero-body-fat fit, although he never seems to exercise. He lives in paradise, but he almost never goes outside.

Dr. Luke checked Twitter, retweeting a couple of tweets from his artists. He was edgy because he was expecting a call from Katy Perry's manager, Bradford Cobb, about a song for her forthcoming album, *Prism*, which Dr. Luke and Max Martin had written seven songs for and also executive-produced. Their previous album with Perry, *Teenage Dream*, had tied Michael Jackson's *Bad* for most number ones on a single album, ever—five. Now, with *Prism* about to appear, they were set to extend their amazing run of hits. Or not.

Cirkut, Dr. Luke's latest protégé and co-producer, worked beside him in the studio, serving both as a collaborator and as a sort of musical scrivener. Part of Cirkut's job (the more engineering-oriented part) involves taking down the rhythmic and melodic ideas that issue from Dr. Luke day and night (and sometimes well into the next day), and moving them inside the box. Dr. Luke will say, "Let's redo the 'right-nows,' because they should be simple, but everything else should be ornate, like a lead. Do the 'ooh-oohs' first. Get eight falsetto ones, then eight full-voice ones, and I don't know if we'll Auto-Tune all of them or just some." And Cirkut gets right to work, fingers chattering lickety-split over the keys, translating the doctor's orders into Pro Tools, manipulating the colorful rectangles that represent sonic blocks. Then he hits Playback with a flourish, and they listen.

Part of Dr. Luke's talent is finding talent. Ambitious DJs and beat makers like Cirkut are constantly sending him tapes, and he listens to most of them. When he hears something interesting, Dr. Luke wants to work with that person right away. Benny Blanco, the Dr. Luke protégé who had become a major hit maker by the tender age of twenty-five, was nineteen when he met his mentor. Blanco recalls, "I knew nothing about pop music. I didn't even *think* about pop music—that wasn't part of my realm. . . . I made him a CD of my stuff, and then at the end of our meeting he was like, 'No, I don't need the CD.' So I left, and I was like, 'The guy doesn't like me.' And then he calls me up and he's like 'Yo, want to come out to L.A. and make some music?' And I was like, 'Uhhhhh, I thought you hated me, man.' And he was like, 'No, man, I just liked your stuff so much I knew I didn't need a CD.'"

Dr. Luke said he wanted Benny to come to L.A. the next day. Benny was scared of flying, so he drove across the country. As soon as he arrived, Dr. Luke wanted to get started.

"I had just got there after six or seven days of driving," Benny recalls, "and Luke goes, 'Come into the studio!'

"'Luke I'm so tired.'

"'Come into the studio, everyone wants to see you.'

"'But I'm exhausted!'

"'I want to show you this new guitar I got!'

"So I go in, and he was showing me this new guitar, and then he goes, 'Let's just start a beat.'

"And I'm like, 'Dude, I'm so tired!'

"So we made two beats that night, and one become 'California Gurls' and the other became 'Teenage Dream.'" Benny adds, "The guy has the best kind of screw loose."

Dr. Luke keeps half a dozen or so beat-up-looking electric and acoustic guitars propped up around the studio, and noodles on them frequently. He can be heard riffing and shredding on many of the tracks he has produced. The '80s, when electronic song-making machines became common, are a frequent source of inspiration. "If you listen to Tears for Fears, they had great melodies and less rigid cut-and-paste," he says, adding, "My problem with eighties songs is they take too long to get to the chorus."

Working with different teams, Dr. Luke composes about twenty songs a year. They accrue slowly, sometimes over many months and hundreds of tracks, as he and his collaborators tinker with different ideas, putting half-finished projects aside to address imminent deadlines, then coming back to them. That summer he had seven or eight songs in various states of completion. "I've got Juicy J—he's my rapper; he had the biggest urban record last year. We have two songs we have to finish for him. No, three songs. Plus a Justin Timberlake record with Juicy J on it coming in right now. Sometimes I don't even like to look at the list, because it stresses me out."

Because of the vagaries of working with artists, Dr. Luke rarely schedules sessions more than a day ahead. "Their plans always change," he says, trying not to sound irritated. "An artist is sick. Or an artist was going to work this week, but she got a corporate gig in Saudi Arabia and the guy is going to pay her a million dollars. I mean, a zillion things." His voice goes up high with frustration. "Their boyfriend broke up with them. They met a guy and they're going away to Hawaii. So planning is sort of useless."

Dr. Luke prefers to delay finishing projects for as long as possible, "because I might hear something I like over the weekend." However, label executives need to plan records months in advance. Inevitably, telephone screaming ensues. Downstairs at the beach house, the air is alive with pings and trills and ringtones, as e-mails and texts and calls arrive from various Sony labels and the artists signed to them, seeking the doctor's medicine. But Dr. Luke, like pop music itself, tends to deal only in the here and now. "I don't do time well," he explains. "There are hard deadlines, and I've learned to recognize what those are, and I can tell the difference in the calls, by the amount of calls, and the tone of voice on the other end, that this really needs to be done now." That pointillist awareness of urgency infuses his songs.

Making music is by no means the only thing that Dr. Luke does in the studio. He is constantly checking on sales, radio, and social-media impact. He pores over Mediabase, a widely relied-on industry database for tracking radio spins. He scours the ever-expanding number of charts purporting to measure a song's popularity, parsing such mysteries as how songs that trail in traditional measurements (sales and spins) can still come out on top of the Hot 100, based on YouTube and Spotify streams, which *Billboard* now counts. "I'm a bit of a numbers junkie," he admits.

His biggest concern at the moment was the upcoming release of *Prism*, the new Katy Perry album. Most of the songs had been written the previous spring, in Santa Barbara, where Perry lives. "Luke and Max came to Santa Barbara," Perry recalls, "and we'd hang out, go to the ocean, have nice dinners. There's this really amazing studio we like to work at called the Secret Garden, and it's in the woods of Montecito. We go there and listen to music, we do a lot of YouTubing; we drink some Chablis. Luke and his protégé Cirkut make these little beds of music for me to listen to—not too long, just kind of appetizer-size—and then they'll do the full entrees if I like them."

Finally the call from Perry's manager came through, and Dr. Luke took it on his cell.

"Hey, man," he said, trying unsuccessfully to sound relaxed. "What's up? Talk to me."

They discussed the idea of getting Drake, the Canadian superstar rapper with an easy-like-Sunday-morning appeal, to write a rap for the bridge on one of Perry's upcoming singles. Neither was sure he would do it, but they wanted to have the track ready so that if Drake were to come into the studio, he could listen to it and record something on the spot.

Hanging up, Dr. Luke instructed Cirkut how to prepare the track. Then, saying, "I will make sure this is what Katy wants," he left the library to call Perry in private, closing the wood-paneled door softly behind him.

. . .

IN 1982, WHEN LUKASZ GOTTWALD was nine, he was living with his bohemian parents in Manhattan—his mother, Laura, an interior designer; and his father, Janusz Jerzy Gottwald, an architect born in Łask, Poland. They had a loft on West Thirtieth Street in Manhattan. Welfare hotels and brothels dotted the neighborhood, and there were crack heads in the lobby. His parents listened to jazz, which he grew to despise.

On Saturdays, his father took him down to the checkerboard stone tables that used to occupy the southwestern corner of Washington Square Park, where the young hustler would challenge adult players to rounds of speed chess. The pace of the games, many played in less than three minutes, suited the boy's OCD-like concentration. (It is no coincidence that his adult life would be consumed with making the best possible three-minute song—a sort of sonic speed chess.) The standard wager was five dollars, and he won frequently.

Grandmaster Flash and the Furious Five's song "The Message" was playing everywhere in the city that year. The funky rhythmic effects and the range of strange electronic sounds, created on a reverb-drenched synthesizer, delighted him. He started playing drums, but his parents wouldn't allow them in the house, so he picked up his older sister's guitar. Soon he was practicing six hours a day. Allan Grigg, who met Gottwald in New York, and is now the Prescription songwriter and producer known as Kool Kojak says, "Whether it was playing chess or learning guitar, Luke always had this almost inhuman focus."

When he was fourteen, Gottwald attended a camp run by the National Guitar Summer Workshop, held at a boarding school in Connecticut. Jarret Myer, a fellow camper, says, "Everyone was, like, 'You got to meet this kid Luke. He shreds—he's so amazing!'" Myer was particularly impressed that for his end-of-camp recital Gottwald considered playing a medley of Run-D.M.C. songs on the guitar. This kid was fresh.

Myer and another camper, Brian Brater, attended Horace Mann, the academically rigorous Bronx private school; both went on to Brown University. Gottwald went to eight different schools, including St. Luke's and the Little Red School House, in Greenwich Village. "We were from different worlds," Myer says. "I can recall Lukasz coming to our houses and seeing all this homework, and being blown away, like, 'What is all this?' And I remember going to his house and he had a duffel bag full of weed. And he was, like, 'Yeah, I deal, this is how I make money.' He was fifteen years old and he had it broken down into a science. And I was, like, 'Wow! I do homework, you do this, but we're friends.'"

Gottwald explains how he got into the weed-selling business: "I started growing some weed in my closet. I got some fluorescent lights from my school, and I hung them on chains, with tinfoil. And every time I watered the plants it would smell like crazy. So one day my dad was, like, 'Dude, you have to get rid of the plants.' And it just so happened that Mother's Day was three days later. And I knew a guy who dealt on Twenty-Second and Eighth. He had a photography studio, but he was really a drug dealer. So I wrapped the weed plants in floral paper, with ribbons on them, and walked right down the street, because he said he'd look after them. A month later, the plants are dead, and he felt bad about it, so he gave me a garbage bag of weed and I could sell whatever I wanted."

He did not invest the same kind of energy in school. "I never could make it to morning classes. I never felt like I needed to do it. I remember being in class, and saying, 'I don't care about this, I don't need to know this.'" (To this day, he boasts, he has yet to finish a book.) He got in trouble for bringing an alphanumeric beeper to class, so that clients (who at one point included his mother) could page him. When he was seventeen, Gottwald recalls, a music teacher of his, the guitarist Adam

Rogers, had a talk with him about dealing. "He said, 'Dude, you got to get serious. If you want to be a real musician, you can't do this.' And I stopped. And from then on I made my money playing guitar."

After high school, Gottwald enrolled at the Manhattan School of Music. Perversely, he decided to study jazz. "The thing that made Luke hilarious back then, apart from the pot smoking, was that he was completely arrogant," David Baron, a producer friend from those days, remembers. "One night, we were out to dinner with a whole group of people, and Luke starts talking about jazz. He's like, 'What is jazz? You learn a chord, you learn a scale, and you just move your fingers up and down the neck—that's it, right?' And everyone is like, 'Um, I think jazz may be more than that. Maybe you should listen to Miles Davis.'" But within a year he was good enough to get a weekly gig playing at Augie's Jazz Bar, on 106th and Broadway.

Gottwald made his first real money writing commercial jingles. He did the music for a popular Nike ad that ran during the 1994 World Cup. He hated it. "I didn't like the people who were deciding things," he says. He wanted to be the decider.

In 1997, Lenny Pickett, the *Saturday Night Live* bandleader, put out the word around music schools that he was looking for a young guitar player for the band. It had to be someone who could sight-read music. As he explains, "We had only two hours for rehearsal, so I needed someone who could pick the music up quickly."

Pickett, who was the tenor sax soloist in the band (before *SNL*, he was a horn player in Tower of Power), auditioned about forty young players. "Lukasz walked in," he recalls, "and—he's hilarious—the first thing he said to me was, 'You can stop the auditions right now.'

"I said, 'What do you mean?'

"He said, 'Because I'm the guy.'

"So I said, 'Sit down and read this music!' He was very sure of himself."

Gottwald was right: he was the guy. "I liked the way he played,"

Pickett continues. "I thought he had a really good rhythmic feel, he played with a lot of confidence, and he had a pretty large bag of guitar-player tricks. And he looked good, which is important on TV. He was thin, with that angular face that looks good on camera."

"Lenny was the coolest boss ever," Gottwald says. "He mentored me. Protected me. I think I was fired five times."

Of his decade-long stint with the *SNL* band, he says, "I played a bunch of styles—Philly Soul, Booker T., the Delfonics. I learned a repertoire. And I learned about how to be a boss. It was fun, and then for me it became not fun. There was something more for me to do."

GOTTWALD'S DISCOGRAPHY BEGINS IN 1995, at Rawkus Records, an underground hip-hop label started by his friends from guitar camp, Jarret Myer and Brian Brater, together with James Murdoch, a son of Rupert's, whom they had met at Horace Mann. Myer, who had not been in touch with Gottwald during his college years, discovered that "Lukasz had applied the same obsessive focus he had brought to the guitar to learning how to make beats." Gottwald had a tiny studio in the basement of a building on West Twenty-First Street, where he rented an apartment, and he would disappear into it for days at a time, and play music at astonishing volume.

"Those guys came to my studio and heard my stuff and said, 'Why don't you put out a twelve-inch?'" Gottwald recalls, "and they started asking me to do remixes. And that's how I learned about producing. I mean, I didn't even know what a producer was. When I was remixing I realized I was producing, but not getting credit for it. You were just fixing someone else's production, you know?"

Gottwald also released several records on Rawkus as an artist, under the moniker "Kasz." His 1998 debut, a twelve-inch single called "Wet Lapse," combines the Chemical Brothers' techno sounds with the more lyrical electronic music made by Fatboy Slim. These records weren't intended to be commercial; at best, they would be heard by a few thousand people in a club where Gottwald was DJing. The idea was to make tracks that one of Rawkus's lineup of rappers, which included Mos Def and Shabaam Sahdeeq, would want to rhyme to. For some reason, rappers rarely chose Gottwald's tracks, perhaps because they didn't sound underground enough. The music was much edgier than his later pop songs—"Wet Lapse" is like the soundtrack to a sci-fi movie in which the aliens win—but it was exquisitely crafted. Myer remembers a remark made by Alchemist, a well-known hip-hop producer. "He said, 'Yo, this dude could be really big.' I never forgot that."

Lenny Pickett says, "He had very good music skills, especially in the areas he needed to have them for producing music. Equally important, he had very good social skills, because if you don't have those, doesn't matter how good your tracks are, you're going to end up being somebody's helper." Pickett goes on: "He would bring tracks in on CDs and hand them to the cast people, and say, 'If you're writing something that fits this, feel free to use it,' and so his tracks started making their way into the show."

It was during the making of one of his last Rawkus records that "Dr. Luke" replaced "Kasz" as Gottwald's disco name. (It is not true, as legend has it, that the name derives from the hit maker's talent for mixing Adderall and Ritalin with coke and MDMA to create the perfect studio cocktail that kept you working through the night.) "I would tell people my name was Kasz, and no one could get it," he says. "And, like, why have a weird name you have to *explain* all the time? So, one day in the studio, Mos Def just said, 'Nah, man, your name's not Kasz. It's Dr. Luke, man,'" and it stuck. Gottwald adds, "The truth is, I don't even like 'Dr. Luke.' I mean, I can't change it now, but if I could I'd think of a cooler name."

He began making his own remixes for his DJ gigs. "When I first started being a producer I was a DJ and I would play all the hits, and then I would sneak in one of my tracks and I would just see, is it working or is it not working? I learned a lot from that."

Could his music succeed beyond the club? "What I thought was, 'Wow, how can I make songs for the biggest audience in the world? Not just do it for the people in front of me, but for everybody.'" That was where Max Martin came in.

DR. LUKE STARTED AS Max Martin's apprentice. He provided impeccable track-making skills and up-to-the-minute beats; Max offered Luke a path to big-time hit making. David Beal, Gottwald's old friend, now a media executive, says, "In the early days, Max had a lot to offer him. And Kasz saw that if he latched on to Max, he could take it to another level." Jarret Myer says, "You can't overstate the influence Max had on Luke. One day he is remixing underground records, and the next day he is doing Kelly Clarkson. After Max, he had no inhibitions."

But Dr. Luke was also exactly what Max Martin needed. Gottwald had the knowledge to make the rock sound Martin Sandberg heard in his head. "He's a better guitar player than me," Max Martin remarked in *Billboard*. "He can travel in many worlds," he added. "With his background as a guitar player, it seems within pop or rock, there's nothing he's not capable of. I think he's more versatile than me, actually."

Most important of all, Gottwald was comfortable with hip-hop, and that was where the pure pop mainstream of the future lay. The Swede had nothing like that in his background. "He's got really deep roots in hip-hop," Max Martin said. "And that's something that's further away from me. Having that in your arsenal makes it cool." In return, Max showed Gottwald how to make the melodies, and how to arrange and produce the vocals, which Max Martin could do at a genius level. Gottwald was a New York City guitar player who wanted to be a hit maker, and Max Martin was the former "sixth Backstreet Boy" who needed a new sound. They clicked.

"I don't know, man," Gottwald replies when asked to describe the chemistry between them. "It happened really fast. It was magical."

David Baron, speaking of the Gottwald he used to know, says, "Nobody knew that Luke was going to become the Beatles of our generation, or whatever he is. He wrote tracks that were pretty awesome, but they were a lot like other people's tracks. And then, when he had that first hit with Kelly Clarkson, it still sounded like Luke, but he had become a great songwriter."

From then on, other people's songs would start to sound like his.

DR. LUKE AND MAX MARTIN followed "Since U Been Gone," their first smash, with two hits for Pink, the Bucks County, Pennsylvania–born pop singer. Both "U + Ur Hand," and "Who Knew," were released in 2006. "U + Ur Hand" sounded a lot like another song, "4ever," that the songwriters had done in 2005 for the Veronicas, an all-girl pop-rock group, and Pink didn't know until someone told her. The artist hasn't worked with Dr. Luke since.

Dr. Luke and Max Martin had their first number one together with a song they did for Avril Lavigne, "Girlfriend." This song also proved contentious. The Rubinoos, a power-pop group, accused the songwriters of using part of their song "I Wanna Be Your Boyfriend" in "Girlfriend." Worse still, Gottwald ran afoul of Butch Walker, the Georgian recording artist and songwriter. Walker came to believe that Luke had stolen his original idea for "Girlfriend," which was a gloss on Toni Basil's '80s hit "Mickey." Walker describes the incident in his memoir, *Drinking in Bars with Strangers*, which includes a thinly veiled portrait of Luke as "Larry." Larry is a jackass. Walker wrote: "I remember him asking me, 'So when you write songs for people, do you even bother with *lyrics* or *melody*? Or do you have someone come in to help you with that? Because I can't do anything with lyrics and melody; I need to bring in outside help.'" Walker is stunned. "*How interesting,*" he thinks. "Hearing this, I was offended and appalled. I wondered, 'If you can't do that, then what the hell do you do?'" Fueled by his rage at the song machine—a rage shared by many of his fellow singer-songwriters, whose melody-and-lyrics approach has been devalued by the track-and-hook method—Butch confronts Larry at a party, but security pulls him off before he can punch him in the nose.

The Asphalt, a rock band, charged Dr. Luke with stealing the hook from their song "Tonight" and using it in Daughtry's 2008 song "Feels Like Tonight." The rapper Chrissy claimed that Dr. Luke knocked off her 2006 song "Slushy" in Kesha's 2009 "Tik Tok." And "Party in the USA," Luke and Claude Kelly's 2009 hit for Miley Cyrus, has a similar drum beat and overall production vibe to the Tom Tom Club's "Genius of Love," and a melody that recalls "I'm Coming Out" by Diana Ross. There is a logic to this: songs that sound like other, already familiar songs can get a jump on Zapoleon's Rule of Three. But although lawsuits were filed in some instances—as Dr. Luke likes to tell his Prescription writers, getting sued is a sure sign you've arrived as a hit maker—none of the suits were successful. Dr. Luke defends himself against these and other accusations, saying, "A lot of things are similar. But you don't get sued for being similar. It needs to be the same thing. 'Almost' doesn't count. Close but no cigar."

Their work with Kelly Clarkson, Avril Lavigne, and Pink established Max Martin and Dr. Luke as go-to hit makers in the second half of the 2000s. But for all of Luke's striving, they had yet to find that one artist who would put their sound over the top; they needed their Britney.

20 | Katy Perry: Altar Call

"I WANT TO BE the American girl for the whole world."

That's how Katy Perry describes her career ambitions to me, and with her enthusiastic embrace of a loopy, Vargas-girl persona—crossed-eyed with peppermint-swirl breasts, part Playboy bunny and part Little Bo Peep—she comes as close to achieving that dubious goal as any pop star in the two thousand teens. In her most famous song, "Teenage Dream"—

> *Let you put your hands on me*
> *In my skin-tight jeans. . . .*

the major chords (G D C) convey the teenage thrill part, but the A-minor chord limns the melancholy reverie of lost youth. No song better demonstrates the repurposing of teen pop for adults. The teening of America was in full *"schwing."*

KATHERYN ELIZABETH HUDSON WAS born in Santa Barbara, California, to evangelical Christian parents, in 1984. Her sheltered upbringing is far from the pop star whose bra squirts whipped cream in the video for "California Gurls." But then again, when you compare swooning fans at Katy's shows to home movies of her father, Pastor Keith, evangelizing in churches, as the congregation falls over, "slain in the spirit," Katy doesn't seem very far removed from her family at all.

Katy's parents, Keith and Mary Hudson, forbade pop music, TV, and Hollywood movies in the house (with the exception of *Sister Act 2*; the original was banned because it featured a hooker). Lucky Charms, the breakfast cereal, was verboten because luck was Lucifer's province. Also, deviled eggs were "angel eggs." At church, Keith spoke in tongues, and Mary interpreted what he was saying for the congregation. "Speaking in tongues is as normal to me as 'Pass the salt,'" Katy later told *Rolling Stone*.

Pastor Keith was a Timothy Leary acolyte before he found Jesus. His future wife, Mary Perry, had been a hippie scenester in the late '60s (she dated Jimi Hendrix), who rebelled against her establishment Southern California family by joining forces with an itinerant Pentecostal minister. When their daughter Katy was young—she was the middle child of three—the parents moved around the country, establishing ministries in California, Arizona, Oklahoma, and Florida. Eventually they settled in Santa Barbara, where Katy entered public high school and first made contact with the secular world.

As a child, Katy Hudson listened to the gospel records her parents played around the house. "Oh Happy Day," "His Eye Is on the Sparrow," and, of course, "Amazing Grace." She sang in church and for Christian-themed civic organizations, social gatherings, and festivals. Later, she accompanied herself on the blue acoustic guitar her church gave her when she turned thirteen, a color she would later adopt for her hair. With her liquid eyes and cute-as-a-button face, she had a talent for touching worshippers' hearts with a song, and she was frequently deployed just before the "altar call"—the climactic, come-to-Jesus part of the service.

David Henley, a local producer who heard Hudson sing in church, invited her to his studio, and made an informal demo of her doing traditional gospel tunes, as well as a few of his original songs for the growing market in Christian pop music. That demo made its way to Dan Michaels, head of A&R for a Christian music label in Nashville called Red Hill Records, a division of Pamplin Music, which was a small part of Pamplin Communication, the business empire run by Robert B. Pamplin Jr., a Christian entrepreneur. Michaels was impressed enough to invite Hudson to Nashville to work with some songwriting pros at a publishing company. He thought she might be that rare Christian with genuine crossover pop appeal, an Amy Grant–like artist who could bring secular fans into the fold. "She had the platform to change the world," Henley said.

Brian White, a professional songwriter, became Hudson's writing partner in Nashville and, more important, her mentor. As he told Chloe Govan, author of *Katy Perry: A Life of Fireworks*, the most thorough of the pop star's biographies, "I wanted to be that friend and voice of reason to help guide her in this first-time experience."

They started writing songs together. White was impressed with Hudson's talents, both as a writer and as a performer. However some of her song lyrics tiptoed into the carnal realm. To avoid any confusion over what the songs were really about, according to Govan, White instructed Hudson to write devotionals for each of them, explaining what parts of scripture she had used for inspiration, and what the song's Christian message was. Of "When There's Nothing Left" she wrote, "This song is a crisp, clean, simple 'love note' to God. . . . I wrote as though I was romantically in love with Him, like I would always give Him all of myself even when I didn't have any more to give." That kind of language did not necessarily endear her to the traditional gospel audience Red Hill courted.

But that was Kooky Katy. She definitely wasn't your typical Christian singer. Her faith, which should have been beyond reproach, given her devout parents and her cloistered upbringing (and the "Jesus" tattoo she wore on her wrist), was sometimes called into question both by her lyrics and by her actions onstage.

Part of the problem was her breasts. As a girl, she had prayed for big ones, and when He generously bestowed on her a splendid pair, she had briefly considered breast reduction. But eventually she decided to display them proudly onstage (after all, they were His), in tight tops that probably caused some single guys in the audience to regret their promise rings.

Her gospel album, *Katy Hudson*, came out in March 2001. She embarked on a nationwide tour that summer with several more established Christian acts, playing for audiences sometimes in the thousands who thrilled to her vocal talents. But Red Hill Records had run into trouble; it declared bankruptcy later that year. Financial problems meant the label could not properly distribute the album; most of the CDs ended up in a landfill. Officially, *Katy Hudson* sold a whopping two hundred copies—now prized possessions on eBay.

Hudson returned to Santa Barbara to live with her parents. She was seventeen, and after two years in Nashville her life was at a crossroads. Should she go back and finish high school? (She had left after her first term freshman year.) Or should she push ahead in her musical career?

In spite of the failure of her Christian album, Katy Hudson was still by any measure among the brightest young Christian stars. She could have easily secured a contract at another label, and probably *would* have given Amy Grant a run for her money as the top female Christian pop artist. Had she remained in the fold, who knows how many non-believers she might have converted. But instead, no sooner was she back home than she set about reinventing herself as a "secular" singer-songwriter. Which, in hindsight, is probably what she wanted to be all along.

Perhaps she asked Him what she should do, and the answer was: *Katy, you're going to Hollywood!*

HUDSON TRAVELED TO TENNESSEE with her mom, to consult a Nashville producer about making demos of her rock songs. When the producer asked her who among contemporary artists she'd like to work with, she was forced to admit she didn't know any. "I was like, 'I really have no idea.'"

Ashamed, "I went back that night with my mom to the hotel," she recalled, and "I turned on VH1"—a violation of the family's broadcast decency standards, but it had been a bad day—"and I saw Glen Ballard talking about Alanis Morissette."

Morissette was a Canadian singer-songwriter whose 1995 album, *Jagged Little Pill*, written with Ballard and mostly recorded in his home studio in L.A., had been an enormous, epoch-making success. Watching Ballard talking about making the album on TV, Hudson thought to herself, "You know what? I want to work with him."

The following day, she recalled in a 2008 interview with *Star Scoop* magazine, "I came into the studio, and I said, 'I want to work with this guy named Glen Ballard.'"

The producer replied, "Okay, well, I can pull all the strings I have and make that happen."

"He got me a meeting with Glen in Los Angeles," Hudson said, "and I had my dad drive me up to L.A."

On arriving outside Ballard's home studio in West Hollywood, Katy told Pastor Keith, "'Dad, stay in the car. I'm just gonna go in, play a song for this guy and come back out.' And I did, and I guess it went well, because I got the call the next day."

BORN IN MISSISSIPPI, Glen Ballard made his way to L.A. soon after graduating from the University of Mississippi, in 1975, to pursue a career in music. He landed a staff songwriting position at MCA Music Publishing, and had his first success writing for the British pop singer Kiki Dee. Quincy Jones liked his work, and took him on as a songwriter and producer at Qwest Records in 1985. Ballard worked with Jones on Michael Jackson's albums *Bad*, and *Thriller*, and, in the ensuing decade, added to an array of hits, both as a songwriter and a producer, including

Jack Wagner's "All I Need," Jackson's "Man in the Mirror," and Wilson Phillips' "Hold On," a number-one hit in 1990. Morissette's publishing company had set the two of them up on the songwriting equivalent of a blind date, and it led to one of the biggest-selling albums of all time.

Ballard recalled in Perry's 2012 film *Part of Me*, "Someone knocked on my door, and I said 'Hello? What do you want? Are you a writer?' She said yes. 'You want to play me a song?' She said yes. Bingo. Two great answers. She opened the guitar case and played a song for me, and it blew me away." On the strength of their collaborations, including the songs "Mirrors" and "Simple," Ballard got Hudson a record deal at Def Jam. By then the artist had become Katy Perry.

Perry wrote "Waking Up in Vegas," in 2003 with Andreas Carlsson, the Cheironite, working with super songwriter-producer Desmond Child. When the songwriters met with the artist for the first time, Child asked why her music sounded so serious, when her personality was so fun and bubbly. Carlsson recalled saying, "'You have all this humor, and you're a little bit crazy,' and that's when we started writing." But their song wouldn't make it onto a record for five more years.

Perry's serious songs, the ones she wrote with Ballard, had the raw vocal delivery of Alanis; she also seemed to be trying at times to channel Fiona Apple. But in the years since those artists had broken through, both with debut records in the mid-'90s, the teen-pop phenomenon had taken hold in the culture, reshaping the pop landscape, busting through the narrow barrier islands that had sheltered delicate idiosyncratic talents like Fiona and Alanis. After Britney, an angsty, Alanis-esque pop act seemed hopelessly out of date. In 2004, Def Jam dropped Perry.

AGAIN, ONE IMAGINES, she prayed. *Heavenly Father, please don't make me go back to Santa Barbara. Make me a star.* And again, it seemed as if He had her back. Perry was given that rarest of gifts in the pop business: a second chance. Columbia signed her in 2005, and she began a new solo project.

At around the same time, Columbia was developing another project with the Matrix, the hit-making trio of two men and a woman who were behind Avril Lavigne's early hits. The hit makers were looking for two singers, a man and a woman, to front a band composed of the three of them. The idea was to record an album of their own songs, and go out on tour to support it. Ballard told Perry about the project; she auditioned to be the girl singer, and got the gig. Adam Longlands, an unknown, became her male counterpart.

Since their success with Avril Lavigne, the Matrix had written songs for Britney Spears, Christina Aguilera, and Ricky Martin. But the hits had started to dry up, and artists had stopped calling. Around the time they joined forces with Perry, the Matrix's Lauren Christy had committed the unforgivable sin of saying publicly that Lavigne did not write her hits—the Matrix did. Artists are supposed to embody the work, and anything that undercuts that illusion is dangerous. ("It's very fucking obvious that the lyrics came from me," Lavigne angrily shot back in *The Mirror*, a UK newspaper.) It was refreshing candor from Christy, but career suicide for any hit maker. So when the offer to make an album as artists came along, the Matrix jumped at it. Christy explained, "Well, for five years we've been behind the scenes doing our own thing very happily and someone is offering us a chance to literally go in and be creative. . . . It was just interesting for the three of us to say, 'What do *we* actually want to say?'"

So they made an album, and picked a first single, "Broken," and had the video ready to go when Columbia decided to shelve the album. It was the only sensible decision about the project anyone made. The video of "Broken," with the three aging hit makers playing instruments in the background while up front Katy Perry does her best Avril Lavigne imitation, is a genuine what-could-they-have-been-thinking moment. Years later, their story would be spoken of around Dr. Luke's studio as a cautionary tale—the producers who mistook themselves for the stars.

After her album with the Matrix was canned, Perry worked on her solo project, but Columbia couldn't figure out how to market her either, and in 2006 she was dropped from a major label for a second time.

By then Perry had spent five years in the dark, satanic song mills of Hollywood. She'd done the hustling and the e-mails, the demo singing and the shitty songwriting hookups. Plus, she was broke. "No money," she says. "Car repossessed. No cell phone. Everything dead and gone. No hope, basically." She got a job at a company called Taxi Music, listening to other people's demos.

But Perry had a powerful ally at Columbia—publicity executive Angelica Cob-Baehler, who had witnessed firsthand the label's inept handling of her career. "They tried to make her into something she wasn't," she said. Disgusted, Cob-Baehler left Columbia and went to work for Jason Flom, who was overseeing Virgin's merger with Capitol Records at EMI, which would itself soon be bought by Universal Music Group.

Flom recalls Cob-Baehler saying, "'There's a girl named Katy Perry who Columbia's going to drop, and I think she's a star and you should meet her.' So I met Katy at the Polo Lounge, and I was immediately taken by her presence and her story. I remember seeing that she had 'Jesus' tattooed on her wrist, and I asked about it, and she gave me the background, and her life story captivated me. Without having heard a note of music, I was sure that Katy was indeed destined for stardom. When I listened to the music—I heard the record she had made for Columbia—I got even more excited. But when I went back to New York and played it for my staff, they were not enthused at all. One of my executives actually said to me, 'Please don't saddle us with this crap.' I remember getting a very negative reaction from everyone. So I started to second-guess myself, and I put the deal on hold. Several weeks later on my Christmas break, I was listening to Katy on my iPod while working out in my garage in

Aspen, and I said to myself, 'I just made a giant mistake, I can't imagine why I didn't sign her!' I called her up immediately—fortunately she was still working at that Taxi place—and I said, 'I want to sign you.'"

Flom made a deal with Columbia to get the masters of the songs Perry had done for her solo project; those cuts became a significant part of her first Capitol album, *One of the Boys*. He also wanted Andreas Carlsson's and Desmond Child's "Waking Up in Vegas" on the album, and he commissioned a few more songs. Perry came in with a song called "Ur So Gay," which she had written with songwriter Greg Wells, and the label put it out as a single. It didn't sell, but the song generated a lot of controversy, both from Perry's former fans in the Christian music world, and from gay groups (offending two such philosophically opposed communities with the same song takes some doing) and the publicity helped Perry get noticed.

But Flom still felt that the album needed one or two potential hits, and suggested Perry try writing with Dr. Luke. "We kind of hung out and really vibed well," Perry says. "And he brought in Max Martin. It was a combination pack. I really liked them together. They have great taste, and I have an intuition that has never failed me. I am very lyrics-based, and Max is very melody-based, and Luke is very track-based, so put the combination of us together and you get that ultimate pop song."

Together with Cathy Dennis, a British dance-pop singer turned songwriter who helped with the lyrics, they wrote "I Kissed a Girl." Max and Luke did most of the music and production in Luke's West Twenty-First Street studio in New York City, working late at night. The title hook, according to Perry, came to her in a dream. "The chorus actually popped into my head when I woke up," she said in a 2008 interview with the BBC. "It was one of those moments where you hear artists talking about songs they get in dreams or in the middle of the night."

The song's verses have a Cars-like guitar vibe; in the chorus the guitar becomes a Slayer riff. The production isn't the hit makers' most inspired, but the lyric sold the song, and no two lines did the melodic math better than the hook:

> *I kissed a girl and I liked it*
> *Taste of her cherry Chapstick*

Released at the end of April 2008 as the album's lead single, "I Kissed a Girl" went to number one and spent seven weeks at the top; it also topped the charts in the United Kingdom, Germany, Canada, and Australia. (The second single, another Max Martin and Dr. Luke song called "Hot n Cold," was also a big hit.) As he had done for Britney Spears with ". . . Baby One More Time," and for Kelly Clarkson with "Since U Been Gone," Max Martin wrote Katy Perry's "career record"—the song that made her a star.

The first time Katy's mother heard her daughter's song on the radio, "I was in total shock," she said in an interview with the *Daily Mail*. "It clearly promotes homosexuality and its message is shameful and disgusting." Whenever the song comes on the radio, "I bow my head and pray," she went on, adding, "Katy is our daughter and we love her but we strongly disagree with how she is conducting herself at the moment."

Again there were murmurs of plagiarism. "I Kissed a Girl" happens to be the name of a 1995 song by folkie singer-songwriter Jill Sobule. Sobule's song, a minor hit, is a clever tale of two women who in talking about their boyfriends end up getting it on. Sung by a gay artist, it comes across as a lesbian anthem, rather than as a tease to men, like Perry's song. In a July 2009 interview in *The Rumpus*, an online magazine, Sobule said, "When Katy Perry's song came out I started getting tons of inquiries about what I thought. Some folks (and protective friends) were angry, and wondered why she took my title and made it into this kind of 'Girls Gone Wild' thing." She continued, "As a musician I have always refrained from criticizing another artist. I was like, 'Well, good for her.'

It did bug me a little bit, however, when she said she came up with the idea for the title in a dream. In truth, she wrote it with a team of professional writers and was signed by the very same guy that signed me in 1995." That is, Jason Flom.

Tongue not altogether in cheek, Sobule added, "Okay, maybe, if I really think about it, there were a few jealous and pissed-off moments. So here goes, for the first time in an interview: Fuck you Katy Perry, you fucking stupid, maybe 'not good for the gays,' title-thieving, haven't heard much else, so not quite sure if you're talented, fucking little slut.

"God that felt good."

21 | Melodic Math

ONE AFTERNOON, Dr. Luke and Cirkut were joined in the beach house by Bonnie McKee, a Prescription Songs lyricist. Dr. Luke doesn't enjoy writing lyrics—"it's not fun," he says—and so people like McKee and J. Kash, another Prescription lyricist, are in high demand.

McKee, who was twenty-nine, had Hollywood heartbreak in her backstory. Like Katy Perry, she was a talented child performer who enjoyed the attention of being onstage. She arrived in Hollywood around the same time as Perry, and got a lucrative record contract on the Warner Bros label. The album *Trouble*, was released in 2004, when McKee was twenty.

"Things didn't go as I planned," she tells me out on the patio of Gottwald's beach house over the crashing of the waves. "I came out at a weird time, right before Tower Records shut down, and iTunes was just getting going. Plus it was a mature record for a teenager." As soon as it was clear that the album was a failure—virtually overnight—McKee became damaged goods. "Basically I went from industry darling to no one answering my phone calls. It was brutal. I felt like I was already washed up before I got started." But although the record stiffed, Warner did not drop her right away; instead, they kept her under contract but wouldn't commit to another record, leaving her "in purgatory."

That lasted about a year, until McKee had an idea: "I made a CD of my best songs, and bought a dagger at a smoke shop that had a tiger on the handle, and a jewel for an eye, and went to the CEO of Warner Brothers' house in the middle of the night and stabbed the CD into a tree right by his front door, and I wrote 'Platinum Baby!' in lipstick on his car. The next day was his kid's first day at school, so there was pandemonium—everyone thought a maniac had come in the middle of the night." In a way, one had. "Needless to say, I got dropped."

After that, she says, "I went into a terrible downward spiral for a while, but I put it all into my writing." She was broke. She was addicted to crystal meth. She was in and out of shitty relationships. Her family wanted her to come home. Meanwhile, her brother Yates was on his way to becoming a writer and an art critic. Her life wasn't supposed to be going like this.

One day, McKee was selling clothes for money to eat, when she met a singer-songwriter from Santa Barbara named Katy Perry who was similarly broke, and they became friends. "I met her at a thrift store on Melrose called Wasteland. She'd heard of me and I'd kind of heard of her, and we were both in the same purgatory, and we just hit it off. We had this weird simpatico thing, and shared each other's deep dark secrets."

In 2008, Katy became world famous; Bonnie got another year older. Katy departed the L.A. party circuit to tour the world, and when she returned she relocated to Santa Barbara, to be nearer her parents. McKee remained behind, "in the trenches of Hollywood," writing and recording songs "in shithole studios behind Carl's Jr." She didn't get that second chance, much less a third.

Early in 2010, Dr. Luke and Max Martin were in the midst of planning Perry's follow-up album, *Teenage Dream*. They needed to prove she was more than a singer of gay-themed novelty songs. They had one of the two tracks that Benny Blanco had come up with that sleep-deprived night he arrived in L.A. And they had a melody that had actually been written by Dr. Luke, not Max Martin.

The song was a breakthrough for Gottwald. Max Martin recalled how it happened. "Benny Blanco did a track," he said, "and then Luke just started singing"—sounds and nonsense words—"and he had this flow, where everything that came out was great, including the chorus. He was just standing there and screaming, and it just wrote itself."

What they did not have were words—the part of a song neither Dr. Luke nor Max Martin can handle alone. In thinking back to her own teenage years in L.A., Perry remembered her friend Bonnie McKee. She called and asked if Bonnie would listen to the track and take a shot at the lyrics. "She had just gotten engaged," McKee says, "and she was in the honeymoon phase of being in love."

Bonnie and Katy wrote the song five or six times. For Perry, this was annoying, but for McKee, it was a matter of life and death. One version was more in Katy's wacky vein. It included the line "And the next thing you know/You're a mom in a minivan." Max Martin and Dr. Luke rejected it. One version used the metaphor of "trying me on," as a sort of double entendre for sex. Max and Luke rejected that, too. In *Katy Perry: The Teenage Dream*, a 2012 book by C. Duthel, McKee explained, "Luke always makes us 'Benny Proof' everything. He says that if Benny doesn't get it, America won't get it." Benny didn't get it.

They looked at each other "with dread," McKee says, "knowing we had to start all over again. We were both so over it." But they tried one more time. "I thought about my own adolescent years," McKee says, "my own first love. I thought about watching Baz Luhrmann's *Romeo and Juliet* and putting on a little mini disco ball light and just dreaming of Leo. I was like, 'teenager' . . . that's such a great word. It packs a lot of emotion and imagery into three syllables." She added the word "dream" and that was the hook. She went back to the concept "trying me on" and the oft-heard "skin-tight jeans" lines emerged.

"I finished it and I drove up the coast to Santa Barbara," McKee says, "to pitch it to Luke and Max and Katy, and I got there and sang it and everyone was like, 'Hell, yeah!'" And I went to my hotel and got into the bathtub and I just cried and cried. I was just so relieved." "Teenage Dream," the second single from the album of the same name, went to number one and spent two weeks on top.

After that breakthrough in 2010, McKee went on to help Perry write lyrics to five more huge hits, including her best song, "Wide Awake," written after her short marriage to Russell Brand dissolved. McKee also collaborated on "Dynamite," with Taio Cruz, and on "Hold It Against Me," with Britney Spears, both smashes. But McKee still hadn't realized her own teenage dream.

Now, thanks to Dr. Luke, McKee was getting that illusive second chance. He had signed her to Kemosabe, his label, as an artist, and a Bonnie McKee album was forthcoming. The video for the first single, "American Girl," had just dropped.

AT THE BEACH HOUSE that day, McKee was wearing her American Girl outfit from the video—cut-off denim short shorts, gray leggings, and a black leather jacket that was partly covered with metallic spikes. Her lengthy mane was a Roman candle of flame-colored streaks. She was coming from an appearance at an L.A. pop station, where she had performed a four-and-a-half minute medley of her six number ones for other artists, mashed together, a stunt she also performs at her own shows.

Dr. Luke greeted McKee warmly in the open-plan kitchen, which looked out at the ocean. A vast array of hot-sauce bottles took up part of the counter. There were children's toys scattered around, including a nifty-looking car that Luke's older kid could sit in and drive by twisting the steering wheel. Also present was the somewhat terrifying Irene Richter, his majordomo.

Dr. Luke was sipping a glass of the extremely powerful cold-pressed coffee that he kept in a half-gallon glass jug in the fridge. "I have crazy coffee," he says. "It's cold and black. We travel an hour to get this coffee." He adds, "It's all I have left," making reference to the healthy California lifestyle he now pursues, his druggy New York days long behind him. "I can't even smoke pot anymore. I get paranoid and start worrying about e-mails."

The video of "American Girl" had gone up on YouTube the day before. Did Dr. Luke release it? Did someone leak it? Did it matter? In Dr. Luke's world, a "soft launch"—leaking the song on YouTube and hoping it will go viral—was often the best approach. "I just put all these things out there," he says, "and if something catches, we focus our efforts around that." His basic strategy is to have no basic strategy.

Katy Perry, Kesha, Taio Cruz, and Adam Lambert, among others, all appear in the video—Dr. Luke called in a lot of favors—lip-synching to McKee's voice, a clever inversion of the usual arrangement, in which she helped them with their words.

"What're your views at now?" Dr. Luke asked her.

"Two hundred thousand." McKee checked again on her phone. "Like, two oh one."

"Did Katy tweet it?"

"Yes, she tweeted it. Kesha hasn't tweeted it yet, though."

"You know what?" Dr. Luke glanced out the windows at the beach, where the shadows were growing longer. "It's almost better if Kesha doesn't, and waits a couple days and does it."

"And you know Katy has thirty million followers and Kesha has, like—"

"Three," Dr. Luke said sourly.

What was happening with Kesha?

Dr. Luke shrugged, but his shoulders were too tense to elevate much. "I haven't heard from her in a while."

In writing lyrics, McKee adheres to Max Martin's school of pop songwriting. Words are there to serve the melody. "Max doesn't really care about the lyrics because he's Swedish," she says, "so I have to work around that. I can write something I think is so clever and be proud of that, but if it doesn't hit the ear right then he doesn't like it. He's also really stubborn about syllables. A line has to have a certain number of syllables, and they have to be mirror images of each other—it's very mathematical. The syllables in the first part of the chorus have to repeat in the second part. Like 'Cal-i-forn-ia girls un-for-get-ta-ble/Dai-sy Dukes bi-kinis on top'—if you add a syllable, or take it away, it's a completely different melody to him. I remember I wrote him a song and I was so proud of it, and he was like, 'Why are the melodies completely different in the first and second verse?' I was like, 'What do you mean? It's the same melody.' But I had added three or four syllables. He was right, he's always right, as much as it drives me crazy sometimes, he's always right."

But don't Martin's strictures make the songs formulaic? I wonder.

McKee doesn't think so. "Things are changing in pop music and people have caught on to his formulas, to an extent. So you have to break the rules a bit and, as Max says, 'let art win.'" But in general, she adds, "People like hearing songs that sound like something they've heard before, that's reminiscent of their childhood, and of what their parents listened to. I mean, every once in a while something new will happen, like dubstep, where it's like, 'This is robot future music!,' but most people still just want to hear about love and partying."

On writing for Perry, McKee says, "When we're writing for her, we sit down and talk to her and find out what's going on in her life, and try to find out the kernel of truth. I want her to sing about something she cares about, so we talk about her life and what she's going through, and try to weave it into something powerful and visual."

How are Max and Luke different as co-writers? I ask. "They are very similar. But Max has that Swedish politeness," she says.

Dr. Luke turned to Richter. (Before Richter, Dr. Luke had used a jungle survivalist named Barry Silver as his main gatekeeper; he would literally emerge from the wilderness, spend six months organizing Dr. Luke's affairs, then return to trekking again.) "Can you send an e-mail from me to Larry Rudolph and ask if he can get Britney and Miley to tweet the

Bonnie video?" he asked. Rudolph manages both Spears and Cyrus. "Tell him Katy's already done it twice, and use Jewish guilt. Say, 'I know they weren't able to be in the video, so at the very least could they tweet it.'"

"How is it Jewish guilt if neither of them are Jewish?" McKee asked.

"Because *I'm* Jewish."

"Oh, it's contagious!"

Should they offer the track for sale or let it spread virally for free? Should they upload "American Girl" to Vevo, the industry's music-video channel, even though that would cannibalize views from YouTube? It probably didn't matter, but this kind of stuff obsessed Dr. Luke. If they did a soft launch on iTunes and the song didn't sell, might that hurt them with program directors, when they took it to radio? So many uncertainties for Dr. Luke to obsess over, and not one really mattered, because it was already clear, twenty-four hours in, that "American Girl" was not going to make Bonnie McKee a pop star. It would get to number sixty-seven on the charts, then quickly fall back. The lyricist wouldn't be quitting her day job anytime soon.

It was a reminder that for all their talent and experience, even Dr. Luke and Max Martin couldn't guarantee a hit. Neither are they sure they have one until the public hears the song. Hit making remains a tricky, unpredictable endeavor. Dr. Luke often falls back on the hoary truism that it's all a matter of "the right artist with the right song at the right time." Take "Wrecking Ball," a ballad Dr. Luke and Cirkut created sans Max Martin for Miley Cyrus. It seemed like a certain hit; Doug Morris predicted it would be one of the biggest songs of the year. But Luke wasn't sure, and he bet against the song, telling Cyrus he would buy her a Numi toilet like his, the state of the art in potty technology (it has a Bluetooth receiver that can stream music from a smart phone), if it went to number one. When "Wrecking Ball" did hit number one, I asked Cyrus for a comment. "Contrary to what he thinks," she says, "Dr. Luke isn't always right. Now he has to buy me a ten-thousand-dollar toilet. I'll be thinking of him every time I go."

McKee was at the beach house that day to record vocals for another song from her album, "Right Now," an anthem that Dr. Luke and Cirkut were producing for her. They went upstairs to the studio, and Cirkut played back what they had done so far. Dr. Luke asked her to imagine the song when they put the chorus on it. He explained that he planned to record a sing-along in his garage, next door, to give the song an anthemic feel. His plan was to mix people who could sing with people who couldn't, so that it sounded more like a stadium sing-along.

"Interesting!" McKee said.

In the production, Luke went on, "I want to go with guitars and be Def Leppard big. You know what I mean?"

"You're speaking my language!" McKee replied perkily.

She went into the vocal booth, a converted closet concealed behind the paneling, and sang the opening lines of the song about a dozen times. It contained the hook "right now," twice, embedded in a suet of mixed metaphors. "There is a fire in my heart, right now, ready like a loaded gun, heart is like a battle drum, there isn't time to fall apart, right now."

Later Cirkut would painstakingly comp all the takes, comparing them syllable-by-syllable, and stitch them together into the best possible vocal. Comping was so mind-numbingly boring that even Dr. Luke couldn't tolerate it. However, "Max loves comping," Luke says. "He'll do it for hours."

A DREAM TEAM WROTE and produced the second Katy Perry album, *Teenage Dream*, including Benny Blanco (now living back in New York and well launched on a major hit-making career of his own), as well as Stargate, Ester Dean, and Tricky Stewart. "Firework," the smash ballad from the album, was a classic Stargate-Dean collaboration. It had the ectomorphs' signature rise in the pre, that builds toward Ester's hook.

Boom boom boom
Even brighter than the moon moon moon.

The lyrical concept came from Perry herself. Russell Brand had pointed out to her the great passage in Jack Kerouac's *On the Road* in which the narrator expresses his admiration for people like Neal Cassady who "burn, burn, burn like fabulous yellow roman candles exploding like spiders across the stars," and Perry turned it into an inspirational pop ballad. (Brand turned out to be one such firework; he texted her that their marriage was over just as the song was exploding across the charts.)

The re-released version of the album contained "Part of Me," one of Max Martin and Dr. Luke's best compositions, and perhaps the purest example of their chemistry. Luke had created a track—a solid one, but like all tracks a bit repetitious without a topline. When he and Max got together, Max played Luke a melody that he had come up with; it fit perfectly with the track and, with Bonnie McKee helping out on lyrics, "Part of Me" was written.

Taken as a whole, *Teenage Dream* was a state-of-the-art pop album, and it showed what a hit factory is capable of when functioning at its peak. But no matter how many hits Dr. Luke had with Katy Perry, it wasn't the same, economically or reputationally, as having hits with an artist he had signed himself to Kemosabe. Capitol got the record sales, and Capitol was part of Universal, not Sony. If Dr. Luke wanted to take the next step from writer-producer to record mogul—a master of the universe—he would need to use both his musical and his entrepreneurial skills, and create a superstar. That was what Kesha was supposed to be—his very own teenage dream.

22 | Kesha: Teenage Nightmare

DR. LUKE AND MAX MARTIN had come across Kesha's demo in 2005, while working their way through a stack of a hundred or so, listening for something that caught their interest. Eighteen-year-old Kesha Rose Sebert, of Nashville, Tennessee, had made the two-song demo with her mother, Pebe Sebert, a professional songwriter, and Samantha Cox, a musical director at BMI, the artists' rights organization. The first song was a conventional country ballad; the second was bizarre rap.

I'm a white girl/From the 'Ville/Nashville, bitch. Uhh. Uhhhhh.

"That's when I was like, 'OK, I like this girl's personality,'" Dr. Luke told *Billboard* in 2010. "When you're listening to a hundred CDs, that kind of bravado and chutzpah stands out."

Dr. Luke wanted Kesha Rose to come out to L.A. immediately. She was a high-school senior in Nashville, a good student with excellent SATs who was planning to attend college the following year. Dr. Luke, no great believer in formal education—the lack of it certainly hadn't held him back—persuaded the teenager to drop out of high school and move to L.A., where she signed with his production company, Kasz Money. He also signed her to a publishing deal with Prescription Songs. Kesha first lived in Luke's house in Hollywood, which he was renting with his girlfriend; later she moved into a series of cheap rentals with other struggling musicians.

Dr. Luke's plan was to develop Kesha, write some songs for her, and shop her to the labels, hoping to get a deal. But the plan was derailed when a friend introduced Kesha to a prominent manager, David Sonenberg, who had bad blood with Gottwald going back years to his Kasz days, when Sonenberg's offer to manage him was turned down. Sonenberg examined Kesha's contracts with Kasz Money, and reportedly told her and her mother, "This contract is worse than the one Lou Pearlman made with the Backstreet Boys." Sonenberg managed to get Kesha out of her contract with Kasz Money, and worked on getting her a major-label deal himself; she gave Sonenberg a year to get one. When he failed, Kesha signed again with Dr. Luke (Sonenberg subsequently sued both of them), and later, when Gottwald got his label deal with Sony, Kesha became Kemosabe's first artist.

KESHA'S BREAKTHROUGH WAS "Right Round," Flo Rida's 2009 hit (the song that began the Boy's protracted DJ set in the car). The original idea for the song came from Aaron Bay-Schuck, an up-and-coming A&R man at Atlantic Records. He wanted his artist Flo Rida to do a rap that sampled "You Spin Me Round (Like a Record)" by Dead Or Alive, the mid-'80s hit created by the SAW hit factory. "It's gotta happen. It could be huge," Bay-Schuck kept saying. But his attempts to realize the song had so far fallen short. Bruno Mars and his writing partner, Phil Smeeze, had taken a crack at it, but the song still wasn't working. So Bay-Schuck gave it to Dr. Luke, and Luke brought in another key early collaborator, Kool Kojak.

"Dr. Luke and I both had success with the shuffle beat," Kojak recalls, "starting back in 1999 when I composed the song 'Sao Paulo' for my band Supla Zoo." The song's swung eighth-note triplet later featured in "I Kissed a Girl." Kojak: "We rode that bitch hard and we were about to put her to pasture with her greatest incarnation ever," which was "Right Round."

Late in 2008, Bay-Schuck had booked Conway Recording Studios, a fancy oasis of song making in slummy east Hollywood. Flo Rida showed up with an entourage that included E Dub, a former football star; De Vante, from the '90s R&B group Jodeci, who was smoking an enormous blunt; and Cubana Lust, an exotic dancer. Strippers and their patrons are important arbiters of hip-hop music, because the music is often too raunchy to play on the radio. Strip joints are the only establishments where the uncensored songs can be heard by the public. Accordingly, "Strip clubs have become the main breaking place for records, especially in the South," Jermaine Dupri, president of urban music for Virgin Records, told *Billboard* in 2008.

Cubana Lust "walked in the studio and flashed a really charming smile," Kojak remembers. "Then she turned around and all I could hear were air horns. Like, big tugboat air horns. Two denim watermelons. Cubana Lust had that bam-bam. Not like these injected phony buttocksed rappers who are popular today, with their scrawny chicken legs and impossibly buoyant inflata-booties. She was the real deal." That booty was the inspiration for the song. It was the ass that launched Kesha's thousand ships.

At this point, "Round Round" as Flo Rida called it, consisted of Flo's rapped verses over an '80s-sounding beat. It was embarrassing. "We all got in the control room, and Aaron played the demo," Kojak goes on. "It wasn't even ten seconds before Cubana Lust broke out cackling, '*Yo! Ain't no niggaz gonna fuck wid dat shit! Hahahahaha y'all trippppppin! Fuck deez niggaz!*' All the homies started hooting and hollering. I was like, 'Fuck that.' Me and Luke looked at each other like, 'Yo, we ain't goin' out like that!'"

They got Flo to rewrite his verses, and the producers dug in. "The stress was like a trash compactor," Kojak says. "We made the beat in a weekend, between bouts of me sleeping on the studio floor, waking up, plugging in the KAOS pad and the Casio VL-Tone. Luke looked like he was defusing a bomb. We were in the zone. Sunday we jumped in the pool and knew we'd busted out a real banger."

They still needed something extra on the hook, and Dr. Luke thought of Kesha, who had by then disentangled herself from Sonenberg. Kojak was dispatched to find her. She had recently jumped in Dr. Luke's pool with her cell phone in her pocket, and her e-mail was bouncing. She had no fixed address, and was living out of two cars, a gray Honda and an early '80s gold Mercedes sedan. Both were teeming with fast-food wrappers, bottles of whatever, cheap headphones, unmatched boots, high heels, and garbage bags full of clothes. The young lady from the 'Ville would roll up in front of parties in the Hollywood Hills to which she was not invited, emerge from her garbage scow in a heavy-metal shirt, tiny shorts, boots, and a vintage fur coat, and stride right in and up to the bar, parting the seas like Moses.

Kojak eventually located Kesha in a rental house in Echo Park known as the Drunk Tank. "The walls were literally crumbling," he recalls—"nicotine stains, cigarette butts everywhere, old pizza boxes, blacked-out windows, filth. The place was nightmarish." Amid the debris sat Kesha, drinking beers and cranking tunes.

"Luke texted me: 'What up????'"

"I'm like—'Yo! I found her!'"

Kojak turned to Kesha.

"C'mon girl, time to go make you a star!"

The studio was still packed when they returned: Flo, Luke, Bay-Schuck, the engineer, the homies, and Cubana Lust, who was resting on her moneymaker. Kesha walked into the room slugging whiskey from a plastic water bottle. She sat next to Flo and they played her the song. "The glint from her gold-capped tooth blinked in the dark," Kojak remembers. "She loved it—the song, the attention, the rapper, people jumping off the walls. She goes, 'I love strippers! I love boners! Let's do this!'"

Cubana Lust just shook her head. *"Y'all niggaz cray-zee!"*

Kesha waltzed into the booth and warbled the hook a few times.

> *You spin my head right round right round*
> *When you go down when you go down down*

It didn't sound great, but when Kojak activated the Auto-Tune everybody went wild.

"Bro!" Bay-Schuck was screaming. "Worldwide number one, bro!"

"It sounded huge!" Kojak says.

Kesha's contribution to "Right Round" was the single most memorable detail in the song, and it launched her into superstardom. However, Dr. Luke didn't give her a songwriting credit, so she earned nothing from the smash. It was around this time that she changed the "s" in her name to "$."

"RIGHT ROUND" WAS ALSO a breakthrough song for Dr. Luke. Not only was it his first pop rap chart-topper; it was his first number one without Max Martin. The track is edgier than those on his Max jams; the sound is closer to the space-alien vibe of his early Kasz days. And, of course, the song introduced his Kemosabe artist Kesha to hits radio, launching his new career as a mogul. His next task was to create a Kesha album that would fully realize her raggedly joyous sound.

Dr. Luke tried to explain to me the kind of music he wanted to make. "If you listen to hip hop in the '80s and '90s," he says, "you can hear that at a certain point people discovered that if you're rapping, and then someone sings a hook—that works. You know? And the reason that works is that it does a lot of the things you have to do in songwriting. One of the most important things in songwriting is melodic rhythm."

What is melodic rhythm? I ask.

"OK, say that you have a verse, and it's done in eighth notes, and everything is starting on the one—DAH-*ut da-ut da-ut da-ut DAH-ut*

. . . Right? OK then when you go to the pre-chorus you probably don't want to start on the one, and you don't want to do eighth notes. So you come in on the two, or on the upbeats, or go to long notes, so it stays fresh."

The same principle works in reverse. In a song that's mostly singing, a sixteen-bar rap provides new texture. The key is to switch up the feel to keep things lively. "That's why rapping in songs is interesting," he goes on. "Intrinsically, if you're rapping, and then you're singing, you've created a new part. There's no question about which part is the chorus—it's the sung part. When you're doing something without rapping, you still have to make that distinction, but you do it all with melody and rhythm. And that is fundamentally what songwriting is."

"TIK TOK" (2010) WAS Kesha's first solo number one, a monster smash that established her as the louche pop-rap queen—more Lady Gaga than Katy Perry. (In fact, "Tik Tok"'s melody is strongly reminiscent of Lady Gaga's "Just Dance," but not quite similar enough: another case of "close but no cigar.") The lyrics, an ode to round-the-clock partying, begin with the arresting opening hook: "Wake up in the morning feeling like P. Diddy," followed by Diddy himself giving Kesha a little shout-out: "What up, girl?" In keeping with Luke's songwriting practice, Kesha raps the verses and sings the chorus. Her distinctive vocal personality saturates the record, for example in the odd way she pronounces Mick Jagger's name.

"Tik Tok" also marked the first chart topper for young Benny Blanco, Dr. Luke's songwriting protégé. Blanco recalls, "I went out to L.A. to work with him for the first time and I was only going to be there a week and a half and I stayed nine months." He goes on, "There was no one else. Now he has like thirty or forty people. But then it was just me and him, and we were just making songs every day." It was the beginning of Benny's hot streak, and Dr. Luke made the most of it.

After "Tik Tok" came "Your Love Is My Drug" in 2010, which peaked at number four on the Hot 100. Benny co-produced and co-wrote the song with Dr. Luke's next major discovery, a young African American called Ammo, whose real name is Joshua Coleman. Ammo grew up in Baltimore, where his parents were musicians, and began making tracks and rapping over them when he was twelve. His first job, loading trucks in a Saks Fifth Avenue warehouse, was not to his liking and hardened his resolve to be a musician. He interested Jim Edmunds, an A&R man at Epic Records, in some of his beats, and Edmunds played a couple for Dr. Luke. Luke invited Ammo to come to New York and meet him in the Sony Building, where they went out for sushi. Ammo had never eaten sushi before. Later they went back to the office and Luke played Ammo some tracks he was working on with Benny—"super next-level stuff," as Ammo describes it. Inspired, Ammo returned to Baltimore, stayed up all night making beats, and e-mailed ten of them to Dr. Luke, who called the next day and offered him a publishing deal, which included a nice advance. "He gets a piece of my publishing and I get to be in the room with some of the biggest talents in the world," Ammo says proudly.

After Blanco headed back east—he doesn't care for the pressure that Dr. Luke likes to work under—Ammo took over his spot at Luke's right hand, as well as Benny's air mattress on Luke's floor. Luke and Max gave Ammo "Your Love Is My Drug" to work on. Ammo explains his process: "I listened to Kesha's last record a lot, trying to figure out those sounds—how to do it, but make it a bit different, like take those same thirds and put them over a kick pattern. I put my best verse melody together with a chorus melody and a pre-chorus melody, and played it for Max. At first he was quiet. He went outside, then he came back and took the tag from the second half and put it in the first half and that was it! That song was my landmark and I graduated from track guy to songwriter." Ammo followed that hit with an even bigger smash—"We R Who We R," which debuted at the top of the Hot 100.

. . .

RELATIONS BETWEEN THE LABEL head and his biggest star soured during the making of Kesha's second full-length album, *Warrior*, in 2011–2012. Kesha wanted this album to establish her rock bona fides. Her reputation as a fun-loving pop rap queen might be good for Dr. Luke's overall market share—after all, with Katy and Avril and Pink, Luke and Max had the pop-rock genre covered—but Kesha wasn't really a rapper. She was a rocker, and she wanted to make a dirty-sounding '70s rock record à la the Rolling Stones—the kind of album her mother always wanted to make. "People say that rock and roll is dead," Kesha stated in *Billboard*, "and it is my mission and my goal to resurrect it in the form of my pop music." She added, "We'll see what happens. That's a very ambitious and lofty goal, but that's my goal." She added, "Some will also be excited to know that I don't just do silly white-girl rap," though possibly those people did not include Dr. Luke, who had signed her to do just that.

Kesha and her mother wrote a clutch of rock songs for the sophomore album, all of which Dr. Luke eventually rejected. He and Kesha also spent a couple months in L.A. working together, but the sessions didn't yield anything that sounded like a radio hit. Kesha brought Luke and his crew to Nashville, trying to get a Southern-rock vibe onto a record. Benny, Ammo, Kool Kojak, and Bonnie McKee were all brought in to help. Young Cirkut, who had only recently arrived, also worked on the album. The factory was running at full capacity. But still the hits wouldn't come.

Max Martin summoned Kesha to Sweden, to record a song called "All That Matters (The Beautiful Life)" that he had written with *his* latest protégé, Johan Schuster, a former death-metal rocker who calls himself Shellback. Together the pair would go on to write huge hits for Pink ("Raise Your Glass," "Fuckin' Perfect") and Taylor Swift ("We Are Never Ever Getting Back Together," "I Knew You Were Trouble," "Shake It Off," and "Blank Space"). But "All That Matters" wasn't a hit.

Warrior was supposed to come out at the end of 2011, but the album was delayed because, Kesha explained to *Billboard*, "I want to take enough time to make sure it's the reinvention of pop music. That's the ultimate goal, to reinvent pop music." That would take another six months, she reckoned. "May sounds right," she said. But May came and went with no album. Kesha took some time apart from Luke, and she and Pebe wrote some more songs. Dr. Luke supported her, but he also reminded Kesha, somewhat ominously, that the more songs they wrote, the more would have to be cut, ultimately. In the end, only one of the songs Kesha wrote with Pebe made it onto the album.

Finally, Dr. Luke put his foot down: *Warrior* would continue the Kesha as party-girl vein. Together with Benny, Cirkut, and Nate Ruess from the band Fun, Dr. Luke wrote and produced "Die Young," and released it as the first single, in the fall of 2012, with the refrain:

> *Let's make the most of the night*
> *Like we're gonna die young*

The song topped some charts, but immediately after the December 14 Newtown school massacre it all but disappeared from the radio, and the Kesha haters went into a frenzy on Twitter.

Kesha had previously claimed to have written the lyrics by herself. In her book *My Crazy Beautiful Life* she said, "I rewrote the words a thousand times until I found something simple that felt right." She added, "When I sing, 'Like we're gonna die young,' I'm promising that no matter how old I get I'm never going to lose my youthful spirit.'" But on December 18, four days after the Newtown massacre, she tweeted, "I did NOT want to sing those lyrics and I was FORCED to." Who had forced her? Kesha's fans thought they had a pretty good idea.

In September 2013, a super fan named Rebecca Pimmel started an online petition to "Free Kesha" from Dr. Luke's clutches. The petition accused the producer of stifling the artist's creativity by making her sing the same generic, predictable, recycled pop songs. It was a tune as old as Phil and Ronnie Spector, but social media gave it wings. "It's no surprise that Ke$ha is 'forced' to work with the same collective group of people, through each record," Pimmel wrote in her petition. "Dr. Luke is controlling Ke$ha like a puppet. . . ."

In January 2014, Kesha checked into a rehab clinic to treat an eating disorder, allegedly brought on by Dr. Luke telling her that she looked like "fat fucking refrigerator."

The artist remained out of sight for most of 2014, but in October remerged in the tabloids in a very big way. Kesha and her mother and their attorneys filed suit against Dr. Luke, charging him with sexual assault. The wording of the lawsuit combines *Hollywood Babylon* and *Tess of the d'Urbervilles*, and the spectre of Spector hovers over the accusations. "At eighteen years old [Kesha] was an intelligent, family-oriented, and joyful young woman," the suit reads. "Ms. Sebert excelled academically and had a bright future ahead of her." Dr. Luke "showered her with promises of fame and fortune," and persuaded her to move to L.A. to pursue "a glamorous music career under his auspices." However, once she was in L.A. in the fall of 2005, "Dr. Luke displayed despicable conduct in front of Ms. Sebert. Specifically, Dr. Luke would boast and brag to Ms. Sebert about how he liked to take girls out on a first date, get them as drunk as possible, and 'fuck them in the ass.'"

Soon, claims the suit, Gottwald turned his charms on Kesha herself, forcing drugs and alcohol on her "in order to take advantage of her sexually while she was intoxicated." The plaintiffs also claim that one night, after drinking with Kesha, Dr. Luke gave her a pill, which he said would sober her up, but which was actually a roofie. He then raped her (reportedly she was a virgin at the time) when she was unconscious in his hotelroom bed. The next day, Dr. Luke allegedly took her down to the beach and made it clear that if she said anything about what had happened, he would "shut her career down, take away all her publishing and recording rights, and destroy not only her life but her entire family's lives as well," all of which Kesha supposedly reported to her mother. The lawsuit also gives examples of cutting remarks the producer would routinely make to his star, such as, "I don't give a shit if you don't want to sing it, get in there and do it," and "Go finish the song so I can buy a yacht," and "You are nothing without me."

Dr. Luke's camp released their own countersuit the same day, denying the Seberts' claims, and alleging defamation and breach of contract. The countersuit accuses Kesha's mother of pressuring Dr. Luke into letting Kesha out of her contract by threatening to tell a blogger about Kesha's alleged rape. Dr. Luke's suit also points out that both Kesha and her mother swore under oath in depositions for Sonenberg's 2011 lawsuit that the drug and rape accusations, which Sonenberg had heard about, were in fact not true.

Perhaps, as Kesha and Pebe maintained, Luke had forced them to lie under oath then. But Dr. Luke's camp doesn't see it that way. An associate of the hit maker's argues: Wouldn't a young girl's mother, on hearing her daughter had been drugged and raped by her boss, immediately call the police? Why would she wait eight years to file charges, a period during which she and her daughter signed a publishing deal with Dr. Luke's company, and re-signed with Luke as an artist? And, he points out, why would the only remedy they seek be in a civil lawsuit for termination of Kesha's contract—surely they should be pressing for a criminal prosecution if the charges were true.

EVEN BEFORE THE ONGOING Kesha drama, Dr. Luke's peers were undecided about how far his unique combination of musical skills and ambition would carry him in the record business. Doug Morris thinks he is the Jimmy Iovine of his generation. "He is certainly one of the most talented people," Morris says. "He's had so many hits, and that really is the heart of what the record business is all about—the people who can deliver hit after hit after hit. Creatures like that are enormously rare. He's already the top producer-writer, and he'll evolve into a top executive—he can go as far as he wants to go. He's as good as it gets." Could he have Morris's job one day? "Oh, absolutely. You know, these kinds of people come along very rarely, and they're driven and brilliant and they go as far as they can and sometimes they go so far it's shocking."

But could Dr. Luke continue to be closely involved with the creative process of songwriting, developing hit songs for artists, while also running the label that was releasing the artist's work? It was one thing for a label chief to reject an artist's songs, as Clive Davis did Kelly Clarkson's; it's another for the boss to force the artist to sing his own songs, so that he can get the publishing royalties too. As Luke's boyhood friend Jarret Myer observes, "A lot of his personality is still tied to making sure he gets the right margin on dime bags. Sometimes he doesn't let things go. Because if you're going to make your margin on dime bags, you can't let things go."

WITH KESHA'S CAREER IN TURMOIL, Dr. Luke was fully engaged in launching the career Becky G, a sixteen-year-old Mexican American artist he had signed to Kemosabe in 2011. He first spotted her in a YouTube video, rapping over a Kanye West and Jay-Z song called "Otis." He arranged a meeting and signed her on the spot.

Dr. Luke invited me to the set of a video shoot for Becky G's first single, a fun number called "Play It Again." The shoot was in Becky's 'hood, the Inglewood neighborhood in southwest L.A. Lots of relatives and school friends of Becky's had turned out, mingling with a troupe of professional hip-hop dancers—muscular dudes doing strenuous athletic moves.

"She's got it," Dr. Luke says, watching his artist sing along to the track. "A lot of these young kids are too *Star Search*-y—they've got a mother who has been hauling them off to auditions since they were little. But Becky isn't like that. Whatever she has, she got on her own, from watching videos." He gestured toward the girl's mother, who was watching intently as an assistant touched up her daughter's makeup, adding, "Becky G is a very nice, respectful girl who was brought up right by her parents with solid values." Plus, she was easy to work with, which is not always the case with rappers. But whether or not a nice, respectful girl who followed orders would appeal to a hip-hop audience remained to be seen.

Becky G, née Rebecca Gomez, was scheduled to come by the beach house late on a Friday morning. Dr. Luke wanted her to write a rap to the bridge in a song he had co-written for Jessie J, the British pop star. Young Becky arrived on time, modestly attired in a tracksuit. She is petite, with high cheekbones and a gap-toothed smile that is sassy-friendly. Dr. Luke nodded toward Cirkut, and the Jessie J song "Excuse My Rude," began to play. The hook was "Excuse my rude but I really fucking hate you." Everyone nodded in silence to the beat. At the end, Dr. Luke said, "It's a dope song. I think you can go hard on it."

"Oh, yeah," Gomez said. "For sure. Make it gorilla!"

Luke wanted her to tap into a sense of anger and outrage. "I know no one ever does anything bad to you because everyone loves you, but just imagine."

"I'll just go on YouTube and read comments."

"Anonymous haters."

"Yeah."

Gomez noted that her mother didn't allow her to swear in her raps.

"I think swearing, though it sounds cool, is overrated," Dr. Luke says. "Usually, when you make the clean version, you have to think, and most of the time that one's better."

Becky went outside on the patio to work on her rap, the Jessie J song playing in her headphones, as the surf beat its own rhythm on the beach. Inside, Luke instructed an assistant to order lunch from a nearby takeout spot. When it arrived Becky came back in. Dr. Luke was seated at the head of the table, the barefoot paterfamilias of a pop empire, his turkey burger with avocado waiting behind a selection of hot sauces.

Becky G, spying the toy car belonging to Dr. Luke's older child, sat down in it and, scrunching up her knees, began to drive in circles around the living space, childish delight in her face. Dr. Luke looked on, beaming.

BEFORE I LEFT THE beach house, Dr. Luke wanted me to hear a song. "Here, I'll play you something from the new Katy album. This is the first single." He nodded in the direction of Cirkut, who punched up the song on the keyboard. It started to play.

> *I used to bite my tongue and hold my breath*
> *Scared to rock the boat and make a mess*

As the song played, I was thinking, Oh, man, what am I going to say? This is a *terrible* song! It's way too slow! Luke and Max have really lost their mojo! I was cycling through the studio ejaculations I had picked up in my time with the pros. Dope? Cray-zee? Sick? A real banger?

In the end, I just went with "Cool!"

"Thanks," says Luke, with a show of gratitude that, like his other attempts to be sincere, had a slightly forced quality. As did my compliments, no doubt—especially since they definitely weren't sincere.

"That's the first single?"

"Yep."

"Huh! What's it called?"

"'Roar.'"

CHORUS
SPOTIFY

23 | The Moment Space

DANIEL EK, SPOTIFY'S founder, is pale, boyish, cerebral, and calm. *Jantelagen*, the Scandinavian code of humility and restraint, is strong in him. He is a rock star of the tech world, but he isn't long on charisma. No firm handshake is offered from behind an imposing desk; he doesn't use a desk. He sprawls on a couch with his laptop, like a teenager doing his homework. Wandering the office floors, around the open core of a big building on Birger Jarlsgatan, in central Stockholm, he says he likes to encourage "random encounters," which Ek once read was Steve Jobs's plan in laying out Pixar's offices.

Ek's phlegmatic Swedish manner makes his unshakable, almost spiritual belief in Spotify, the Netflix of streaming music service, burn all the more brightly. His vision, that Spotify is a force for good in the world of music, is almost Swedenborgian: salvation in the form of a fully licensed streaming-music service where you can find every record ever made. Spotify doesn't sell music; it sells access to it. Instead of buying songs and albums, you pay a monthly subscription fee ($9.99), or get served an ad every few songs if you're on the free tier. You can listen to anything on the service—the Beatles (as with iTunes, the surviving members are not rushing in) and Taylor Swift (who left the service in a blaze of publicity) notwithstanding. There is an astonishing amount of music on Spotify. It's a music nerd's dream, which may be why the user population on Spotify tends to lie outside the mainstream. On Spotify, the Pixies' top songs have about four times as many streams as Neil Diamond's biggest hits.

Spotify launched in Sweden and part of Europe in 2008, nine years after Napster. In some respects, Spotify was Napster—a site where you could find almost any song you wanted, for free. Ek was even one of the pirate band. Before starting the company, he had briefly been the CEO of uTorrent, which made money in part by monetizing pirated music and movies on BitTorrent, a major file-sharing protocol. Later, the Napster co-founder Sean Parker, for years public enemy number one to record-company executives, joined forces with Ek. Who would have imagined, as one label head put it, that "your enemy could become your friend"?

One factor in the evolution of the labels' thinking was Apple, which had proved to be an unsatisfactory business partner. The iTunes store, the industry's attempt, in partnership with Apple, to build a digital record shop, opened in 2003 to sell downloads, but that didn't alter the downward trajectory of sales revenues; indeed, by unbundling tracks from the album so that buyers could cherry-pick their favorite songs, Apple arguably hastened the decline. Music had been an important part of Apple's business when Steve Jobs first negotiated the iTunes licenses, back in 2002—the music helped sell the iPod. But by 2011 music was more important to the Apple brand than to its business. Apple would not even let Android users, who represent more than 80 percent of the global mobile business, have iTunes on their phones, because it wanted to sell iPhones. Spotify offered a way out of a troubled marriage.

By 2014, Spotify was in more than fifty-eight countries. (Canada, its latest market, got the service that September.) It had raised more than half a billion dollars from investors, including Goldman Sachs, to fund its expansion, and there were rumors of an IPO in its future, to raise more. Spotify's user base exceeded 50 million globally, with

12.5 million paying subscribers. At the current rate of growth, that number could reach 40 million subscribers by the end of the decade. It had paid out more than $2 billion to the record labels, publishers, distributors, and artists who own the rights to the songs. "I'm very bullish on it," Tom Corson, the president of RCA Records, says. "The all-you-can-eat access model is starting to make sense to people. And we expect that free is going to roll into subscription and that is going to be a really huge part of our business."

ON SPOTIFY, THE SONG is once again king, just as it was in my maternal ancestors' time. Yes, you can listen to albums if you want to—it's the same price as listening to a song, after all—but that's not the way the system is organized. Instead you are pushed to listen to playlists of songs by different artists, often ranging across traditional genres, made by Spotify's own curators and editors, as well as by Spotify users. In enabling Spotify's playlist culture, Ek has done as much as his countryman Max Martin to break down traditional genres like R&B, rock, hip-hop, and pop.

The playlist is the album of the streaming world. Ek thinks top artists will start making their own playlists. They will be organized around activities and moods—"moments" Ek calls them—rather than around the artist's creative vision, as it was in the age of rock 'n' roll. "A workout playlist that is a collaboration between Avicii and Usain Bolt," for example, Ek says.

You can design your own Spotify day. You wake to the "Early Morning Rise" playlist (Midnight Faces, Zella Day), and get ready with "Songs to Sing in the Shower" ("I'm hooked on a feeling/I'm high on believing"). Depending on how much work you have, there's "Deep Focus," "Brain Food," or "Intense Studying." By eleven thirty, you've hit "Caffeine Rush," and, after a sandwich at your desk ("Love That Lazy Lunch"), it's time to "Re-Energize" (Skrillex, Deorro) for the afternoon.

A late-in-the-day "Mood Booster" (Meghan Trainor) gets you pumped for your workout (there's a "House Workout," a "Hip Hop Workout," and a "CrossFit Mix," to name just a few). Then it's "Happy to Be Home" (Feist, the Postal Service). After "Beer 'n Burgers" (rockabilly) or "Taco Tuesday" (Celia Cruz), you "Calm Down" (Wilco, the National) and then, depending on your love life, click on "Sexy Beats" or "Better Off Without You" (or maybe "Bedtime Stories," for the kids), followed by "Sleep" (heavy on Brian Eno, king of the z's).

"We're not in the music space—we're in the moment space," Ek declares, with the slight air of spiritual superiority that tech visionaries sometimes give off. The moments are created by Spotify programmers, using song analytics and user data to help them select the right songs for certain activities or moods, and build playlists for those moments. In 2014, Spotify bought a Boston-based startup called the Echo Nest, which has developed a form of artificial music intelligence—a kind of AI hipster that finds cool music for you. The Echo Nest powers Spotify's automated radio stations and is also behind an in-house programming tool called Truffle Pig, which can be told to sniff out music with combinations of more than fifty parameters, such as "speechiness" and "acoustic-ness." Now that the Echo Nest is part of Spotify, its team has access to the enormous amount of data generated by Spotify users showing how they consume music. Spotify knows what time of day users listen to certain songs, and in many cases their location, so programmers can infer what they are probably doing—studying, exercising, driving to work. Brian Whitman, an Echo Nest co-founder, told me that programmers also hope to learn more about listeners by factoring in data such as "what the weather is like, what your relationship status is now on Facebook." (In 2011, Facebook entered into a partnership with Spotify.) He added, "We've cracked the nut as far as knowing as much about the music as we possibly can automatically, and we see the next frontier as knowing as much as we possibly can about the listener."

Playlists can be customized according to an individual user's "taste profile." You just broke up with your boyfriend, you're in a bad mood, and Justin Timberlake's "Cry Me a River," from the "Better Off Without You" playlist, starts. Are you playing the music, or is the music playing you?

BY THE TIME HE turned twenty-two, Daniel Ek had achieved his life's ambition: he was rich. A gifted programmer, he had been making money by working on Internet-based tech products since he was fourteen. After selling an Internet advertising company called Advertigo, in 2006, he retired. He rented a big place in Stockholm. He bought a red Ferrari and drove it to nightclubs, where he arranged for good tables for friends and attractive female companions, whom he plied with expensive Champagne. He lived like this for a year or so, until one morning he awoke to a startling realization. "I was completely depressed," he says.

"I realized the girls I was with weren't very nice people," Ek goes on, "that they were just using me, and that my friends weren't real friends. They were people who were there for the good times, but if it ever turned ugly they'd leave me in a heartbeat. I had always wanted to belong and I had been thinking that this was going to get solved when I had money, and instead I had no idea how I wanted to live my life. And no one teaches you what to do after you achieve financial independence. So I had to confront that."

Ek describes himself as "missionary," by which he means he likes to formulate five-year missions for himself. "That's how I think about life," he says. "Five years is long enough for me to achieve something meaningful but short enough so I can change my mind every few years. I'm on my second five-year commitment on Spotify. In two years, I will have to make my next one. I will need to ask myself if I still enjoy what I'm doing. I'm kind of unusual that way, but it gives me clarity and purpose."

Ek sold the Ferrari, got rid of the apartment, and moved to a cabin near his parents' place in Ragsved, a Stockholm suburb, where he meditated about what to do with his life. He had soul-searching conversations with Martin Lorentzon, the Swedish entrepreneur who had bought Ek's advertising company, and was himself looking for a new project. "And we always came back to the music industry," Ek says.

Like many teenagers around the turn of the millennium, Ek had become infatuated with Napster—in particular, with the idea of a site where all the world's music was available for free. Radio offered free music too, of course, but radio wasn't interactive; you couldn't pursue your own interests, the way you could on Napster. Ek says, "Before that, I was listening to Roxette," the Swedish pop-rock band from the '80s. "I discovered Metallica and learned that they were inspired by Led Zeppelin, and King Crimson, and then I got into the Beatles. And from there I went to Bowie and the whole British scene from the Eurythmics to the Sex Pistols. Hearing the anger and frustration of the Sex Pistols or the Clash made you feel like you were in the seventies. You started to understand culture. It was pretty magical."

Ek goes on, "It came back to me constantly that Napster was such an amazing consumer experience, and I wanted to see if it could be a viable business. We said, 'The problem with the music industry is piracy. Great consumer product, not a great business model. But you can't beat technology. Technology always wins. But what if you can make a better product than piracy?'" Ek continues: "Piracy was kind of hard. It took a few minutes to download a song, it was kind of cumbersome, you had to worry about viruses. It's not like people want to be pirates. They just want a great experience. So we started sketching what that would look like."

Their "product vision," in tech parlance, was that the service had to give the impression that the music was already on your hard drive. "What would it feel like?" Ek asks. "That was the emotion we were trying to invoke." The key was to build something that worked instantly. Streaming, whether audio or video, tends to have built-in delays while you wait for the file, which is stored on a server in the cloud. But if the music starts in two hundred milliseconds or less—about half the time it takes, on average, to blink—people don't seem to perceive a delay. That became Ek's design standard. He told his lead engineer, Ludvig Strigeus, a brilliant programmer he had worked with before, "I don't accept anything that isn't below two hundred milliseconds."

Strigeus responded, "It can't be done. The Internet isn't built like that."

"You have to figure it out," Ek insisted.

The solution involved designing a streaming protocol that worked faster than the standard one, as well as building their own peer-to-peer network, a decentralized architecture in which all the computers on it can communicate with one another. In four months, they had a working prototype.

"And I knew when we had it that it was going to be very special," Ek says.

Ek's original idea was to launch Spotify in the United States at the same time that he launched the service in Europe. Ken Parks, Spotify's chief content officer, says, "Daniel thought he could just go down to the corner store in Stockholm and pick up a global license." He didn't realize that he would have to negotiate directly with all the different copyright holders, a herculean task. Not surprisingly, the labels weren't interested. Ek was an outsider—a techie, and a Swedish one at that.

Parks, an attorney who'd worked at EMI recalls, "We needed to overcome the music-is-free mentality that Spotify represented." Of the labels' attitude, he continues, "If you have something you've invested a ton of money in, and you've been selling it for a lot, and you feel raped by piracy—to say to that person, 'The only way to beat this is to co-opt the people who are stealing from you,' that was a challenge." Ek says, "If anyone had told me going into this that it would be three years of crashing my head against the wall, I wouldn't have done it."

Eventually, Ek decided to start regionally and prove that his concept worked. "And I invested all of my personal money in it," he says, "saying, you know, here's my balls on the table. For them, the risk of trying it was kind of zero." Swedish labels, gutted by piracy, literally had nothing to lose.

SEAN PARKER WAS LIVING in the Plaza Hotel, in a private residence in the northeast corner of the building, looking out at Fifth Avenue and Central Park South. His townhouse in the Village was undergoing long-term renovation. The grand, high-ceilinged dining room had commanding views in both directions, and it was there that the thirty-four-year-old billionaire was sitting on a warm fall afternoon, dressed in jeans and rust-colored high-tops, drinking tea from a white china cup. It was a setting that would have impressed Edith Wharton, even if the owner's attire might not have.

Parker recalled the end of Napster, and the havoc that followed in its wake, as illegal file-sharing sites bloomed. As for him, "I went off and did other things." He became president of Facebook in 2004, and helped turn it into a company, which helped turn him into a billionaire. "But in the back of my mind I was thinking about the untimely fate that Napster had met. That aborted mission." He had watched while other entrepreneurs tried to realize the dream that was Napster. "They'd try to negotiate with the record labels and they really didn't speak the language and they'd end up adapting their product vision to the terms they were able to get," he says. In 2009, a friend told him about a Swedish service called Spotify. Parker had never heard of it. He sent Daniel Ek an email, and they arranged to meet.

"The thing that made Spotify very different when I first met Daniel and Martin was that they had this incredible stubbornness," Parker goes on. "In a good way. They were willing to let the product vision lead the business deals." He agreed to invest in the company and help Ek in his negotiations to enter the US market. "Daniel said, 'I think it's going to take six weeks to get our licenses complete.' It ended up taking two years." Of the four global music companies at that time—EMI, Sony,

Warner Music, and Universal—Ek had managed to get EMI and Sony on board, but Universal and Warner were holdouts. The latter was led by Edgar Bronfman Jr., who had spearheaded the move to close Parker and Fanning down back in 2001.

This time, Parker was more persuasive. "He did know a lot of people," one top label executive says. "Daniel Ek didn't. And he worked it nonstop." The Swedish trial period, during which piracy plummeted, was key. The record industry's total revenues in Sweden grew by more than one-third between 2008 and 2011. As the label executive recalls, "It was like—OK, proof of concept, we should be doing this if we can get the right license."

Thomas Hesse, who led the negotiations for Sony, says, "The main reason it took so long for Daniel to get all the majors on board was that he had this free tier, where all the music was on demand. Was that going to cannibalize the download world?" In the end, the free tier was limited to personal computers, so users would have to pay for subscriptions in order to listen on their mobile devices, a major incentive to convert to the paid tier. Nevertheless, Hesse continues, there was "a lot of discussion about how much Spotify needed to pay for the free streaming and how many paying subscribers it could potentially guarantee."

After Universal made a licensing agreement with Spotify, Warner was virtually compelled to join the other major labels in negotiating. At the time, the company was also looking for a buyer. Parker says that he tendered an offer to buy Warner with Ron Burkle, the Los Angeles–based venture capitalist. When another buyer, the Russian oligarch Len Blavatnik, expressed interest, Parker recalls telling him, "Look, if you make Spotify contingent on the deal, I will withdraw my offer and you'll get the company." In 2011, Blavatnik bought Warner, for $3.3 billion. Parker became a Spotify board member and helped broker its partnership with Facebook.

The exact terms of the licensing deals that Spotify made with the label groups are not known; all parties signed nondisclosure agreements.

In addition to sharing with other rights holders nearly 70 percent of the money Spotify earns from subscriptions and ad sales—about the same revenue split that Apple provides on iTunes sales—the labels also got equity in Spotify, making them business partners; collectively, they own close to 15 percent of the company. Some analysts have questioned whether Spotify's business model is sustainable. The company pays out so much of its revenues in fees that it barely makes a profit. It operated at a loss before 2013. (The company maintains that its focus has been on growth and expansion.) The contracts are renegotiated every two or three years, so the better Spotify does, the more, in theory, the labels could ask for. This makes Spotify unlike many Internet companies, in which the fixed costs of doing business become relatively smaller with scale. For Spotify, scale doesn't diminish the licensing fees.

When Spotify began in the United States, in the middle of 2011, labels demanded up-front payments as the price of getting in the game. These payments were not always passed along to the content creators, even though it is their work that makes the catalogues valuable in the first place. Month by month, Spotify pays the major labels lump sums for the entire market share of their catalogues. How the labels decide to parcel these payments out to their artists isn't transparent, because, while Spotify gives detailed data to the labels, the labels ultimately decide how to share that information with their artists. The arrangement is similar on the publishing side. Artists and songwriters basically have to trust that labels and publishers will deal with them honestly, which history suggests is a sucker's bet. As one music-industry leader puts it, "It's like you go to your bank, and the bank says, 'Here's your salary,' and you say, 'But what is my employer paying me? I work for them, not you!' And the bank says, 'We are not going to tell you, but this is what we think you should get paid.'"

Parker's tea had grown cold, and he poured some hot water into it. The October light dimmed in the high Plaza windows. He pondered the progress of the tide of humanity flowing up and down Fifth Avenue. For him, he tells me, Spotify is a do-over—a second chance to get Napster right. And that felt "very vindicating."

THE QUESTION OF WHETHER Spotify is good for artists is wickedly vexed. The service has been dogged by accusations that it doesn't value musicians highly enough. In 2013, Radiohead's Thom Yorke memorably called Spotify "the last desperate fart of a dying corpse," a remark that "saddened" Ek. Taylor Swift wrote in a *Wall Street Journal* editorial, "In my opinion, the value of an album is, and will continue to be, based on the amount of heart and soul an artist has bled into a body of work." For Swift, streaming is not much different from piracy. "Piracy, file sharing and streaming have shrunk the numbers of paid album sales drastically, and every artist has handled this blow differently," she wrote. But was pulling her music from Spotify a gesture of artistic solidarity, or, as one insider put it, "a stunt to wring the last drop of blood out of what is a dying model"—that is, album sales?

Ek's answer to the question of whether Spotify is good for artists tends toward the tautological. If it's good for listeners—and almost everyone who uses Spotify likes it—then it must be good for artists, because by encouraging more listening it will "increase the over-all pie." Many music-business people think he's right. Richard Jones, the Pixies' manager, says, "Particularly for artists who are established with solid catalogues and are big live-touring acts, streaming services can be extremely beneficial. I'm a massive supporter." He says of Taylor Swift's decision to pull her music, "It's purely PR-driven, which is fine. But let's not pretend it's artist-friendly. Because actually the most artist-friendly thing here is for everyone to make streaming into something that is widespread."

But for a lot of musicians, Spotify has further eroded their CD and download sales, without coming close to making up the difference in streaming revenues. Ek acknowledges that the switch from a sales model to a streaming model could be bumpy for some artists. "In Sweden, there was one tough year and then the debate changed," he says. "That will happen in the larger markets. The end goal is to increase the entire pool of music. Anything else is part of the transition." He adds, "This is the single biggest shift since the beginning of recorded music, so it's not surprising that it takes time to educate artists about what this future means."

Two artists who are part of that transition are Marc Ribot, an esteemed jazz guitarist, and Rosanne Cash, whose work has won two Grammys and received twelve nominations. Both are midlevel, mid-career musicians who are a vital part of the New York City music scene. Both have worked with major labels. The long tail is supposed to bene-fit artists like Ribot and Cash, and Spotify's payment system is a good example of why it hasn't, so far. You can spend all your Spotify time in the tail, listening to Ribot and Cash, but 90 percent of your subscription fee is still going to the megastars in the head, because that's how Spoti-fy's share-based system works.

They got together in New York one afternoon in October to talk to me about Spotify. Ribot and Cash brought along their Spotify num-bers. In the past eighteen months, Ribot reported, his band made a $187 from 68,000 streams of his latest album, available on Spotify in Europe and the United States. Cash had made $104 from 600,000 streams. The math doesn't fit Spotify's benchmarks, but that is how their labels and publishers did the accounting.

On hearing that both Ek and Parker seemed to be sincere in their desire to help artists, Ribot said he and his fellow musicians had been hearing this for almost fifteen years now. "Our 'friends' in the online-distribution business have helped artists to go from a fourteen-billion-dollar domestic record business to a seven-billion-dollar one, and now Spotify wants to help us reduce it even further. With friends like that, give me the old Brill Building system."

Ribot goes on, "Here's the simple fact that no one wants to talk about. Spotify says it pays out seventy percent of its revenues to rights holders. Well, that's very nice, that's lovely. But if I'm making a shoe, and it costs me a hundred dollars to make it, and the retailer is selling that shoe for ten dollars, then I don't care if he gives me seventy percent; I don't care if he gives me one hundred percent—I'm going out of business. Dead is dead."

Cash says, "I don't think any of us want to make the streaming services go away. We are not Luddites. We just want to be paid fairly."

"And we're not going to say a model is viable unless it's viable for the creators," Ribot adds. "I know Daniel Ek is going to do just fine. I don't know that about the people in my band."

"And, if the artist can't afford to work, the music is going to suffer," Cash puts in, with feeling. "Spotify is not acting in its own self-interest by obliterating us."

At least Ribot and Cash can go on the road. Nonperforming songwriters don't have that option. AM/FM radio pays the writer of the song on a per-play basis, but gives the performer and the owner of the recording of the song—generally, the record label—nothing. On most streaming services, the situation is nearly reversed: the owners of the recording get most of the performance royalty money, while the owners of the publishing get only a fraction of it. The reason for this, as one music publisher explains, is because "Basically, the major music corporations sold out their publishing companies in order to save their record labels. Universal Music Publishing took a terrible rate from streaming services like Spotify in order to help Universal Records. Which, in the end, means that the songwriter gets screwed."

You could obliterate the Ribots and Cashes of the music world, and the labels would do just fine. But if songwriters can't afford to work, then the whole hit-making apparatus of the song machine is doomed. Aloe Blacc, one of the songwriters of Avicii's smash "Wake Me Up" (as well as a vocalist on the track) received only a small fraction of the song's millions in Spotify earnings. As we have seen, the artists don't write, by and large, which makes it easier to control them in the production of hits.

The writers, for their part, already share songwriting credit with a half dozen or so other writers, because of the way song production has been industrialized since the early '90s. And now that share is threatened by services like Spotify, because the labels are keeping more of the money for themselves. "If streaming is the future," songwriter Savan Kotecha says, "no young songwriter will be able to make a living."

OR MAYBE SPOTIFY ITSELF will get obliterated. Apple, Amazon, and Google are all in the on-demand streaming market. Spotify's advantage, Ek maintains, is its data and its ability to analyze that information. "We've been doing this for years," he says. "And what we've built is the largest set of data of the most engaged music customers. I think it would be really hard for anyone to come in and do what we do better. Maybe someone could lower the cost of a streaming service and make it hard for us to survive. But am I concerned that someone will build a better product? No, because they can't."

James McQuivey, an analyst with the Boston-based Forrester Research, is less optimistic about the company's prospects. "Spotify has shown people the value of streaming," he says, "and that means somewhere someone could use that value in a bigger chess game. Someone like an Apple or a Google is already realizing how valuable music is as a customer-engagement tool and will offer something quite similar to this, without making you pay for it, the way Amazon has included video in the Prime membership without expressly charging. And then suddenly you've disrupted Spotify." He adds, "If I have to say yes or no will Spotify be as big and strong as it is five years from now, the answer will be no."

Apple could pose a real threat to Spotify by preinstalling its service—Apple Music—on a future generation of iPhones and including the price of a subscription in the plan. Siri could be your DJ. That would ensure a paying user base in the hundreds of millions almost instantly, easily eclipsing Spotify's. And since Apple makes money primarily from its hardware, it could afford to undercut Spotify on the price of a subscription—a scheme it was promoting to the labels. Of course, that would require the support of the labels, and they are Spotify's business partners in streaming.

"You might want to take a discount in a business you have equity in," one label head says. "You might not want to take a discount in a business you don't have equity in. Would we subsidize Apple with no real upside for us? We did that once before. It was called unbundling the album." In any case, the downward pressure on price from increased competition seems likely to diminish the pot of money that the rights holders get to divide.

Even if Spotify does manage to survive Apple, it would take years to complete the paradigm shift to streaming. Meanwhile, album sales would continue to decline—even albums recorded by Taylor Swift. Although *1989* was by far the biggest-selling album of 2014, its first-week sales, 1.3 million, were far short of the 2.4 million first-week sales of 'N Sync's 2000 album *No Strings Attached*. The labels, feeling the pinch in their bottom line, may try to squeeze more money out of Spotify, imperiling its future growth. They may even try to cash in their equity stakes. Proving that, while your enemies can indeed become your friends, the reverse can also be true.

OUTRO
SONGWORM

24 | "Roar"

"ROAR," OF COURSE, was a stupendous hit. It was everything a CHR song could be. How could I have been so wrong? The song that I had hated, on first hearing in Dr. Luke's beach house studio—had laughed about, like Denniz PoP and Douglas Carr on hearing Ace of Base for the first time in Denniz's Nissan Micra—became unavoidable. What I did not realize, and presumably Max Martin did, because he'd learned it from Denniz and taught it to Dr. Luke, was that by the time I'd been forced to hear "Roar" ten times—trapped in the Nissan Micra of contemporary hits radio—I'd come to like it too. Still, I was troubled by the possibility that I had been right the first time.

Apparently, I never really had a chance. According to a 2011 research project based on a fMRI study of people listening to music, familiarity with a song reflexively causes emotional engagement; it doesn't matter what you think of the song. In "Music and Emotions in the Brain: Familiarity Matters," lead author Carlos Silva Pereira and his collaborators write that familiarity is a "crucial factor" in how emotionally engaged listeners are with a song.

But why does hearing a song over and over again make us like it? In her 2014 book *On Repeat: How Music Plays the Mind*, Elizabeth Margulis, who is the director of the Music Cognition Lab at the University of Arkansas, explores this topic. She explains, "When we know what's coming next in a tune, we lean forward when listening, imagining the next bit before it actually comes. This kind of listening ahead builds a sense of participation with the music." The songs in heavy rotation are "executing our volition after the fact." The imagined participation encouraged by familiar music, she adds, is experienced by many people as highly pleasurable, since it mimics a kind of social communion.

That's a sobering thought. If Margulis is right, it means that the real controller of the song machine isn't the labels, nor is it radio stations or the hit makers. At the end of the day, the true puppet master is the human brain.

NOT ONLY WAS "ROAR" a smash—thanks to its inspirational theme, it has become something of an anthem for little girls. Which is why, less than a year after I first heard the song, I found myself escorting the Girl to her friend's sixth birthday party at a Manhattan recording studio, where the birthday treat was to make a real-life professional recording of "Roar!" The song was like the party's piñata.

I helped the Girl prepare for the session by running through the tune with her on an acoustic guitar. (She's a fan, unlike others in the house.) It turns out that some of the biggest hits, stripped of their glossy synths and sick beats, hold up really well as acoustic songs. "Brave," "Wrecking Ball," "We Can't Stop," and "Summertime Sadness" have all become part of our repertoire. "Roar" is too minimalist for a sing-along, but I enjoyed learning the subtle chord progression. And I had fun with the '80s shout-out: "I GOT THE EYE OF THE TIGER . . ."

At the studio, on East Twenty-Eighth Street in Manhattan, the girls lined up in the vocal booth, three to a mike. The studio techs played the song, explaining that the birthday girl and her friends were going to sing to a track—they would be the vocalists. A karaoke video of "Roar" started to play. Images of Katy Perry in a variety of wacky costumes—

Katy as a peppermint patty, Katy as a fruit salad—flashed across the screen. The little girls stared at the screen, glassy-eyed, mouthing the superimposed words of the song.

On the Internet, much was made of the similarity of "Roar" to "Brave," by Sara Bareilles, which had come out four months earlier. "Brave" is also in the key of B flat, and it begins with the same tempo— eighth notes, played on the piano. The songs also share similarly inspirational hooks: "You're gonna hear me roar," versus "I wanna see you be brave."

Dr. Luke insists that he and Max Martin wrote "Roar" first. The buzz over the controversy gave "Brave" a second chance on the charts, and it became a much bigger hit than it was the first time, featured in Microsoft tablet commercials, presumably because it took real bravery to purchase hardware from the creators of the Windows Phone and the Zune.

THE HEART OF THE old Cheiron crew is in L.A. these days. Andreas Carlsson has a baronial mansion in the Hollywood Hills, and Jörgen Elofsson is in Santa Monica; Kristian Lundin lives in Pacific Palisades. The hit-making methods developed at Cheiron by Denniz PoP have spread throughout the UK and the United States. Swedish hitmakers, once a crazy dream of Denniz PoP's, supplied one quarter of all the hits on the Billboard Hot 100 in 2014. The Swedes have become a driving force in K-pop as well. Swedes turn out to be just as good at working within Asian musical genres.

But as malleable as the Swedish musical genius seems to be, for the Swedes themselves, adapting to American songwriting culture isn't always easy. Savan Kotecha says, of L.A., "With producers here, it's all about the hype in the room. Here, you gotta jump up and down and go, 'It's a smash! It's a smash!' Whereas the Swedes are like, 'I think this could be better.' If Max Martin says something is really good, then you know it's a hit. But he doesn't go, 'It's amazing!' like people do here. He'll go, 'That's really good.' In America you don't want to be the negative guy in the room—that guy who, when everyone else is going 'It's a smash!' is going 'Mmm, maybe not.' Whereas in Sweden, everyone's negative."

Max Martin lives in L.A. too, for a large part of the year. He is tanned and buff now—Martin White, the doughy, whey-faced front man of the band It's Alive, has been hitting the gym. Max doesn't have his own label, and he doesn't have an investment in high-end bottled water, either. Perhaps because he comes from a social democratic country in which everyone is assured of a decent standard of living, and displays of excessive wealth is frowned upon, the Swede seems content to focus on his craft and not worry about making all the money. Kotecha says, "I always think in my head, if Max Martin was an American, he would have fizzled out a long time ago. He would have believed his own hype. But because he's Swedish, he's able to contain himself. He just focuses on being the best writer and producer and mentor he can be."

Max has moved through three genres of music: R&B, rock, and hip-hop, co-opting each for his purposes, and now he's taking on Taylor Swift; her album *1989* has no fewer than nine tracks co-written or co-produced by Max Martin. In Swift, the Swedish master may have found his ultimate collaborator: an artist strong enough to stand up for her vision, but canny enough to appreciate his genius. Still, for the first time Swift's hit songs sound like anyone could have sung them. The singer-songwriter whom the Boy and I had bonded with four years earlier was gone.

THE BOY, I AM pleased to report, hated "Roar." (He also hated "Brave," which I loved.) He did like the third single from *Prism*, "Dark Horse," which also went to number one and featured an inspired rap by Dr. Luke's Kemosabe artist Juicy J, who was a comer. ("Dark Horse" also brought a copyright-infringement suit from the creators of "Joyful Noise," a 2008 Christian song by the rapper Flame.) And I think he liked "Birthday," the fourth single from *Prism*, which only got to number seventeen.

The truth is we don't listen to a lot of music together anymore. After his first year in Salk School of Science, the Boy was old enough to take the subway into Manhattan by himself, and our morning car rides came to an end. On longer family trips in the car, he sits in the back with his Beats headphones plugged into his iPhone, keeping his music to himself.

We got a new car, and it has satellite radio in it. SiriusXM makes the "Comfortably Numb" groove easy to settle back into. If the "Classic Rewind" channel isn't playing a tune I want to hear, there's always "Classic Vinyl" and "Deep Tracks" right next door. Still, I often find myself surfing up the Sirius dial to the two CHR channels, "Hits" and "Venus." Just like the waitresses in that coffee shop in Omaha, when given the choice, sometimes I just want to listen to what everyone else is listening to.

As one of the current hits starts to play, I watch the Boy's face in the rearview mirror. I see the moment the radio penetrates his headphones, and his eyes flick up from his phone to the Sirius display showing the song and artist. Then, information duly logged, his eyes drift back to the phone.

ALTHOUGH I DON'T GET to listen to much music with the Boy anymore, I am aware of what he's listening to, or at least what he chooses to purchase, because he does so with my iTunes account. He may be the very last person to use iTunes.

Recently, he's started buying rock songs. It began with AC/DC's album *Highway to Hell*. Then the Clash's *London Calling*. (Be still my heart.) Then the Smiths' album *The Queen Is Dead*—one of my personal favorites. Not long after that, while I was lecturing him on the dangers of fame (now he's at LaGuardia High School, aka the "*Fame* school," as an actor), I quoted the lines about fatal fame playing hideous tricks on the brain from the Smiths' "Frankly, Mr. Shankly." Without missing a beat, he added the next lines:

> *But still I'd rather be famous*
> *Than righteous or holy*

That rocked my world.

Is it possible that, thanks to some Freaky Friday–like switcheroo, we've changed places—I'm the teen-pop fan now, and he's the rock guy? Or maybe I am the Boy, and I always have been.

> *Oh, the movie never ends*
> *It goes on and on and on and on*

Of course he knows that one too. That's my boy.

Afterword

I THOUGHT THAT I was writing *The Song Machine* about the end of something—a particularly long pure pop period, one that would inevitably give way to the doldrums, and then to the extremes, according to Guy Zapoleon's theory of the pop cycle, as outlined in Chapter 11. Now I wonder whether I was describing the beginning of something new—a permanent pure pop that spreads from the center to the edges, less cyclical than osmotic.

The eye at the center of this expanding ring of influence is Max Martin. The Swedish master, and the school of collaborators he has gathered around him at MXM, his publishing and production company in Los Angeles, are more a part of our everyday listening experience than ever. In 2012, when I began writing the book, Martin had already gone on not one but two spectacular hit-making runs, the first from Ace of Base through the Backstreet Boys and 'N Sync to Britney Spears, and the second from Kelly Clarkson through Pink to Katy Perry's *Teenage Dream*, the album he executive-produced with Dr. Luke, which produced a whopping five number ones. Even then he had already surpassed most of the greatest songwriters in history, in output (he now has at least sixty-five top ten hits, of which twenty-two are number ones) and longevity (eighteen years between number ones; most Top 40 hitmakers get only six years at most).

I didn't expect Martin to become any more successful than he already was in 2012. But as I was working on the book, Martin and his new writing partner, the former death metal drummer Shellback, were embarking on a third run of hits—the ongoing hot streak of smashes with Taylor Swift, Ariana Grande, and the Weeknd.

Martin and Shellback's collaboration with Swift was starting around the same time I was starting the book. It began auspiciously, as Martin later explained to journalist Jan Gradvall on stage in Stockholm, the night before Martin received Sweden's 2016 Polar Music Prize.

Me and Shellback had our first date with her at Conway Studios. I was a little nervous, the good kind of nervous. Maroon 5 was recording in the studio next door. And this guy shows up, a friend of theirs; we hadn't started the session yet. He comes up and goes, "Hey I heard Taylor Swift is here. I got to say hello."

And I say, "Really?"

"Oh no, I totally know her, it's fine. We're friends."

So he walks in, and it turns out he didn't know her, and I was vouching for this guy!

"Here's . . . as you know."

"No, I don't know."

So I started sweating. It was really messy. And I apologized and said, "Oh I'm so sorry." And she was super cool and said no problem at all.

And then I asked what was it about, and she told me the story of this guy she was dating (and how the interloper was trying to lobby on the ex's behalf), and then she said—

"One thing's for sure: we're never EVER getting back together."

And I was like, "That's pretty harsh."

And she said, "No no, we are never ever EVER getting back together."

And I told her, and we were laughing about it, "That sounds like a song title," ha ha ha. (A dopey-sounding laugh, as if to say, "Isn't that the stupidest idea ever?") And then we went on to something else.

The next day, she came in, and she said, "I thought about what you said." And she played us this idea, and that became the song.

I had been so mad at this guy, and it turned into eternal love. Thank you! Because that song would never have happened if he hadn't come in. So I love that guy.

The song, "We Are Never Ever Getting Back Together," hit number one in August 2012. And boom, Max was off on another run.

I kept having to revise the manuscript and the galleys as the book moved closer to publication and Martin's hot streak blazed on. "Shake It Off" was his eighteenth number one; "Blank Space" made nineteen; and with "Bad Blood" it was an even twenty. We just got that change in before the presses rolled.

In August 2015, as warehouses were getting the finished books, "Can't Feel My Face" made it twenty-one. The book was not even published, and Max Martin had already dated it.

And as I was working on this update, Martin got number twenty-two, with Justin Timberlake's "Can't Stop the Feeling!" I suspect this number will also be out of date before next week.

MXM is the embodiment of the crazy dream that Denniz PoP had in 1987—a Swedish songwriting factory that creates hits for American artists. Denniz would have found it amusing that the recording studio is inside what used to be Frank Sinatra's West Hollywood house, and is now the home of Max Martin.

MXM includes Martin's protégé, Swedish-trained but American-born (to Indian parents) Savan Kotecha, who co-wrote "Love Me Like You Do" for Ellie Goulding and "Problem" (with Martin) for Ariana Grande. He also worked with the Weeknd on the Torontonian R&B singer's new album, MXM's next big project. Kotecha and other younger MXM writers ensure that if and when the master finally does lose his touch his protégés can carry on making hits under his auspices and brand, employing the methods of songwriting formulated at Denniz PoP's studio, Cheiron, in Stockholm in the early '90s.

AS MAX MARTIN'S FORTUNES have soared, his former protégé and partner Dr. Luke's have plummeted, as a result of his ongoing legal battle with Kesha.

There is something mythic about Dr. Luke and Kesha: the artist who, in her desire for fame, becomes deeply connected to a producer with his own powerful set of ambitions for himself and his company. He can make her a star; she can make him a mogul. But it all goes wrong and now they are locked in a mutually destructive career death spiral, all played out amid a vibrant subculture on social media.

Dr. Luke is reportedly isolated in his many mansions. Many top female artists won't work with him anymore—effectively cutting off the blood flow to his songwriting career. He is distracted, leaving the Prescription songwriters and producers whom he had assembled into a hit factory leaderless and demoralized. It isn't surprising that MXM, and not Prescription, are getting all the best projects. As one of Luke's collaborators put it, "The only thing he can do now is go away for a long time, hang out in Maui, and come back as someone else. Dr. Luke is finished." The good news is that Gottwald never liked the name Dr. Luke anyway.

It should be noted that my reporting with Dr. Luke at his beach house studio occurred in June of 2013, a year and a half before the Kesha scandal broke. At that time Kesha was rumored to be unhappy about the songs Luke was creating for her to sing, and I asked about that, but no one was talking about sexual assault. Several months after the article "The Doctor Is In" appeared in *The New Yorker*, in October 2013, Kesha entered rehab for bulimia, an eating disorder brought on—according to Kesha's mother, Pebe Sebert—by Dr. Luke's caustic remarks about Kesha's body.

Kesha's lawsuit, accusing Dr. Luke of drugging and raping her starting in 2005, when she signed her contract at age 18, was filed in October 2014. Dr. Luke immediately countersued for defamation and alleged breach of contract, claiming Kesha was "publishing false and shocking accounts" as a way of extorting Dr. Luke to let her out of her contract.

In February 2016, five months after the hardcover edition of this book came out, Kesha lost her motion for a preliminary injunction in connection with her bid to terminate her contract. She was photographed in tears at the courtroom in New York. Taylor Swift offered her $250,000 to pay her legal bills, and Lady Gaga and Kelly Clarkson, among others, offered support. On social media, #FreeKesha became not just a cry for Kesha's artistic freedom over Dr. Luke, but also for justice for all women who are victims of assault or abuse. The artist's image with the words "Free Kesha" were projected onto the former Sony Building on Madison Avenue at a protest in March 2016. In a letter to fans, Kesha wrote: "All I ever wanted was to be able to make music without being afraid, scared, or abused. This case has never been about a renegotiation of my record contract—it was never about getting a bigger, or a better deal. This is about being free from my abuser. I would be willing to work with Sony if they do the right thing and break all ties that bind me to my abuser."

Dr. Luke remained quiet, except for a series of tweets sent over the course of an hour on February 22, 2016, in which he denied her accusations. "I didn't rape Kesha and I have never had sex with her," he wrote. "Kesha and I were friends for many years and she was like my little sister." Among other things he said he was a feminist, and raised by a "feminist mom"—Laura—"Who raised me right."

No one from the songwriting community spoke up in support, including Dr. Luke's old mentor and partner, Max Martin.

While Sony is not a party to Dr. Luke's contract with Kesha, it did have its own business arrangement with the hitmaker. Sony invested $60 million in Kemosabe, Dr. Luke's label, in 2011. So far, that investment has not paid off—and now Dr. Luke has blown up his best shot at a real payday with Kesha. Becky G, Dr. Luke's bid for a teen pop star, is neither Selena Gomez nor Demi Lovato. (Note again the shaping hand of Disney, which has molded so many of the artists in the book.) The smart move for Sony would be to take the financial hit and bid the good doctor adieu.

In April 2016, *Pitchfork* reported that Kemosabe was downsizing. Some of its functions as a record company would be handled by Sony. A spokesperson told *Pitchfork* that the cuts had "nothing to do with" Dr. Luke's legal problems. Six months later, Kesha dropped her sexual assault case against Dr. Luke in California, but pressed on with what remains over the contract dispute in New York.

If there is any good to come out of the Kesha's struggle with Dr. Luke, it is the light it has thrown on the plight faced by young women who go into the music business hoping to be artists. As soon as you show a glimmer of talent, some manager or producer or A&R person finds you and wants to turn you into a star. One could argue that forcing teen-agers to sign six-album contracts, which is standard industry practice, is itself abusive.

ANOTHER MAJOR DEVELOPMENT IN the music world since I finished the book is Apple Music, which was officially unveiled in June 2015. Confusing to use, it did not prove the Spotify-killer some thought it might be. Apple Music has arguably helped Spotify so far, as Daniel Ek predicted it would. Spotify now has 30 million subscribers; Apple Music has 15 million. Apple is once again in the underdog position it was in for so long, in the '80s and '90s, a position the company no doubt relishes.

My plea in the Note on Sources notwithstanding, Taylor Swift has not returned to Spotify, which continues to stick by the free, ad-supported tier she objects to. Swift's music is available on Apple Music, which does not have a free tier; you have to subscribe, for $9.99 a month. Limiting superstar artists' availability, as well as so-called "windowed releases"—when an album is unavailable for streaming for a period of time—have become more common lately, except on Spotify, which opposes them. "We're not really in the business of paying for exclusives, because we think they're bad for artists and they're bad for fans," Jonathan Prince, Spotify's head of communications, told *The Verge*.

Tidal, the Jay Z–owned high-fidelity streaming service—which had a somewhat rocky start but has begun to gain traction—has used exclusives to quickly establish itself as a serious rival to both Spotify and Apple, attracting a respectable 4 million subscribers. (Apple has been rumored to be interested in purchasing Tidal.) Tidal had Rihanna's album *ANTI* exclusive for a week, which helped Tidal but arguably cost *ANTI* the top spot in the Billboard Hot 200, the album chart. When, in February 2016, Kanye West announced that his much-anticipated album *The Life of Pablo* would be exclusive to Tidal, he tweeted "My album will never never never be on Apple," it caused a surge in $20-a-month subscriptions. So when *Pablo* came out on Apple six weeks later, some of those subscribers were irate enough to start a class action suit against Tidal, and against Kanye West personally for misrepresentation and fraud.

As Stephen Witt, the author of *How Music Got Free*—my book's Amazon algorithmic buddy—pointed out on NewYorker.com, the practice of windowing and exclusives is undermined by that fact that in most cases artists, even those as omnipotent as Kanye West, don't own their masters—their record companies do. And while the rights holders may agree to a temporary period of windowing, ultimately they want the record on as many platforms as possible. Until a streaming service becomes a full-fledged label, that weakness in the windowing strategy will persist.

There is no sign that the unsettled landscape of streaming is going to resolve itself any time soon. (Soundcloud, the Berlin-based streaming service that has built up a base of 40 million users by cultivating artists, but not paying them much, recently launched a premium subscription version called Soundcloud Go and is itself rumored to be for sale.). Nor is it clear that Spotify's dominant position will last long. Its revenues grew 80 percent in 2015, to more than $2.12 billion, but losses also hit a new peak at $188.7 million, raising the question of whether Spotify will ever be sustainable. (The company has lost $698 million since it was founded in 2008.) Apple Music, of course, might not be sustainable either, but it is hardly more than a rounding error for Apple.

For most artists and songwriters, music streaming continues to cut into CD sales—and pathetic streaming royalty payouts don't even come close to making up the difference. In 2015, the revenues from vinyl record sales, $416 million, were more than the revenues from YouTube and all other ad-supported on-demand services ($385 million). Perhaps the greatest outrage, apart from the primal sense that the services are picking the artists' pockets, is directed at the corporations benefitting most from streaming music—Google, Amazon, Apple—which are among the wealthiest on earth. They use music to draw traffic to their sites and keep people within their ecosystems. In 2015, according to the International Federation of the Phonographic Industry (IFPI), the global music-copyright industry brought in $15 billion, about 6 percent of Apple's revenues for the year. Operating under rules designed in part to prevent songwriters from monopolizing the market, composers are now in the Kafkaesque situation of being compelled to license their songs to these monopolistic behemoths at absurdly low rates.

CATCHING UP WITH OTHER figures from the book, Kelly Clarkson had another baby, and she had another big hit, "Heartbeat Song." Clive Davis, her former antagonist, moved out of his palatial office at the top of the Sony Building, along with the rest of Sony; they are now in considerably more humble circumstances closer to Union Square. Stargate left Roc-the-Mic on West 27th Street, where I saw Ester Dean at work early in 2012, at the beginning of the project that became *The Song Machine*, and relocated their families to Los Angeles, to be nearer the action. Theirs was the last studio left in New York that regularly turned out hits. Tin Pan Alley may have come to an end (it was a blind alley, after all) eerily close to where it started, on West 28th Street.

Rihanna's album *ANTI* was created by a crew of some fifty composers, writers, and engineers—a whole song camp's worth—overseen by Robyn "Rihanna" Fenty, who is credited as "composer, Creative Director, Executive Producer, primary artist, poetry." Notably absent from the list was Stargate. But the lanky Norwegians are doing just fine, with recent hits such as "Worth It" for Fifth Harmony and "Same Old Love" for Selena Gomez.

Britney Spears has established a successful Las Vegas residency, and seems to have gotten her life back in order. However, under the court-sanctioned conservatorship, her father, Jamie Spears, has control of her assets and manages all the important decisions, including her children. His care is overseen by a state-appointed lawyer. In May 2016, a *New York Times* article suggested the conservatorship was no longer necessary, but that the people who could end it, the doctors and conservators, pocket handsome fees for keeping it going.

Ester Dean has continued to find great hooks in the simplest phrases, as in the 2015 Selena Gomez hit "Come & Get It" ("Nah na-nah nah / nah na-nah nah"), and her work on David Guetta's "Hey Mama" ("Hey MaMaMa / Hey MaMaMa") featuring Nicki Minaj.

Girls' Generation have yet to break through in the United States and it feels like their time has come and gone. Here, the influence of K-pop is still seen more in hip-hop than in pop, and it's more a matter of style than music. It is not that big a leap from G-Dragon, a member of BIG-BANG who has a solo career as well, to Young Thug, the Atlanta rapper.

"Roar," the song Max Martin and Dr. Luke did with Katy Perry, which I dismissed as a stinker on first hearing it in Luke's studio, has gone on to become one of Hillary Clinton's campaign songs. Katy Perry performed it just before Hillary accepted the Democratic nomination for president; it was as though it had been written for the occasion. And what did America hear just before the balloons dropped? Stargate and Ester Dean's hook, "Baby you're a firework . . . ."

I sent Lou Pearlman a book, with a note, and the Texarkana Federal Penitentiary sent the package back, opened. Pearlman died in prison in August 2016.

THE GIRL, NOW EIGHT, whose musical preferences were starting to make themselves known at the end of the book, has since developed a strong interest in hip-hop. The profanity and misogyny of much of today's hip-hop is problematic for any parent—and the constant repetition of the "N" word poses a special dilemma for the white parents of a black child (the Girl was born in Haiti). Still, we are exceptionally fortunate that Lin-Manuel Miranda's *Hamilton* is widely available on the streaming services, and the Girl listens to little else now, commanding Alexa, Amazon's household A.I., to play favorite songs again and again (and again). Musically, hip-hop is still the most vibrant, inventive, and exhilarating popular music of our time, but its potential has been stunted by an unimaginative devotion to keeping it real. *Hamilton* shows us what hip-hop is capable of when it takes on subjects other than life in the streets.

The Boy continues to follow modern pop—Zayn Malik, formerly of his beloved One Direction; Taylor, of course, though he may be turning on her; and Ellie Goulding, who may have replaced Taylor in his heart— all the while continuing to accumulate a stealthy mastery of my music through our shared iTunes account. He doesn't seem to mind that I used him as a character in my book—in fact I think he likes it. But he does sometimes seem nostalgic for those golden days before I got interested in the songwriters and producers behind his music (thanks in large part to him)—those salad days when he innocently assumed that the songs were created by the artists who sang them. "I sort of wish you hadn't told me this stuff," he said, when we talked after the book came out. "It's kind of disillusioning."

ACKNOWLEDGMENTS

The author is grateful for the help and support of the people who made this book possible.

At the *New Yorker*, where portions of the *The Song Machine* first appeared in a different form—Stargate/Ester Dean, K-Pop, Dr. Luke, and Spotify—thanks to Cressida Leyshon (possibly the world's best editor), David Remnick, Daniel Zalewski, Henry Finder, Dorothy Wickenden, Susan Morrison, Nicholas Thompson, Lizzie Widdecombe, Roger Angell, Virginia Cannon (who suggested the title), Jiayang Fan, Andrew Marantz, Neima Jahromi, Lev Mendes, Carolyn Kormann, Rhonda Sherman, Pam McCarthy, Bruce Diones, Peter Canby, and the magazine's copy- and style editors and query proofreaders who(m?) I am privileged to work with—Ann Goldstein, Elizabeth Pearson-Griffiths, Mary Norris, Carol Anderson, and Mary Hawthorne, among others. And as always, C. S. Ledbetter III. Yo, the *New Yorker*.

At Norton: Tom Mayer—it's all you, baby. Plus thanks to Ryan Harrington, Laura Goldin (P '81), Steve Colca, Meredith McGinnis, Alice Rha, and Rachel Salzman, and Rachelle Mandik, for great copyediting. Also, thanks to Leah Clark for her work on johnseabrook.com.

For interviews, insight, and support in Sweden: *tack* to Douglas Carr, StoneBridge, Anders "Snake" Hannegård, Jeanette von der Burg, Kristian Lundin, Andreas Carlsson, Rami Yacoub, Carl Falk, Ulf Ekberg, Dr. Alban, Karin Jihde, Diana Esposito, STV, Swedish Radio, Klas Ahlund, Per Magnusson, Herbie Crichlow, Jacob Schulze, Jörgen Elofsson, Jens von Reis, Annabelle Jönsson, Marie Ledin, Daniel Ek, Graham James, Louise Shwebel, Jan Gradvall, and Martin Dodd. Fredrik Eliasson's 2008 Swedish Radio documentary, *The Cheiron Saga*, was a priceless resource.

In Korea: *gomawo* to Jessica, Tiffany, Max Hole, Neil Jacobson, Melody Kim, John Kim, Jon Toth, Alex Wright, Dominic Rodriguez, Jinsop Lee, Grace Lee, Mark Russell, and Ted Chung.

In New York, L.A., London, Atlanta, Orlando, Nashville, and Vermont: *ta very much* to Tor Hermansen, Mikkel Eriksen, Tim Blacksmith, Danny D, Ester Dean, Aubry Delaine, Tricky Stewart, Mark Stewart, Kuk Harrell, Teddy Riley, Lukasz Gottwald, Laura Gottwald, Kool Kojak, Cirkut, Bonnie McKee, Ammo, Becky G, Mark Beaven, Steve Lunt, Dave McPherson, Clive Davis, Sean Cassidy, Barry Weiss, Jason Flom, Jay Brown, Katy Perry, Lou Pearlman, Tom Poleman, Steve Blatter, Andy Schuon, Judy McGrath, Guy Zapoleon, Savan Kotecha, Tom Corson, Peter Edge, Mika El-Baz, Benny Blanco, Evan Bogart, Evan Rogers, Carl Sturken, Gabriel Rossman, Drake, Ne-Yo, Miley Cyrus, Paul Williams, Lauren Lossa, Bobbi Marcus, ASCAP, Doug Morris, Jarret Myer, Brian Brater, Lenny Pickett, David Beal, David Baron, Brian Whitman, Sean Parker, Ken Parks, Will Page, Thomas Hesse, Liz Penta, Willard Ahdritz, Daniel Glass, Richard Jones, Marc Ribot, Rosanne Cash, James McQuivey, Elizabeth Margulis, Rebecca Chace, Lisa Spiegel, Norman Janis, Hychem Benali, Horst Dresler and Alex Kim at Anything Printed in Taftsville, Vermont, and the Sequoias—rock on.

And the amazing Billy Mann, musical genius and Philly bro.

For kindly reading early versions of *The Song Machine* and helping me correct and improve the manuscript: shout-outs to Roy Horan,

Scott "Babydaddy" Hoffman, Jon Regen, Kool Kojak, Peter Grigg, Rob Buchanan, Eric Beall, Justine Neubarth, Eric Schlosser, Ken Auletta, Walter Isaacson, Bob Spitz, Terry Reed, and Harry Seabrook.

Toe-Dah to Ruth Margalit, for fact-checking.

Thanks to my wonderful and patient agent, Joy Harris, and to Adam Reed.

And most of all Lisa Claire Reed. I still want to hold your hand.

INDEX